CAMBRIDGE CONCISE HISTORIES

This is a new series of illustrated 'concise histories' of selected individual countries, intended both as university and college textbooks and as general historical introductions for general readers, travellers and members of the business community.

First titles in the series:

A Concise History of Australia
STUART MACINTYRE

A Concise History of Bolivia
HERBERT KLEIN

A Concise History of Brazil
BORIS FAUSTO

A Concise History of Britain, 1707–1975
W. A. SPECK

A Concise History of Bulgaria
R. J. CRAMPTON

A Concise History of France
ROGER PRICE

A Concise History of Germany
MARY FULBROOK

A Concise History of Greece
RICHARD CLOGG

A Concise History of Hungary
MIKLÓS MOLNÁR, TRANSLATED BY ANNA MAGYAR

A Concise History of India
BARBARA D. METCALF, THOMAS R. METCALF

A Concise History of Italy
CHRISTOPHER DUGGAN

A Concise History of Mexico
BRIAN R. HAMNETT

A Concise History of Poland
JERZY LUKOWSKI, HUBERT ZAWADZKI

A Concise History of Portugal
DAVID BIRMINGHAM

A Concise History of South Africa
ROBERT ROSS

Other titles are in preparation

A CONCISE HISTORY OF
NEW ZEALAND

New Zealand was the last major landmass, other than Antarctica, to be settled by humans. The story of this rugged and dynamic land is beautifully narrated, from its origins in Gondwana some 80 million years ago to the twenty-first century. Philippa Mein Smith highlights the effects of the country's smallness and isolation, from its late settlement by Polynesian voyagers and colonisation by Europeans – and the exchanges that made these people Maori and Pakeha – to the dramatic struggles over land and more recent efforts to manage global economic forces. In the late twentieth century, new upheavals saw governments demolish institutions that had once defined New Zealand, and economic problems damage a country dependent on exports.

A Concise History of New Zealand places New Zealand in its global and regional context, linked to Britain, immersed in the Pacific and part of Australasia. It unravels the key moments – the signing of the Treaty of Waitangi, the Anzac landing at Gallipoli, the sinking of the *Rainbow Warrior* – showing their role as nation-building myths and connecting them with the less dramatic forces, economic and social, that have also shaped contemporary New Zealand.

PHILIPPA MEIN SMITH is Associate Professor of History at the University of Canterbury. She is the author of *Maternity in Dispute: New Zealand 1920–1939* (1986), *Mothers and King Baby: Infant Survival and Welfare in an Imperial World: Australia 1880–1950* (1997) and co-author of *A History of Australia, New Zealand and the Pacific*.

A Concise History of
New Zealand

PHILIPPA MEIN SMITH

CAMBRIDGE
UNIVERSITY PRESS

CAMBRIDGE UNIVERSITY PRESS
Cambridge, New York, Melbourne, Madrid, Cape Town, Singapore, São Paulo

Cambridge University Press
477 Williamstown Road, Port Melbourne, VIC 3207, Australia

Published in the United States of America by Cambridge University Press, New York

www.cambridge.org
Information on this title: www.cambridge.org/9780521834384

First published by Cambridge University Press 2005
Reprinted 2007, 2008

Printed in Australia by Ligare Pty Ltd

A catalogue record for this book is available from the British Library

National Library of Australia Cataloguing in Publication data

Mein Smith, Philippa.
A concise history of New Zealand.
ISBN-13 978-0-521-83438-4 hardback
ISBN-10 0-521-83438-4 hardback
ISBN-13 978-0-521-54228-9 paperback
ISBN-10 0-521-54228-6 paperback
Bibliography.
Includes index.
ISBN 0 521 83438 4 (hbk).
ISBN 0 521 54228 6 (pbk).
1. New Zealand – History. I. Title.

993

ISBN-13 978-0-521-83438-4 hardback
ISBN-10 0-521-83438-4 hardback

ISBN-13 978-0-521-54228-9 paperback
ISBN-10 0-521-54228-6 paperback

In memory of my mother Barbara Ann Staff
whose stories and library
contributed to this book

CONTENTS

List of illustrations   *page* x
Acknowledgements   xv
Preface   xvii

 1 Waka across a watery world   1

 2 Beachcrossers 1769–1839   21

 3 Claiming the land 1840–1860   45

 4 Remoter Australasia 1861–1890   70

 5 Managing globalisation 1891–1913   95

 6 'All flesh is as grass' 1914–1929   123

 7 Making New Zealand 1930–1949   150

 8 Golden weather 1950–1973   176

 9 Latest experiments 1974–1996   201

10 Treaty revival 1974–2003   226

   Epilogue   249

Glossary of Maori words   254
Timeline   256
Sources of quotations   265
Guide to further reading   277
Index   295

ILLUSTRATIONS

MAPS AND FIGURES

1.1   New Zealand: principal mountains, regions and towns, cartographer Tim Nolan   *page* 2

1.2   From Gondwana to New Zealand's emergence, cartographer Tim Nolan   3

1.3   A watery world, cartographer Tim Nolan   8

2.1   Maori tribes (iwi), *c.*1839, cartographer Tim Nolan   22

2.2   Carte de la Nle Zélande visitée en 1769 et 1770 par le Lieutenant J. Cook Commandant d l'Endeavour vaisseau de sa Majesté. Paris: Saillant et Nyon, 1774. The French version of Cook's chart. MapColl 830atc/1769–70 (1774)/Acc.39323, Alexander Turnbull Library, Wellington.   24

2.3   Lieutenant George F. Dashwood, Maoris, 1832, Sydney. Wash drawing from the albums of Lt George Dashwood. Ref. PXA 1679/vol. 2/f. 89b, Mitchell Library, State Library of New South Wales.   31

2.4   James Barry, The Rev. Thomas Kendall and the Maori chiefs Hongi and Waikato, London, 1820. Ref. G-618, Alexander Turnbull Library, Wellington.   33

2.5   George F. Angas, Motupoi [Motuopuhi] Pah with [Mt] Tongariro, 1844. Ref. A-196-022, Alexander Turnbull Library, Wellington.   40

3.1.1   Patuone, Treaty of Waitangi signatory. Courtesy of Benjamin Pittman.   46

3.1.2 Tamati Waka Nene, Treaty of Waitangi signatory and
Patuone's brother. Courtesy of Benjamin Pittman. 46

3.2 The Treaty of Waitangi: English translation of Maori
text, 1865. J. Noble Coleman, *A Memoir of the Rev.
Richard Davis*, London, 1865, 455–6. 48

3.3 William Mein Smith, From the Pah Pipitea, Port
Nicholson, December 1840. Ref. C-011-005, Alexander
Turnbull Library, Wellington. 58

3.4 William Strutt, Settler putting out chimney fire, 1855 or
1856. Ref. E-453-f-003, Alexander Turnbull Library,
Wellington. 60

3.5 Thomas B. Collinson, Hosey's Battle, 1847. Capt[ain]
Henderson, Capt[ain E.] Stanley, R. N., Tamati Waka
Nene, Te Wherowhero Potatau (the future Maori king).
Ref. A-292-058, Alexander Turnbull Library, Wellington. 66

4.1 P. E. jnr, 'For Diver's reasons'. *Wellington Advertiser
Supplement*, 19 November 1881. Bryce is carving up the
protester, who wears the white feather headdress of Te
Whiti's followers and lies down in passive resistance.
Ref. A-095-038, Alexander Turnbull Library, Wellington. 76

4.2 Population growth. Marney Brosnan, after Phil Briggs,
Looking at the Numbers, Wellington: NZ Institute of
Economic Research, 2003, 21. 79

4.3 Population pyramids 1874, 1891 (European only). Tim
Nolan, based on Statistics NZ data. 80

4.4 Sew Hoy dredge gold mining. Burton Brothers
Collection, C.014896, Burton Brothers ref. BB N5220,
Museum of New Zealand Te Papa Tongarewa,
Wellington. 83

4.5 Helen Connon, MA Hons 1881. University of
Canterbury. 89

5.1 House in Bealey Avenue, Christchurch, possibly the
Minson family home near the Carlton Mill Bridge. This
spacious villa represented the suburban house to which
most New Zealanders aspired. Photographed c.1897.
Ref. F-145266-1/2, PAColl-6051, Alexander Turnbull
Library, Wellington. 101

5.2 The Summit at Last. *New Zealand Graphic and Ladies
Journal*, 1894. Amazonian womanhood assisted to
the summit. Ref. PUBL-0126-1894-01, Alexander
Turnbull Library, Wellington. 104

5.3   Scatz, How we see it. *New Zealand Graphic*, 20 October
      1900. Zealandia, Britannia's daughter, wearing an
      indigenous feather cloak, holds hands with the noble
      savage. She fends off the ogre of convict Australia to
      protect her indigenous ward (depicted as a Pacific
      Islander rather than Maori), and so opts for a separate
      destiny in the Pacific. Ref. J-040-002, Alexander
      Turnbull Library, Wellington.   113
5.4   John C. Blomfield, Still they come. *Free Lance*, 17 Jan-
      uary 1905. Chinese or Japanese (to xenophobes they
      were indistinguishable), depicted as coolies, pole-vaulting
      into New Zealand over the barrier of immigration
      restrictions, aided by, as opposed to in spite of, the poll
      tax to the chagrin of Premier Richard Seddon. Ref.
      A-315-3-042, Alexander Turnbull Library, Wellington.   118
6.1   'Row on row'. Lijssenthoek Military Cemetery, the
      second largest New Zealand cemetery in Belgium, 6 June
      2004. Photographer Richard Tremewan.   130
6.2   A. Rule, "In Blighty!" A thing we dream about. *Shell
      Shocks: By the New Zealanders in France*, London:
      Jarrold & Sons, 1916, 29. Courtesy of Jack Tait.   131
6.3.1 Capt. P. P. Tahiwi, Sling Camp, July 1916. Photographer
      H. S. Tremewan.   132
6.3.2 Mrs M. Mylrea YMCA and Capt. H. S. Tremewan, Sling
      Camp, July 1916. Tremewan album.   132
6.4   Eat more milk, health class, 1926. Ministry of Health,
      Wellington.   139
6.5   Californian bungalow, Wakefield, Nelson. Photographer
      Jeff Mein Smith.   142
6.6   Milk for muscles: drain layers, Christchurch *c.*1920s
      milking the cow for morning tea. Ref. 2000.198.452,
      Pheloung Collection, Canterbury Historical Association
      Collection, Canterbury Museum, Christchurch.   144
7.1   Unemployed women organise: a May Day unemployed
      workers' demonstration led by a small band of women,
      Christchurch, 1932. c/n E3254/72, Hocken Library,
      Dunedin.   153
7.2   G. E. G. Minhinnick, The Medicine Man, *New Zealand
      Herald*, 18 August 1938. Savage has had to resort to
      distributing medicines himself. Ref. H-723-005,

	Alexander Turnbull Library, Wellington. Courtesy of Dion Minhinnick and *NZ Herald*.	158
7.3	'Got his man'. All soldiers were souvenir collectors. Here men from 28 (Maori) Battalion perform for their Australian photographer. Alexandria, 1 June 1941. Negative no. 007783, Australian War Memorial, Canberra.	166
7.4	*Making New Zealand*. Wellington: Government Printer, 1939–40. Photographer Duncan Shaw-Brown.	173
7.5	The invincibility of the All Blacks. In C. V. Smith, illustrated by G. E. Minhinnick, *From N to Z*, Wellington: Hicks Smith & Wright, c.1947. Family collection.	174
8.1	Nevile S. Lodge, Needmore Power Project, 1963 or 1964. Ref. PUBL-0206-081-1, Alexander Turnbull Library, Wellington. Courtesy of Mrs Pat Lodge.	183
8.2	Toddler in sandpit, Palmerston North, c.1959: for the under-five set in a new house in a new subdivision, the sandpit took precedence over making a garden in an undeveloped backyard. Family collection.	189
8.3	Eric W. Heath, Big 3 ANZUS meeting, 'Is there some reason we can't all support a nuclear free zone, gentlemen?' 27 February 1974. Ref. C-132-124, Alexander Turnbull Library, Wellington. Courtesy of Eric Heath.	194
8.4	G. E. G. Minhinnick, Tails you lose! *New Zealand Herald*, 3 February 1966. Courtesy of *NZ Herald*.	198
9.1	Trading partners: proportion of total exports going to different markets, 1860–1989. *New Zealand Official 1990 Yearbook*, Wellington: Department of Statistics, 1990, 599.	203
9.2	Robert Muldoon and Malcolm Fraser. Copyright unknown.	206
9.3	Eric W. Heath, ANZUS, 5 February 1985. Ref. B-143-009, Alexander Turnbull Library, Wellington. Courtesy of Eric Heath.	220
9.4	The stricken *Rainbow Warrior* in Auckland Harbour, July 1985. Courtesy of *NZ Herald*.	222
10.1	Justice Edward Taihakurei Durie, Chair of the Waitangi Tribunal, 1981–2003. Courtesy of Donna Durie Hall.	232

10.2   Prime Minister Helen Clark on Hochstetter Dome,
        Mt Cook National Park, 5 July 2003. Courtesy of the
        Office of the Prime Minister and photographer Gottlieb
        Braun-Elwert.   239

TABLES

4.1   Population trends and Maori land ownership. In Mason
        Durie, *Whaiora: Maori Health Development*. 2nd edn.
        Auckland: Oxford University Press, 1998, 36.   78
9.1   What did New Zealanders want? From *Defence and
        Security: What New Zealanders Want*, Wellington:
        Defence Committee of Enquiry, 1986.   223

ACKNOWLEDGEMENTS

A concise history incurs many debts. To my extended family I owe the largest: especially to Richard Tremewan; to Tanya Tremewan, who read and edited the first draft of the manuscript; to Edna, Christine and Peter Tremewan, Philip Tremewan and Trish Hall, and Janis Brooker; to my late mother Barbara, to whom this book is dedicated; and to my brothers Jeff and Alastair. I also thank my second cousin Barry for papers supplied years ago. Readers may notice that in some ways this is a family history.

I am grateful to Kim Armitage, my Cambridge editor, who commissioned a book proposal and gave advice on the draft manuscript, to Karen Hildebrandt, and the Cambridge team in Melbourne. I owe thanks to the anonymous referees who approved the proposal, and in doing so sent me on an enjoyable journey. Colleagues in New Zealand history will see the extent of reliance on their work, and the endnotes and guide to further reading suggest my principal obligations. Colleagues in the School of History at the University of Canterbury provided support, among whom I am especially indebted to Katie Pickles and Miles Fairburn, who read and discussed draft chapters. Ashley Sparrow in the School of Biological Sciences lent lecture outlines to assist with chapter 1, and Elizabeth Gordon taught me about the origins of New Zealand English. Most of the book was written while I was on sabbatical leave in 2004, which allowed the peace and time to write. Thanks are also due to the Marsden Fund of the Royal Society of New Zealand, whose research grant for a project on ties between Australia and New Zealand supported some of the research underpinning this book.

The link between research and teaching is a precious one, and I thank my students, tutors in New Zealand history and postgraduates, beginning with Chris Brickell, Hayley Brown, Philip Ferguson, Matt Morris, Linda Moore, Rebecca Priestley, Tracy Tulloch, and Megan Woods. I continue to value the friendship of my own thesis supervisors, Len Richardson, Ken Inglis and Barry Smith, and other colleagues in Australia, whose work informs my own. Beyond the university, brief service on a research co-ordinating committee at the Waitangi Tribunal increased my appreciation of the tribunal's enormous task.

I had terrific fun finding illustrations, an exercise eased by the expertise of Marian Minson and David Small at the Alexander Turnbull Library. Duncan Shaw-Brown turned images into digital files, while Tim Nolan and Marney Brosnan prepared maps and graphs. I am especially grateful to copyright holders for permission to reproduce material. Benjamin Pittman and Donna Hall supplied family photographs, and the late Jack Tait lent me his father's 'soldier' magazines. Special thanks are due to the Christchurch Art Gallery and to Bill Hammond, whose painting 'The Fall of Icarus', on the cover, conveys the sense of isolation felt by New Zealanders.

Philippa Mein Smith
August 2004

PREFACE

It is a pleasure to introduce this history to readers who may know little about New Zealand other than that it is located in the Southern Hemisphere, somewhere near Australia. Often people are surprised to find how far New Zealand is from Australia. They may know the country from film, sometimes from art, music or novels, or sport, or business that takes them there; or travel. Some are familiar with national brands, such as Anchor butter and the All Blacks.

Local readers have their own expectations of how the country's history is, or ought to be, written. The basic narrative that they require is of equal relevance to the visitor. I wrote this concise history for my students, so that I could comprehend the story of New Zealand, and explain its significance to them; I also kept in mind friends overseas, and people I have met while travelling. Emphases reflect my understanding and interests; but they also indicate where gaps exist in existing histories of New Zealand. Certain themes, such as literature, are already expertly covered elsewhere. This is not an alternative history, but a broadening of the histories that have already been written.

Neither is this an isolated history; the aim is to place New Zealand history in global and Pacific context. This requires a comparative element, especially concerning parallels with Australia. Globalisation is a core theme of this book. One objective is to explore the persistent tension in New Zealand's short history between domestic politics and global and regional pressures and to examine the importance of the effects of smallness and isolation.

Health and social issues are central to this country's past (and present) international reputation, and continue to inform beliefs about national identity. Childbirth is one example of how this small country tracks international trends. Demographic contours are too often ignored; here population and defence issues are treated together, alongside economic problems that have consistently beleaguered a country dependent on exports. Maori–European interactions are pivotal in all histories, but their internal dynamics, prominent at home, need to be balanced by an external regard for foreign affairs.

My approach is to highlight themes that explain what has happened. I try to unravel the way in which key moments and episodes in New Zealand history contribute to the country's national myths. Such events include the Treaty of Waitangi signing, the Anzac landing at Gallipoli, and the sinking of the *Rainbow Warrior*. But there is more to history than war – sex (women and children, fertility) and money (economic history) drive societies. There is more to myth-making than war. Migrants know little of Anzac legends, but often come here because of myths about New Zealand as a good place to bring up children, as an Arcadia and a social laboratory. Since these are frequently the stuff of marketing exercises, it is often these myths of New Zealand that people overseas first encounter. They therefore beg to be explained, or at least investigated.

I

Waka across a watery world

How and when did New Zealand begin? Geologically the archipelago dates back 80 million years when it separated from Gondwana. Other than Antarctica, New Zealand was the last major landmass settled by humans. The first settlers, ancestors of the indigenous people, the Maori, are now thought to have arrived in the thirteenth century, whereas people inhabited the rest of the Pacific Rim from 12,000 to an estimated 60,000 years ago. Europeans arrived very late indeed, with planned settlements only from 1840. The two waves of people from Polynesia and Europe in a flash of time transformed the land and remade the landscapes. These simple facts of place and time explain why the environment is so much associated with the nation's culture and identity.

TIME BEFORE HUMANS

Geographically, New Zealand is an archipelago of many islands, from Raoul in the Kermadec group to Campbell Island, although the three main islands account for almost 99 per cent of the land area of 270,000 square kilometres. Its comparable size to the British Isles is important in a once dominant version of the country's history. Ancestral New Zealand, so scientists tell us, was once part of the great southern continent of Gondwana, its rocks forming a mountainous area stretching along Gondwana's eastern margin, 100 million years ago. Then what is known as the Rangitata landmass broke away and headed eastwards into the Pacific. Ancestral

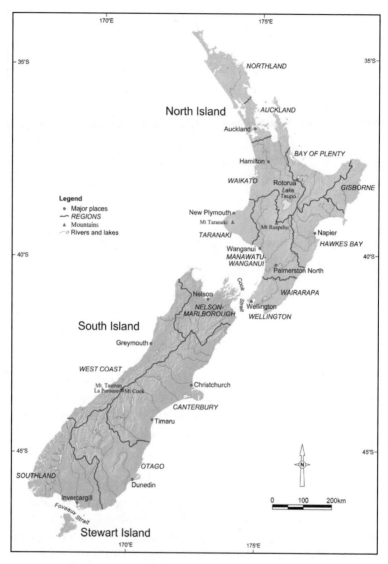

1.1 New Zealand: principal mountains, regions and towns

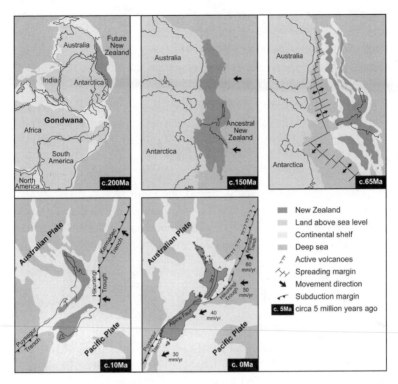

1.2 From Gondwana to New Zealand's emergence

New Zealand was on its own. Flora and fauna have not migrated overland for the last 80 million years, and movement and sea floor spreading ceased about 55 million years ago when the Tasman Sea reached its full width, separating the New Zealand landmass from south-eastern Australia.

The area that would become New Zealand had eroded to low plains by 65 million years ago. Shifting, swampy and geologically unstable, the low-lying land slowly sank. By about 35 million years ago, in the Oligocene, most of this Gondwanan fragment was under water. Dinosaurs lived on the chain of small islands – drowned remnants of the Rangitata mountains – that remained above water, as did crocodiles, frogs and tuatara. The mountains thrust upwards millions of years later, and various parts of New Zealand shifted around, moved by plate tectonics as the continental crust of the

Pacific Plate began to collide with the Australian Plate underneath the archipelago, from about 25 million years ago. Gondwanan rocks, the oldest segments of New Zealand's crust, are now confined to the west coast of the South Island, from west Nelson to Fiordland. In the east the land is new. While the South Island evolved through mountain building and glacial activity, the North Island acquired its contours from volcanoes that erupted as the crust crumpled.

The land continues to be in a state of upheaval. New Zealanders live in a dynamic environment, on the margin of the Pacific and Australian plates, amidst one of the Earth's fastest rising mountain systems: in the South Island, the Alpine Fault system marks where the Australian and Pacific plates slide past each other; the island's two segments have moved by an estimated 500 kilometres relative to each other along the Alpine Fault in the last 25 million years. As the colliding plates squeezed New Zealand's crust, high mountains formed right at the coast. Geologists believe that mountain building along the Southern Alps has accelerated in the last five million years, matched by rapid erosion. As recently as 1991 the distinctive tip of New Zealand's highest peak, Mt Cook – increasingly known by its Maori name of Aoraki, and named on road signs Aoraki Mt Cook, to signpost New Zealand's official stance as a bicultural, bilingual nation – tumbled into the Tasman Glacier below.

So much for the certainty imparted to schoolchildren that Mt Cook stood 12,349 ft before metric replaced imperial measures in the 1960s. Even the phrase 'solid as rock' calls for local scepticism when the key national icon, an environmental feature, can be shortened by 10.5 metres in an avalanche. Site and self are shaken: the summit shifts, and with it the vista, the imaginary, the image, that which is sacred.

Because of this seismic history, New Zealand is no ancient Gondwanan ark. Certainly it was a Gondwanan fragment, at least in the west and south of the South Island, its forests populated by podocarps under whose ancestors dinosaurs might have sought shelter. But the land itself represents a dynamic force, anything but solid and permanent, which – problematically – sank in the Oligocene before the mountains thrust skywards. Pollen records suggest that almost all New Zealand's flora arrived after the underlying landmass had drifted off into isolation. The native flora is the result of recolonisation since the breakup of Gondwana, suggesting a pattern of plant dispersal from Australia followed by radiation through adaptation to local ecological and climatic conditions, and then by extinction for some plants. Botanists have found that Tasmania and New Zealand share 200 plant species, while the case of the *Nothofagus* beech, which has Gondwanan origins, can be explained by long-distance dispersal. The origins of the beech tree remain contested. Many animals were recent migrants too, and are migratory; for example, seabirds regularly cross the Tasman Sea.

Palaeontologists, however, have questioned how New Zealand's fauna thrived in isolation for 80 million years, and why that fauna proved so vulnerable to humans. New Zealand was a land of birds, many of them uniquely large, naïve and flightless. Prominent among them are the kiwi, adopted as an informal national symbol in the twentieth century, and the moa, whose fossils fascinated Europeans since their first discovery, in the 1840s, of the earlier existence of various species. As for who, or what, killed the moa, naturalists in the nineteenth century thought that people did. By the 1950s the accepted view was that climate change had rendered the moa and other flightless birds extinct before the first people arrived. Today, however, zoologists consider that the continental focus of Northern Hemisphere-trained scientists overrode the initial insights into the disappearance of island faunas. In their view, about half of New Zealand's post-glacial bird species became extinct after humans disturbed their environment. That is, predators were responsible – the first people and the rats that accompanied them in their voyaging waka (canoes).

NAVIGATORS UNDER THE SOUTHERN CROSS

The tangata whenua (people of the land, a concept with maritime kin connections throughout the Pacific) were Polynesian venturers whose great journeys denoted one of the last stages of human colonisation of the Pacific region. While Europeans were sailing along familiar coasts to trade with and invade neighbours, Polynesian navigators struck out north and south in search of new lands across millions of square kilometres of the Pacific Ocean. In diverse traditions about migrations to and within New Zealand, generations passed on stories of dangerous voyages from the ancestral homeland of Hawaiki, and of arrival, dispersal and settlement in these southern islands. To establish their mana whenua (authority over the land) settlers 'brought with them the intellectual order, the mental maps, of the Polynesian world', peopling the spiritual fabric of the new land with their own gods and creation stories.

The North Island, the first landing place, they named Te Ika a Maui (the fish of Maui). In the myth derived from Polynesia, Maui stood on the South Island and hooked a great fish, which the sun turned solid. The eye of the fish is Lake Taupo and the tail is Northland (see 1.1). The South Island became Te Wai Pounamu (water or river of greenstone) because of the precious jade found in its rushing West Coast rivers, which artists carved into tools such as fine chisels, weapons and ornaments. People who migrated there called the South Island Te Waka o Aoraki, the canoe of Aoraki, the name of their ancestor and the highest mountain. Stewart Island took the name Rakiura, which in the latest restatement of propinquity has become the name of the national park on this third largest island.

Tangata whenua – themselves a diversity of people, cultures and histories – subsequently became Maori in their encounter with Europe. They were boat people, a role and experience with which the European migrants could identify. Their feats of ocean navigation, voyages and settlement from eastern Polynesia to New Zealand and the Chatham Islands continue to generate scholarly debate about when, how and from where the first Polynesian navigators arrived. Latest studies in western science matched against tribal genealogies suggest a story of multiple and deliberate, rather than accidental, voyages.

Anthropologists surmise that the first navigators from eastern Polynesia settled New Zealand only relatively recently. There are three competing hypotheses about the time of settlement: that New Zealand has been peopled for about 2000 years; that the first people arrived between 800 and 1000 AD; and that the Polynesians reached New Zealand late, between 1200 and 1400 AD. Current understanding is that the Polynesian ancestors of the Maori landed between 1250 and 1300 AD. Archaeologists argue that there is no evidence of human habitation before about 1250. Subsequently New

Zealand Polynesians migrated to the Chatham Islands in the four-teenth or fifteenth century.

The first settlers set out from a place called Hawaiki, a homeland that recurs in stories throughout Polynesia. Hawaiki was probably an island group or zone that was possibly a referent for the Marque-sas or Society Islands and perhaps for the southern Cook Islands. The first settlers were descended from Austronesians who sailed eastwards from Southeast Asia into the Pacific Ocean 4000 years ago. Like other eastern Polynesians, the first New Zealanders were more direct descendants of Lapita people in the central Pacific, who were agriculturalists and maritime traders. An 'ancestral genetic trail' can be traced from Southeast Asia to New Guinea/Near Oceania to the central and eastern Pacific islands. Eastern Polynesia, the site of Hawaiki, was settled about 2200 years ago. Ventures east to Easter Island about 300 AD, north to Hawaii 100 years later, and after another 1000 years, south to the cold and treacher-ous waters around New Zealand completed this remarkable oceanic exploration.

Three developments made possible the last Polynesian odyssey. The first was maritime technology in the form of the dugout canoe, stabilised by outriggers, and with a lateen sail, that allowed long-distance travel across the Pacific. The second was expertise in agri-culture in the use of crops and domesticated animals. The third was the drive to explore and migrate, the reasons for which are in dis-pute. Whether the urge was religious, entrepreneurial, or motivated by scarcity, it took more than technology for Maori ancestors to navigate such a watery world.

Polynesian navigators had to be resilient and experienced in read-ing environmental cues to reach Aotearoa in the south-west Pacific. Their voyaging and navigation were astonishingly skilled feats. They followed the paths of migratory land-based birds, observed the cur-rents and 'lapa', the phenomenon of underwater phosphorescence that appeared as flashes or streaks of light 50 to 130 kilometres from land, and watched the clouds that appeared stationary above islands (hence the name Aotearoa, the 'land of the long white cloud'). The Southern Cross was their guide south of the Equator, and they voy-aged south in the summer, when the winds were favourable. Sailing down a narrow corridor of stars, they took their main direction from

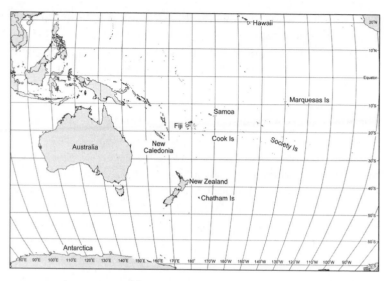

1.3 A watery world

Venus, with the Southern Cross to the port side, always pointing to Aotearoa.

The first settlers may not have used this name for New Zealand because they had no word for the country as a whole, instead giving names to islands. This alternative name for the North Island only became accepted as the Maori name for New Zealand in the twentieth century. Naming is a political act; and what matters is that Aotearoa has become the Maori term for New Zealand. It is now common, the word used in oral traditions that express emotions and show affinity to place, and provide a template for life in the present.

The early navigators conveyed their seafaring knowledge through oral culture, and stored it in waka traditions. It is said in one story that the navigator of the Te Arawa canoe (from which the iwi (tribe) Te Arawa takes its name) 'understood the language of the stars, the children of the lord of light, Tane-nui-a-rangi; he conversed with the moon, Hinauri; and he kept the prow of Te Arawa pointed in a direction that was a little to the left of the setting sun'. Scholars now believe that settlements were the result of deliberate exploration, with at least one return voyage to Polynesia before the planned migrations. Traditional stories told of return voyaging by the mythical ancestor Kupe, who returned to Hawaiki and reported his discovery of a land inhabited only by birds. When he heard such stories in 1769, Tupaia, a Tahitian traveller who sailed with Captain James Cook, was sceptical about the likelihood of two-way voyages, because the tangata whenua's ancestors did not bring their prized pigs back with them. But the absence of pigs does not preclude a pattern of return, or multiple, voyages, because pigs did not make it to New Zealand the first time let alone the second or third. Only rats and dogs survived the oceanic voyages from Hawaiki with the first people; Cook, perhaps 500 years later, supplied the pork.

In the 1980s independent teams of scholar-sailors reconstructed Polynesian outrigger canoes, determined to rebut the thesis of accidental voyaging in vogue in the mid-twentieth century. The team that left Rarotonga in better weather conditions reached northern New Zealand in little more than two weeks. It could be done, strengthening the likelihood that sailor ancestors succeeded in navigating a course in the summer. Only a 'landlubber', the modern sailors asserted, could theorise that the first people were blown off course rather than charting their way to New Zealand, using their knowledge of astronomy and seasonal winds. Maori traditions matched the seasonal evidence, that the best time of year to sail to Aotearoa was in summer, when the red-flowered pohutukawa, the New Zealand Christmas tree, was in bloom.

TRADITIONAL STORIES

The tangata whenua's world was determined by genealogy (whakapapa), which they used to interpret and interact with their landscape. Whakapapa ordered space and time differently from European models, and bound the living with the dead, as Te Maire Tau, a Ngai Tahu historian, explained:

If whakapapa was the backbone, oral traditions, chants, wananga, incantations and other arts could attach themselves as the flesh to the skeletal structure of genealogy. Thus, the earth (Papatuanuku) and sky (Raki) were understood as the original parents of humankind, with the sea, flora, fauna and other elements of the natural world connected by a web of kinship.

As is the way of culture, oral traditions explained kin relationships with the land and nature. A big problem for Te Maire Tau's
tribe, in the present, is that people immersed in the 'old' world view
know that traditions are not irrefutable accounts of actual historical events, or forever unchanged, whereas new entrants returning
to the tribe want traditions to affirm their discovery of indigenous
identity. A question for the here and now is: should an iwi commit
to the 'old' or 'new' knowledge system? Indigenous knowledge can
be applied most effectively in its local context, in terms of knowing
the environment, for example how and when to catch eels or birds.

Waka traditions were not just origin stories but prescribed boundary markers of identity, proprietorship and kin networks. Stories
of origin, settlement and exploration contained archetypes from
Polynesian mythology, providing role models whose exploits set the
pattern for people to follow. They did not distinguish between the
supernatural and the human, between the earliest ancestral 'gods'
and later 'heroes' because all were remembered as tupuna (ancestors), who continued to walk by their side.

Polynesians carried their stories with them, peopling each island
with their own genealogy to establish a cosmological and social
order. Laid as a mental map across the land, whakapapa acted as a
cultural marker, so that the land also became the people's ancestor.
The landing places of canoes helped to establish people's authority
in a region. Claiming the land began with naming, where the people
planted 'archetypal images from Polynesian mythology' across the
landscape and became tangata whenua in the process. The interac-
tion of tradition and landmark reinforced their beliefs. While myths
explained the presence of a landmark, the existence of a landmark
associated with a story of waka migration from Hawaiki confirmed
that myth or story's truth.

Stories at least 2000 years old evolved as narrators adapted them
to fit their new environments and to record the local landmarks as
they travelled. The consistencies are striking despite diversities of
detail in each place. Accounts across Polynesia shared the names
of Hawaiki and important figures, for example Maui the navigator who fished up the land. But names acquired new meanings as
traditions shifted and stretched to cover diverse landscapes. Ngai
Tahu leader Sir Tipene O'Regan elaborated: 'Each time we voyaged

onwards we rolled up our legends, our whakapapa and our place names, and carried them with us to be unrolled in a new place and fitted to a new landscape'.

This world view also reflects the belief that ancestors marched alongside people. The ancestors were both women and men in waka traditions, indicative of deliberate voyages by pioneers to start lives anew. As historical narratives expanded to include women as well as men in the late twentieth century, historians of gender grew conscious that male narrators of stories – Maori and Pakeha – selected masculine heroes and captains for preference. Traditional stories cast women as helpmeets associated with the natural world, as when they brought fire and planted kumara. Alternatively, waka women unleashed disaster and violence. The beautiful and the brave, however, are remembered the most, as in Te Arawa stories about the heroine Wairakei who saved a canoe.

Traditions of his Ngati Porou people collected by Sir Apirana Ngata, the pre-eminent twentieth-century Maori leader, relate how their ancestor Maui fished the North Island out of the ocean, naming it Te Ika a Maui. Kupe is remembered as a founding ancestor in the west of the North Island, and Toi in the east. In Te Arawa traditions, from around Rotorua, Toi was an ancestor living in Hawaiki before the mariner Tama Te Kapua and his people sailed to New Zealand. In other traditions, Toi lived in New Zealand and was associated with fetching kumara from Hawaiki. He is also known in Rarotonga.

All stories about Paikea, the great founding ancestor of the North Island's East Coast tribes, have in common that he travelled to New Zealand on the back of a whale and landed at Whangara. In the most accepted version of the story, a vessel set sail from Hawaiki with 70 sons of chiefs on board, only to be deceived by the paramount chief's younger son Ruatapu, who avenged an insult from his father by boring a hole in the hull in an effort to kill his older brother Paikea. When the vessel overturned, only Ruatapu and Paikea did not drown. Paikea survived by invoking his heritage as the son of the sea, and over generations the metaphor of his summoning the sea to 'lift him "as a great fish" to shore' became a whale that bore him through the surf. Eventually Paikea reached home, and later migrated to New Zealand. Similar stories about Paikea are told in the South Island by Ngai Tahu, who have kin links to Ngati Porou.

Most recently the story of the whale rider has been retold by Witi Ihimaera, who is from the East Coast, in his novel *Whalerider* and in the subsequent internationally acclaimed film.

A EUROPEAN SEARCH FOR ORIGINS

Problematically, Europeans imposed their frameworks on traditional stories. Not only did they rename physical features, but they reclassified Pacific peoples as Polynesians (meaning 'of many islands') and Melanesians, and ordered them into hierarchies based on skin colour. According to this racial template New Zealand's tangata whenua, as (brown) Polynesians, ranked more highly than (black) Melanesians, and were far superior to Indigenous Australians who were relegated to the bottom of the ladder. Ethnographers also found power-holding arrangements less obscure among Polynesians, including Maori, whose entrepreneurial qualities led European scholars to liken them to Jews. Europeans developed their own myths about Maori origins that melded diverse stories into tidy legends suitable for use in children's literature.

Influenced by Bible stories that humans were descended from the sons of Noah, missionaries such as Richard Taylor preached that the 'New Zealand race' was 'one of the lost tribes of Israel', an idea taken up by the Mormons and by Maori prophet movements. The model of the Aryan Polynesian and, locally, the Aryan Maori gained common currency in the nineteenth century as Pacific scholars sought clues about human origins. With the rise of Darwinism in the late nineteenth century, the concept of Caucasian Maori replaced the biblical idea of Semitic Maori. Edward Tregear, a surveyor and public servant, claimed that Maori and European shared an Aryan origin in *The Aryan Maori* (1885). This idea persisted with the flowering of the eugenics movement. In 1938 Te Rangi Hiroa (Sir Peter Buck), Director of the Bishop Museum in Honolulu, published his popular *Vikings of the Sunrise*. Buck bestowed mana on the portrayal of Polynesian navigators as Vikings of the Pacific since he was Maori, a medical graduate and a professional anthropologist, who joined the ranks of international scholars.

The idea of shared origins in human antiquity gave mana to Maori as well as Europeans, and usefully asserted New Zealand's distinctive identity as 'Maoriland'. More than anyone, it was the surveyor-general S. Percy Smith who devised the chronology which, in tracing a Maori heritage from India or the Caucasus to the Pacific, placed Polynesians in the 'Caucasian family of the human race'. In his search for origins Percy Smith also assembled and simplified traditional stories. For years, schoolchildren learned his version of Maori history: that the Polynesian 'sea rover', Kupe, discovered New Zealand about 950 AD, and that about 1350 a great fleet followed his instructions to reach the new country far to the south, a feat only possible because Maori ancestors were 'fearless, sea-loving people'.

This chronology is now debunked; but the idea of a planned migration has regained authority, as has the timing of the first settlers' arrival 500 years before Europeans. Scholars now accept that Maori ancestors navigated their way to New Zealand; as in legends, adventurers returned home and reported their discovery of a large southern land before an organised fleet or fleets returned. Probably the people arrived in a series of waka, and together created the first critical mass of population.

'FUTURE EATERS'

The 'cultural habits of humanity' have always made room for environmentalism, or the 'sacredness of nature', and so it is with Maori. During the process of settling claims for redress by iwi in the 1980s for past losses as a result of British colonisation, the Waitangi Tribunal suggested that Maori were more ecologically minded than Pakeha and, significantly, had suffered for that outlook. Tangata whenua saw themselves as part of their environment, not dominating or subduing it; they were its guardians who held resources in trust as taonga (treasures) for future generations. They had to guard and protect the land, lakes, rivers and the sea as gifts from their ancestors. The tribunal stated in 1985:

Although there is some opinion that the Maori did not come to a full environmental awareness until several generations after his arrival in Aotearoa, it also seems clear that the Maori brought with him a magico-religious world view of the environment that readily lent itself to the conservation of the earth's natural resources.

The tribunal had been 'introduced to rules' about how Maori used the sea and land; it was 'told how local tribes taught a respect for the sea' such that Maori treated the sea as a farm, whereas Pakeha cast their waste into it. The people had to be conservationists to survive. Accepting that species were depleted by overuse or accident before Europeans arrived, the Waitangi Tribunal nevertheless concluded that the scale was minor compared to environmental change since 1840.

Ecologists project a different view. They have portrayed the first Polynesian settlers not as environmentalists but as humans who typically exploited nature's bounty; who exterminated the moa, a large flightless bird, and decimated marine life before they intensified food production. In Tim Flannery's ecological history of Australasia, for instance, humans entered territory as 'future eaters'. The late settlement of New Zealand presents a case study of how humans plundered their environment, its flora and fauna, until in the long term they reached an accommodation with it. Australia provides the contrast of humans reconciled to their land and ecosystems because indigenous people have lived there for at least 60,000 years. In this interpretation, New Zealand's first settlers were 'optimal foragers' who hunted moa and seals because this required the least effort for the greatest return. Characteristically, the people raided the environment.

Similarly, evolutionary biologists have attributed Eurasia's global dominance to environments favourable to technological advances. In global history, 'guns, germs and steel' won. Environmental variables determined that people could continue to be agriculturalists or 'hunter-gardeners' and warriors in New Zealand. Other environments were to shape a different future; the people who migrated from Cook Strait to the Chatham Islands, for example, were constrained by the cold to be hunter-gatherers.

Palaeobiologists have concluded that 'the New Zealand avifauna has been decimated by introduced mammalian predators, including people'. After surviving glacial–inter-glacial cycles, ecosystems vanished 'in a geologic instant, after humans arrived'. Key agents in the extinction of indigenous fauna were twelve species of predator foreign to New Zealand's ecosystem, and the humans who brought them, across a time span of 2000 years. First came the Pacific rat from the Cook Islands and Society Islands, and second Polynesian settlers with their dogs 1000 years later; the rest came after Captain Cook arrived. While Europeans brought the most animal predators, Maori precipitated most extinctions of native animals before that. New Zealand therefore serves as a model of how predators acted as agents of extinction on islands. Before European colonisation, the Pacific rat ate the little flightless birds, which had evolved undisturbed by a human presence, and eggs, while the tangata whenua – accustomed to birds as food – initially ate out the largest species, including the moa.

An intriguing aspect of this research is that the Pacific rat could only have arrived courtesy of Polynesian visitors. This animal-centred history has the potential to push back the arrival of the first visitors to New Zealand to nearly 2000 years ago, and this reinforces myths about early mariners who preceded the Polynesian settlers. It also pushes forward the estimated time of Polynesian settlement to just before 1300 AD; and rat DNA studies support the view that humans arrived on more than one trip.

Archaeologists agree with biologists about late settlement. But they are yet to accept that rats landed with early human visitors 1000 years before 'demonstrable' Polynesian colonisation, because there is no corroborating evidence such as 'documented extinction' of any bird species. Partly the disagreement is about method. Biologists model predator behaviour and view archaeological evidence as insufficient because traces of early human food and shelter could have been buried in the sand or eroded, obliterated by shifting coastlines. Archaeologists, on the other hand, look for middens and argue that predator–prey models are too simplistic because they fail to account for the complexity of cultural systems that governed the search for a food supply.

There is general agreement that the first settlers were primarily responsible for the extinction of the moa within 60 to 120 years of human settlement by over-killing and destruction of habitat. Humans also precipitated the disappearance of 40 per cent of the forest cover by fire after 1300, whether deliberately or unintentionally, and the extinction of half the animals before Europeans in turn transformed the landscape. Forests in Aotearoa lacked resistance to fire, unlike in Australia, and climate change could have contributed to deforestation. But fern and tussock thrived with firing, so that human intrusion to ensnare moa, for example, led to forest loss and erosion, especially in the east of the South Island where open forests gave way to tussock grassland. In the north, fire from swidden agriculture transformed the landscape as fern and scrub replaced the forest cover, offering more scope for harvesting bracken fern root and for kumara gardens.

Over time the climate grew harsher. Probably the wind and the weather restricted the initial choice of settlements to a few coastal districts. Patterns of archaeological sites suggest that people were initially drawn to the leeward zone, in the southern North Island and eastern half of the South Island, with their more open landscape, big game and easier foraging. Once human-induced changes to the environment forced people to adapt, however, settlements shifted to the windward, perhaps reinforced by cooler temperatures in the seventeenth century. Continued migrations reversed the pattern, with late migrations into the leeward zone, first into Hawkes Bay and the Wairarapa, then Wellington and across to the South Island. By about the late sixteenth century some Ngati Mamoe had begun to settle in the South Island. Ngati Kahungunu peoples moved into the Wairarapa soon after, motivating others to depart across Cook Strait. Probably at this time the population in general felt pressure on land and resources. After several migrations Ngai Tahu consolidated as an iwi in the South Island in the nineteenth century, to combat threats from the north. These migrations were continuing as Europeans arrived.

CREATING AN INDIGENOUS CULTURE

Who Maori were before they encountered Europe is not the same as who Maori were in the nineteenth or twentieth centuries. Tangata whenua did not become Maori until they engaged with Europeans, and faced being colonised. Conversely, Europeans only gradually became Pakeha. The term 'Maori' entered general use in the 1860s, to distinguish ordinary people from the newcomers, at the very moment when the ordinary folk found themselves outnumbered by Europeans. One problem with history as a discipline is that it begins not just with human societies but with the written record, so that people who possess an oral culture become people without a history. Risk attaches to any attempt to transcribe knowledge transmitted orally, as happened with waka traditions. Consequently the pre-European Maori past was frozen in time. Schooling imparted constructs of *The Maori As He Was* (ethnographer Elsdon Best's book title in 1934), reminiscent of the dying Maori as a museum artefact, not Maori as adaptive, resilient, stubborn survivors, even if Europeans respected the indigenous people as warriors, entrepreneurs and agriculturalists.

A historical best guess is that it took many generations for the first people to learn by trial and error what effort would yield the best return in a seasonal environment, and to develop conservation practices in areas where the climate and environment constrained horticulture. In Aotearoa they found the largest and coldest land in Polynesia, much more diverse than the small tropical islands of their ancestors, with unpredictable seasonal extremes that stretched their adaptability to the limit. Aotearoa proved a graveyard instead of a garden for the standard Polynesian fare of coconut, breadfruit and bananas. Cycles of abundance and dearth demanded inventiveness in adapting tropical agriculture to a temperate climate. Kumara grew no further south than Banks Peninsula on the South Island's east coast and became economically prominent only in the north, where in turn taro and yam only just tolerated the climate.

Kumara became the staple, as in Hawaii, because of adaptations in technique. Originally from Peru, this sweet potato could have been the key to successful settlement when imported tropical foods failed and large game such as moa and sea lions disappeared. The people who became Maori developed unique food storage methods, building insulated underground storage pits to provide kumara for winter meals and for seed tubers to plant in spring. They also warmed the soil to grow kumara by adding gravel, planting the sweet potato under stones covered with soot to absorb the heat. Fish, sea lettuce and wild plants and fruits such as karaka berries were dried and stored, and fish and birds were caught young when they were plump, and stored in their fat to carry the people through seasonal cycles.

There was much regional variation because of New Zealand's size and diversity. Gardening was a communal activity where the women planted, weeded, fetched and carried while the men dug the ground. Where the climate did not allow extensive cultivation, as in the south, the people transformed what were famine foods elsewhere in Polynesia into staples, notably fern root. Bitter, even toxic, plants became 'festive fare' in 'a remarkable example of "added value"', using methods of prolonged cooking and soaking that were practised across the Pacific. Southern Maori practised seasonal harvesting of fish, birds, seals and rats, as well as plants and their fruits, stems and roots. Different groups exchanged foods such as muttonbirds (sooty shearwaters) for a dish made from the head of the ti-kouka and different types of seafood. Throughout New Zealand fish and shellfish formed a major part of the diet and fishing a key part of the economy. In the North Island shellfish and crayfish were especially important.

Part of becoming Maori entailed applying Polynesian crafts to local resources. Women worked the native flax. They selected particular shells to scrape the tough flax leaves, and wove the strands into mats for clothing and to cover floors of houses; they also made baskets, thatch for roofs, rope and netting. Fibre fishing nets could be 1.5 to 3 km long. Men built houses and canoes. The land was abundant in tall timber such as totara and kauri in Northland, ideal for hollowing out logs to build single-hulled canoes. The waka made in New Zealand were long, narrow and fast, designed for river and coastal travel rather than epic oceanic voyages.

By about 1500 the leading features of Maori culture and society had been established. At their core were clearly defined concepts of collective identity with descent as the primary bond, where membership of an iwi or hapu derived from direct descent from a founding ancestor. Ngai Tahu, for example, are descendants of Tahu Potiki of Hawkes Bay. The dynamic culture that evolved mapped boundaries as the population grew, fostering concepts of land ownership and defence. Geographical features such as rivers and mountains, distinctive rock formations or even trees served as boundary markers. The whole of New Zealand and Rakiura became known and explored, bringing new encounters, such as with snow. On the West Coast of the South Island, explorers discovered greenstone which became a treasured item of trade.

From the early sixteenth century, settlements centred on elaborate fortified pa, symptomatic of sporadic warfare, except in the lower half of the South Island where a sparse population were mainly hunter-gatherers. Pa became a distinguishing feature of New Zealand, possibly because the building of pa was associated with developing notions of resource conservation; it became more difficult to feed on flesh or fat because of its scarcity and the evolving warrior culture became more specialised with food storage. With the development of a stratified society there was a flowering of art, especially wood carving, and public buildings such as marae. Maori created a competitive society where iwi competed among themselves, each community held together by land and kinship and by clusters of values that elevated obligations to kin above all else.

While Maori developed into fiercely competitive groups with a warrior class and culture, a splinter group – Moriori – found its way from the South Island to the Chatham Islands some time before 1500. This youngest group of eastern Polynesians gathered food in autumn and summer to preserve in the cold months. The harsh environment limited their food resources and shaped a simplified material culture whose efficiency (like that of Indigenous Australians) both Pakeha and Maori misunderstood. In contrast to Maori, Moriori adapted to be non-violent, sedentary hunter-gatherers who lived among their key resource, the fur seal, supplemented by shellfish, fish, birds, and fern root. These peaceful people were enslaved and butchered by displaced Taranaki Maori in 1835, who arrived on a European brig based at Sydney.

Despite such differences shaped by the environment, the first people spoke one language, although there were minor variations of dialect, and people from alien territories could make themselves understood. Importantly, one language eventually made it easy for tangata whenua to be understood by Europeans.

In the eighteenth century, people lived in hapu-based communities. As far as we know, the traditional dynamics of society centred on hapu before the challenges of colonisation compelled larger groupings of iwi descended from a common ancestor. From the eighteenth century, political and demographic fortunes of descent groups fluctuated. Some tribes such as Tainui, to the south of Auckland, and

Te Arawa, in the central North Island, stayed in the regions where their ancestral canoes had landed. Elsewhere people responded to warfare by migrating to new territory. Generally younger sons and daughters were the ones who moved on. Intermarriage followed between migrants and tangata whenua, with an exchange of women by the highest-ranking men. The next generation inherited their mana over the people from the conquering group of superior warriors, and mana over the land from the tangata whenua.

So it was for Ngati Whatua of Orakei (part of Auckland), who had kin links to many tribes and to several canoes. Through fighting, they extended their long move south to the Orakei area in the eighteenth century, incorporating earlier settlers in their ranks, until unified under a paramount chief, Te Kawau, in the nineteenth century. In the Maori manner, what is now central Auckland became the regrouped people's ancestral land through the recitation of whakapapa. Thus Ngati Whatua established their claim to be the tangata whenua of Auckland, having inherited mana over the people from the 'invading Te Taou line', and mana whenua from the 'ancient Ngaoho occupation'. Marriage networks ensured mana over both the people and the land: equilibrium required women as well as men.

2

Beachcrossers 1769–1839

So deep was Aotearoa in the watery world of the Pacific that it remained for long unknown to Europeans, other than as an imagined part of the mythical great southern land, Terra Australis. Surely there had to be a continent in the South Pacific to balance the weight of land in the Northern Hemisphere? As it proved, there was not. New Zealand is immersed in the Pacific, surrounded for 2000 kilometres by ocean, a fact that is reflected in Maori waka traditions. Only in the late eighteenth century did its full outline register in European consciousness through the process of physical discovery.

In 1500 no European had seen the world's largest ocean. Once they ventured into the Pacific, European sailors had great difficulty navigating its expanse, devoid of landmarks other than scattered islands and numerous uncharted reefs, and unpredictable in its treacherous currents, winds and weather. Geography and navigation remained uncertain. There were no reliable sea routes, other than within the narrow limits of latitude used by Spanish fleets from Acapulco in the Americas to Manila in Southeast Asia. For two centuries Europeans criss-crossed the Pacific Ocean along this track without charting the southern continent that they assumed awaited their discovery.

The European history of New Zealand can be located within a second phase of imperial expansion. Nearly three centuries after the establishment of European hegemony in the Atlantic with the colonisation of the Americas, neo-Europes were transplanted to the Pacific to produce new nations and political forms through colonialism. The delay in incorporating Oceania into European

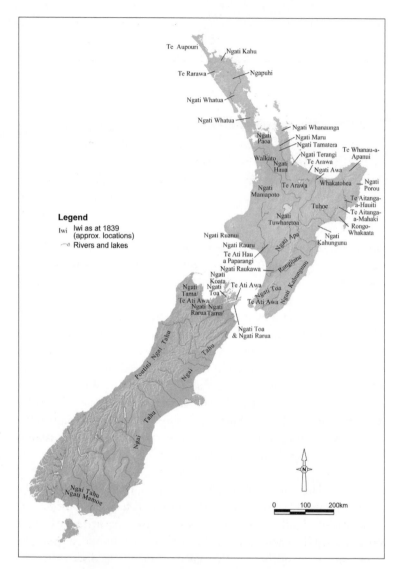

Te Aupouri
Ngati Kahu
Te Rarawa
Ngapuhi
Ngati Whatua
Ngati Whatua
Ngati Whanaunga
Ngati
Paoa
Ngati Maru
Ngati Tamatera
Te Whanau-a-
Apanui
Waikato
Ngati Terangi
Ngati
Haua
Te Arawa
Ngati Awa
Ngati
Maniapoto
Te Arawa
Whakatohea
Ngati
Porou
Te Aitanga-
a-Hauiti
Tuhoe
Te Aitanga-
a-Mahaki
Ngati
Tuwharetoa
Rongo-
Whakaata
Ngati Ruanui
Ngati
Kahungunu
Ngati Apa
Ngati Rauru
Te Ati Hau
a Paparangi
Rangitane
Ngati Raukawa
Ngati
Koata
Ngati
Tama/
Ngati
Toa
Te Ati Awa
Ngati Toa
Te Ati Awa/
Ngati
Rarua
Ngati
Tama/
Te Ati Awa
Ngati Kahungunu

Ngati Toa
& Ngati Rarua

Poutini Ngai Tahu
Tahu
Ngai
Ngai
Tahu
Ngai Tahu
Ngati Mamoe

Legend

Iwi   Iwi as at 1839
(approx. locations)
Rivers and lakes

0   100   200km

N

2.1   Maori tribes (iwi), c.1839

maps and power systems was significant. Spaniards, seeking Terra
Australis from the late sixteenth century, sailed through Torres Strait
without identifying Australia. Their ventures sparked the belief
that sailors from a lost Spanish caravel discovered New Zealand.
Dutch explorers sought Terra Australis in the seventeenth century.

Because of the inaccuracies in establishing coordinates – longitude as well as latitude – in navigation, numerous Dutch East India Company ships were wrecked along the Western Australian coast, far from their objective of Batavia (Jakarta). Only in 1642 did Abel Tasman head eastwards from Batavia to Tasmania, which he named Van Diemen's Land, and from there to New Zealand. Hence New Zealand acquired a Dutch name, and schoolchildren learnt to recite that in 1642 Abel Tasman 'sailed the ocean blue', and discovered New Zealand for Europe.

In one view, it was fortunate for Maori, as for other Pacific people, that they escaped a rapacious first era in European imperialism. Now Europe was obsessed less with conquest than with commerce. But New Zealand scholars argue that Maori were active in postponing their encounter with Europe. In Tasman's experience, Maori controlled the first contact, and so – consistent with his instructions, which distinguished 'civilised' natives from 'wild savages' – he constructed them not as the 'noble savage' but as violent. Tasman's whole object was to learn 'whether there is anything profitable to be got or effected'. He decided the answer was no, interpreting the Maori challenge to fight as evidence that they were the 'opposite-footers' whom Europeans fancied ought to live in the Antipodes. Using speed and surprise, the local people of Golden Bay, which Tasman named Murderers Bay, rammed a boat and killed four sailors. It was this repulsion by the 'Southlanders' that entered European stories, and rendered the Maori frightening to Europe.

CAPTAIN COOK

Unlike Tasman, James Cook actually crossed New Zealand beaches, literally and metaphorically, and became New Zealand's Pakeha storybook ancestor. Like the Maori mythical ancestors such as Maui, Kupe and Paikea, Cook was a great navigator, explorer and supreme leader. This parallel made him a model for nation-building. But his Britishness made him infinitely more suitable than Tasman as a founding ancestor and he has contributed enormously to the country's national myth-making. Lieutenant James Cook (as he was on his first visit) literally put New Zealand on the world map, being the first person to chart its full outline.

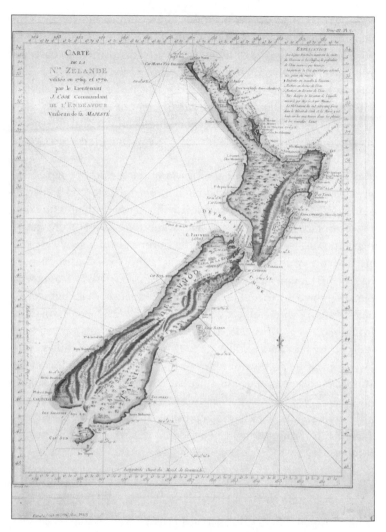

2.2 Carte de la Nle Zélande visitée en 1769 et 1770 par le
Lieutenant J. Cook Commandant d l'Endeavour vaisseau de
sa Majesté. Paris: Saillant et Nyon, 1774, the French version
of Cook's chart.

Cook spent nearly a year exploring the coastline during his four
stays in New Zealand. On his critical first voyage he and his men
stayed six months while he drew his famous chart, which is astonishingly accurate but for the sketch of Stewart Island as a peninsula and
Banks Peninsula as an island (2.2). His maps and journals recording

the land's and the sea's resources in timber, flax and sealife precipitated the process that led to British colonisation. The knowledge which he, the botanist Joseph Banks and ships' artists assembled still informs international scholarship and general understanding of what New Zealand was like in the eighteenth century.

Ostensibly subsequent British settlement, more than his voyages, determined Cook as the founding ancestor, because settlement from the United Kingdom allowed New Zealanders (and Australians) to look back to the *Endeavour* voyage of 1769–70 as the opening chapter of their founding stories. Yet the timing of Cook's epic explorations in itself rendered him a new type of hero for European expansion and Pacific imperialism in the late eighteenth century. Cook was an Enlightenment hero, making him an ideal model for the classroom; he was a Christian paragon of humble origins. A self-made man who represented a New World freedom to get on, he rose to fame through merit and brought a message of free trade, enlarged scientific knowledge and civilised behaviour. As explorer and surveyor, he commanded new technologies, and expanded the contemporary information age by publishing his journals. A plain man, he upgraded homely virtues to evoke professionalism and skill, just in time to become the 'new hero of free and civilised trading'. He embodied the parallel breakthroughs in European printing and exploration, the innovation by a 'large class of mechanical tinkerers' that produced the 'European miracle' of economic development and made the British Empire. His voyages ensured that he did not just belong to New Zealand; he became Cook of Australia, and in Canada, Cook of Quebec, and Cook of coastal British Columbia.

The 'humanist myth' of Cook as a product of the Enlightenment prevalent in New Zealand surprises overseas scholars. The foremost Cook scholars have been New Zealanders, among whom J. C. Beaglehole, editor of Cook's journals and his biographer, is his greatest panegyrist. Beaglehole's Cook was a 'man of action' who left nothing unattempted. He more than fulfilled his instructions, to observe the transit of Venus in Tahiti; to proceed to discover the southern continent; and if that failed, to explore the coast of Tasman's New Zealand. 'He was the genius of the matter of fact', a 'profoundly competent' seaman, 'completely professional' as an explorer; but above all a navigator, who discovered and mapped the country for Britain. He was also humanitarian. Aware that Cook was different on his third voyage, harsh, with outbursts of rage, Beaglehole attributed this conflicting evidence to a physical cause. Geography and navigation were his memorials. The Maori memory of Cook, he concluded, confirmed the view that Cook was a great man.

Equally, this fits well with the belief that New Zealand set an example in race relations. Aided by the Tahitian intermediary Tupaia, Cook and his crew could speak with Maori, who he realised shared a source of origin with other Polynesians. On the first two voyages he tried to act as a man of the Enlightenment, and Maori appeared to respect him as a leader.

Initially remembered as the consummate imperial explorer, memorialised in documents and on the 50c coin (in 1967), he became both a white founding father and a hero for bicultural New Zealand. Maori stories of first meetings focused on Cook; their ancestors had met Cook; his ships connected Maori and other Pacific Islanders to the European world, and 'began the process of making the world a global village'. Captain Cook stories, and places he named, acquired significance for Maori as well as for Pakeha. One example is Young Nick's Head (named for Nicholas Young), whose purchase by an American investor local iwi opposed in 2002, arguing that the headland was a historic site of national importance. In contrast to Indigenous Australians, Maori did not reject Cook's offerings as 'terrible hard biscuits'. Rather they seized Cook's knowledge enthusiastically, just as he and his scholarly passengers keenly observed Maori.

The most famous encounter is that of Horeta Te Taniwha. Every major New Zealand history cites this story of a small boy who was given a nail by Cook; so does a late twentieth-century collection of stories about Maori childhood. In a version written in 1888,

. . . There was one supreme man in that ship. We knew that he was the lord of the whole by his perfect gentlemanly and noble demeanour. He seldom spoke, but some of the goblins spoke much . . . He was a very good man, and came to us – the children – and patted our cheeks, and gently touched our heads.

Critics of the humanist Cook myth argue that this much-repeated story cannot represent reality if only because a missionary first recorded Te Taniwha's account in his extreme old age, more than 80 years after the event. Rather it signifies the triumph of a white over a subaltern voice. Some anthropologists argue that the Horeta Te Taniwha story illustrates the European myth of the apotheosis of Captain Cook; Europeans needed Cook to be a god, and so had him deified by Polynesians. Yet this story is an example of collaboration, as it contains evidence of Maori input and a Maori world view. Cook is certainly remembered as a paternalistic father figure. But it was not he but his ship the *Endeavour* that was described as a god. The 'supreme man', he was perceived as a chief. Significantly, his men were termed goblins. Unlike gods, goblins could be tricked or overpowered; they could be less, not more, than human and therefore easy to manage or dupe.

At times Cook did react violently to the bizarreness of contact and was disconcerted by Maori resistance, even in the face of European firepower. On his first visit, he left without a sailor killed or wounded, while Maori lost ten men killed and many wounded. With colonisation, however, the Enlightenment view gained ground. Its development has a simple explanation: Cook's triumphant first two voyages – especially the first, in 1769–70 – belong more to New Zealand history than his third tragic voyage, during which his ships again anchored in Queen Charlotte Sound in 1777. He died violently in Hawaii two years later, entangled in contradictions.

FRENCH EXPLORERS

A common French view is that Cook brought his fate upon himself through his violent behaviour. This perspective is unsurprising given that France was Britain's enemy until 1815 and a competitor for imperial dominance in the Pacific. French explorers have been neglected in New Zealand. British naming rights decided the hierarchy of the three highest peaks in the Southern Alps visible from the coastline, named in descending order by height Cook, Tasman and La Perouse after the earliest European explorers to see them. While the first two are familiar to New Zealanders, La Perouse is not. Galaup de La Pérouse had sailed from France on a major Pacific voyage in 1785 and received instructions to report on the British penal settlement at Sydney, which he did early in 1788. Then his two ships vanished. Another explorer, D'Entrecasteaux, searched for the lost expedition in the 1790s, tarrying in northern New Zealand in 1793 and finding nothing. The name La Perouse suggests that the best memory of the French is of a vanishing act, or less cynically that French explorers ranked third in importance.

It is often forgotten that a French explorer entered New Zealand waters at the same time as Cook. On an unscheduled visit, Jean-François de Surville sought shelter because his crew were succumbing to scurvy; he sighted Northland in December 1769. By coincidence, Cook was sailing up the opposite coast at the same time. The *St Jean-Baptiste* sailed past the *Endeavour* in a gale without the knowledge of either, the British ship blown north while the French ship veered south.

The resultant encounter between Maori and Surville's crew proved a negative experience for both sides. Angry that Maori removed a yawl washed up on the beach, Surville's men kidnapped a man who had been kind to crew suffering from scurvy, and set fire to buildings in retaliation. They also formed a more negative view of Maori women than did the English sailors, who had been influenced by earlier exposure to Tahiti. When Marion du Fresne landed at the Bay of Islands in 1772, previous experience shaped the encounter on both sides. Du Fresne had already observed and formed negative assumptions about Aboriginal Tasmanians, and the local Maori had experience of Europeans with their guns.

Du Fresne's story has served as a parable for how misunderstanding led to violence. Although the Frenchman was a Maoriphile who made great efforts to befriend the tangata whenua, the chief Te Kauri killed him because he violated a potent death tapu. People throughout Polynesia observed controlling restrictions to order their worlds. In du Fresne's case, he insulted both the living and their ancestors by fishing at a tapu cove, where men had drowned. 'To catch these fish was bad enough, but to eat them was tantamount to cannibalism, an attack on the tapu of the corpses and that of their tribe, and on the mana of their tribal gods.' So – like Cook in Hawaii – du Fresne was killed and eaten, to consume his life force and his mana. Thus overpowered, he could not be celebrated in Maori or European narratives. Rather, histories have tended to imply that, as a Frenchman, he deserved his punishment, killed after a 'series of blunders'. His deputy, Julien Crozet, simply confirmed that the French were inhumane relative to the English by seeking revenge through massacre. Anne Salmond's work on cultural encounter, however, has drawn a more nuanced picture in which du Fresne became caught in Maori rivalries as well as cross-culturally, between worlds.

AUSTRALIAN LINKS

Soon after first contact Maori discovered a larger world that embraced and extended from Australasia. The hub for new networks was Sydney, once Maori became enmeshed in the British strategic decisions to establish the convict settlement of New South Wales. The first Maori to visit Australia were Tuki, a priest, and Huru, a warrior, from the Bay of Islands, in 1793. Having adventurously boarded a supply ship, the two young beachcrossers found themselves transported to Norfolk Island, to fulfil a request for Maori instructors from Philip King, the future Governor of New South Wales, who wanted convicts taught how to dress flax for rope. Dressing flax was women's work. Nevertheless Tuki and Huru's forced overseas trip evolved into what Maori saw as an alliance between King at Sydney and chiefs in the Bay of Islands. Dozens of Maori sailed to Sydney as heads of state, entrepreneurs, tourists and students, to acquire new knowledge and technology.

Inevitably, European mental maps helped to shape Maori perceptions of Indigenous Australians, with negative results. As Governor King recorded in 1806, the northern chief Te Pahi, his guest at Government House, and Tuki before him, showed a 'marked contempt' for the 'natives of this country'. Maori were contemptuous of their 'going naked', and in particular of their 'most trifling mode of warfare'. While King believed in the European race hierarchy, his New Zealand visitors came to share disdain for people whom they perceived as nomads rather than as warriors and agriculturalists. They also shared the British military disdain for European convicts on the basis that they were 'slaves', or war captives. Te Pahi and his four sons returned from Sydney with bricks and a prefabricated house, frontier status symbols.

Visits by young Maori on whaling ships to Sydney stimulated Governor King's interest in New Zealand after 1800. Whalers – hard men on ships from the United States, Sydney, Hobart and later France – were the 'largest group of European agents of contact' with New Zealand. They did a brisk trade with Maori, who supplied ships with pork and potatoes acquired in turn from their diplomatic relations with the colony of New South Wales. Maori themselves became involved in the business of whaling and, because of concern for Maori and Pacific Island crew, arising through stories of kidnap and brutality, Governor King issued a government order in the *Sydney Gazette* in 1805 giving Maori and other Pacific Islanders some of the civil rights of British subjects: they were not to suffer ill-treatment, but were to be protected in property and claims for wages.

In southern New Zealand from the 1790s, sealing gangs – including ex-convicts, escaped convicts and deserters – landed around the coast, to collect skins for the China market. In an effort to protect the British monopoly on trade held by the East India Company as far as Australasia, Governor King banned sealing more than 43 degrees south. But Simeon Lord, a rich ex-convict and now merchant in Sydney, subverted this policy by conniving with American captains and military officers who ran the colonial government. Thus although sealers who discovered a new sealing ground in New Zealand in 1804 at first kept the news to themselves, they soon gained official support. On assuming command after Governor Bligh's overthrow in 1808, the obscure official Joseph Foveaux, after whom Foveaux Strait is named, allowed sealing gangs to head immediately to the strait. Thanks to the military interregnum at Sydney, Stewart Island landmarks bear names from Australia left by the sealing rush.

The Maori response was pragmatic. If the visitors launched unauthorised assaults on their resources, they were attacked. If they were useful in trade, becoming friends, they were found wives. In the process, their children acquired Maori genealogies, particularly around Foveaux Strait, where Ngai Tahu incorporated select sealers and whalers into their communities. Subsequently they intermarried with whalers who established shore whaling stations from the late 1820s, as part of a defence strategy against northern encroachment.

Like whalers and beachcombers such as escaped convicts and crew, the Christian Church reached New Zealand from Australia, initially the Church of England, followed by the Wesleyans. The Anglican mission was delayed when bad relations between whalers and Maori led to trans-Tasman atrocities. Notably the *Boyd* was burnt and her crew killed, news of which reached Sydney in 1810.

2.3 Lieutenant George F. Dashwood, Maoris, 1832, Sydney,
bow of ship with men working on deck: two are wearing top
hats while the carved prow shows a European influence; wash
drawing from the albums of Lt George Dashwood

Sadly, Te Pahi was blamed for this 'massacre', changing in colonial
eyes from a 'friendly chief' to a 'treacherous cannibal'. The British
fiscal-military state reacted by warning whalers to be vigilant in
their dealings with New Zealanders and Pacific Islanders, who were
a 'treacherous race' and 'not to be trusted'. Once again, intersecting
worlds provided scope for Maori agency but also tragedy.

Historians and anthropologists have highlighted Maori initiative
in the missionaries' arrival in New Zealand; in particular, the trans-
Tasman entrepreneur Ruatara of Ngapuhi befriended Samuel Marsden, the Anglican chaplain based at Parramatta in New South Wales.
By negotiating with Marsden, Ruatara secured a monopoly over the
first permanent European settlement in the Bay of Islands, and managed the Anglican mission and missionaries to enhance his mana. In
effect, Ruatara was an early consultant on European relations.

As to Marsden, historians have told of two: Australia's 'flogging
parson', loathed by the convicts for his cruelty, and New Zealand's

humane missionary. The Anglican chaplain is remembered in the Pakeha story as a good man, the first missionary who preached the first Christian sermon to Maori on Christmas Day. He turned to New Zealand in 1814 after failures in the Pacific mission of the Church Missionary Society and among convicts and Indigenous Australians in New South Wales. From Ruatara and other travellers Marsden learnt that rangatira wielded authority over tangata. Among such New Zealand clients he saw both trading prospects and an opportunity for his mission of British order. So did northern chiefs, who had their own motives for a Sydney connection.

Both sides worked to develop that link. To secure imperial sanction for the Anglican mission to New Zealand, Marsden collected a sheaf of complaints about European aggressions in the Pacific that he placed before the Governor. Accordingly, Governor Lachlan Macquarie issued a proclamation in December 1813 that effectively placed Maori 'under the protection of His Majesty' and bound British subjects by British law in their dealings with Maori and Pacific Islanders. The following year, twelve rangatira from the Bay of Islands stayed three months at Parramatta with Marsden, including Ruatara, his half-brother and Ruatara's relative Hongi Hika, a Ngapuhi warrior chief, and Hongi's son, all busy learning English, and about European-style agriculture, gardening and carpentry. This chiefly assemblage returned with Marsden and three missionaries to New Zealand in December 1814.

Architecturally and evangelically, the missionary settlement established at Kerikeri in the Bay of Islands became a 'pocket Parramatta'. The stone store at Parramatta, built in 1809, provided the plan for what is now New Zealand's oldest heritage building, the stone store at Kerikeri; while Marsden's house at Parramatta, 'Old Rangehoo' (Rangihoua, the name of the first missionary base in New Zealand), became the model for the Kerikeri Mission House. Marsden built the Australian Rangihoua in 1819 as a seminary for high-ranking young Maori. The Anglican mission in New Zealand remained marginal until the 1830s, useful more to northern tribes as an entrée to European technology, literacy and commerce. Hongi Hika inherited monopolistic control over the first Anglican missionaries from Ruatara. Missionaries in New Zealand before 1830 had the status of Maori property, over whom Hongi Hika retained

2.4 James Barry, The Rev. Thomas Kendall and the Maori
chiefs Hongi and Waikato, London, 1820. Hongi stands in
the centre. He holds a taiaha (long club) in his right hand and
a mere (club) in his left.

his monopoly until his death. From his seat in the Bay of Islands,
he obliged the missionaries to deal with him on his terms, which
included surreptitious trading in muskets.

For Maori, Hongi Hika is more important than Marsden. The
one-time seminarian was one among dozens of trans-Tasman Maori
travellers and entrepreneurs who engaged closely in trade with colonial New South Wales. Trans-Tasman chiefs are impressive examples
of the Maori presence in Australia since the 1800s.

Hongi Hika became famous in New Zealand, however, by ven-
turing to London in 1820, where he succeeded in his quest to see
King George IV; he also assisted a Cambridge professor to compile
a Maori dictionary. Hongi sailed to England on a whaling schooner,
accompanied by his friend the young lay preacher Thomas Kendall,
and Waikato, his aide-de-camp. Kendall was not authorised to go
but was determined to pursue study of the Maori language as a vehi-
cle for conversion. In England, Hongi was fêted in society, receiving

many valuable gifts, which he traded on the Sydney market the following year for over 300 muskets, powder and shot. But he did not exchange all his gifts; he kept a suit of armour and a helmet that saved his life on several occasions.

THE MUSKET WARS

By the 1800s inter-tribal warfare was intensifying. Some argue that the Maori population peaked about 1800 and the increased scarcity of resources fuelled hostilities. Tougher resource constraints confirm the argument for late settlement of Aotearoa, whereby Maori adapted fast to ecological changes caused by human activity. When competition was already intense among rival hapu, it was inevitable that European contact would overcook things and unleash unprecedented conflict. The process of using warfare to resolve disputes accelerated between 1815 and 1840, abetted by the trans-Tasman connection, the details of which are complex and controversial. Hitherto Maori warfare had been seasonal and highly ritualistic, with relatively few deaths. European guns – muskets, double-barrelled muskets and pistols – were more deadly and produced more devastating effects. The musket wars, as they became known, could just as well be called 'land wars' because so much territory changed hands in their wake. Some scholars also attribute the wars to the white potato which was an easier food to grow and for war parties to carry.

Muskets and potatoes are commonly associated with Hongi Hika because he introduced the musket into inter-tribal warfare. Offensives began in the north, when Hongi equipped an army and laid waste opponents on an unparalleled scale. Long-distance raiding did not require guns and potatoes, however. Customarily warrior victors lived at the expense of their enemies. Hongi aimed to outdo his rivals, not to conquer strangers, and manipulated the new staple items of trade to strengthen Maori values and institutions.

One view is that escaped convicts from Tasmania on the *Venus* triggered the wars in 1806–7, when they kidnapped high-ranking Ngapuhi women – close kin of Hongi Hika and his ally Te Morenga – whom they dumped at various beaches, to be killed by other tribes. Another is that the core element of reciprocity in Maori cultural relations required utu (repayment) for an offence to any group in order to avoid loss of mana and to restore balance and order. Therefore the way the Maori political system operated in seeking restitution for this particular offence, and for earlier wars, explained what happened subsequently. Twelve years later Ngapuhi sought utu from the East Coast peoples, using their new strength in muskets. In 1818 Te Morenga and Hongi Hika led hundreds of warriors on two taua (raids) against hapu in the Bay of Plenty. The very day in 1820 that Hongi left for the United Kingdom, Te Morenga's party returned to the Bay of Islands in 50 canoes with hundreds of dried heads, about 200 slaves, and all the canoes of a chief who had killed one of the women kidnapped years before.

As a result of the wars, three great warrior chiefs became the most powerful figures in New Zealand: Hongi Hika of Ngapuhi, Te Wherowhero of the Waikato and Te Rauparaha of Ngati Toa. The campaigns themselves led Ngati Toa to migrate south first to Taranaki and then to the Wellington region, where Te Rauparaha set out to provide for the future of his people.

Scholars who conceptualise the musket wars in terms of the use of guns and potatoes order the wars into three phases. First, tribes acquired a few muskets, mainly from whalers, enough for a shock effect; second, they acquired hundreds of muskets and built an inventory of food to support large armies, thanks to an agricultural revolution in the cultivation of potatoes; and third, tribes accumulated excess guns. At all phases, muskets were acquired through trade in food, women via sex slavery and prostitution, tattooed heads in the 1820s and, later, dressed flax for the Sydney market. Demand for labour to stockpile trade goods increased the urgency to launch raiding parties who could bring back the slaves required. The embellished workforce in turn made it easier to launch raiding parties as, for a fast-growing food supply, Maori planted potatoes, a job that women or slaves could do while the men went to fight. Not all raid victims were kept for hard labour as a common meat supply for taua was kai-tangata (cannibalism, the term being a combination of the words for food and people), as ritualistic punishment yielded to mass warfare. But the hundreds of surviving slaves, forced to grow more food and earn more weapons, helped tribes to proceed from phase to phase through greater access to Europeans and muskets.

The wars, then, arose from and produced ripple effects. For instance, Hongi Hika returned in 1821 with over 300 muskets bought in Sydney, which made Ngapuhi the most powerful force in New Zealand and left the Auckland area depopulated for fear of raids. In 1822 he invaded the Waikato, forcing Te Rauparaha and his people to migrate. In turn Ngati Toa migrants and their allies launched raid after raid against tangata whenua, and used the fortress island of Kapiti as a base to trade with European ships and mount attacks. In 1824 Ngati Toa leader Te Pehi Kupe emulated Hongi Hika and travelled to England, returning to Kapiti four years later with more arms bought in Sydney. Like Hongi, he traded gifts received in Europe for muskets across the Tasman, which his tribe subsequently used in invasions of the South Island. Ngai Tahu used muskets for the first time in 1825, against other hapu, escalating internal conflict within the tribe. Waikato musket power balanced that of Ngapuhi by 1827, and Hongi Hika's death in 1828 marked the end of unbridled Ngapuhi power. As the pressure pushed southwards, Te Rauparaha invaded the South Island in the summer of 1827–28, causing much bloodshed when he used muskets against traditional weapons. For the next six years he led campaigns south.

Not all inter-tribal wars between 1807 and 1840 were musket wars. To be so they would have had to involve Ngapuhi until the late 1820s. Nor did muskets guarantee victory, as in hand-to-hand combat. Yet the wars were not simply inter-tribal wars. Never before had warfare raged across the entire country. New ideas and strategies apart from gunfire disturbed tribal dynamics and called for new institutions to stabilise society. The wars were not just fought on traditional terms but were a 'modern catastrophe for Maori', demonstrating the full explosive power of native/newcomer relations.

Two infamous episodes involved direct European input. The turning point which hooked New Zealand into the British Empire came in 1830, instigated by Te Rauparaha, who approached the English Captain Stewart for assistance against Ngai Tahu chief Te Maiharanui in revenge for the killing of Te Pehi Kupe. Stewart agreed to transport Te Rauparaha and 70 armed men to Akaroa Harbour on the brig *Elizabeth* in exchange for a cargo of dressed flax. At Akaroa the crew helped lure an unsuspecting Te Maiharanui into the captain's cabin where he was handcuffed. The same evening Te Rauparaha's warriors attacked the pa on shore. The false sense of security engendered in Ngai Tahu by the presence of a European vessel compounded the offence, as did the rape by crew of 'affrighted and fugitive women'. Stewart and the *Elizabeth* transported baskets of cooked human flesh back to Kapiti, with the captive Te Maiharanui and his wife, the former denigrated by restraint in irons. Stewart used the chiefly couple as security for his payment of flax, and on delivery they suffered a terrible death. Te Rauparaha then sought to capitalise on his *Elizabeth* expedition by attacking the Ngai Tahu stronghold at Kaiapoi, north of Christchurch, in the summer of 1831–32. After a siege the pa fell. Te Rauparaha pursued refugees to a pa in Akaroa Harbour, where he used his chiefly captives from Kaiapoi as a ruse to gain entry, ostensibly to discuss peace. Once inside, his warriors opened fire. Unsurprisingly, Ngai Tahu long harboured a desire for utu against Te Rauparaha.

In the second notorious episode, Ngati Mutunga and Ngati Tama from Taranaki invaded the Chatham Islands in 1835, having seized a brig and its captain – whose involvement was this time unwilling – in Wellington Harbour. It took two trips to carry the cargo of about 900 people, seed potatoes and waka to the Chathams. The outcome was tragic. The Moriori formed a peace council in response to the invaders, who misinterpreted it as a war council, limited by their own cultural constructs that could not conceive of non-violence, and embarked on a bloody and ruthless campaign to crush them. The Moriori population numbered 1660 in 1835, and 101 by 1862. Thus encounters with Europe led to displacement of Maori, who in turn used European technology and people to dispossess Moriori. The musket wars finally ended in the Chatham Islands in 1840, when the feuding Maori were themselves separated by land purchases. The wars also had long-term effects in the Wellington region that the invaders had left, because they bequeathed the mana whenua that they claimed in the area, as migrants, to their Te Ati Awa kin Te Wharepouri, who had also led a migration south from Taranaki. Insecure in his rights over the land, Te Wharepouri found it expedient not long afterwards to sell the Wellington district to the New Zealand Company, for a paltry price that included muskets and gunpowder, because the presence of settlers offered protection.

The effects of the musket wars were horrendous. Tribes were redistributed and thousands killed, wounded or displaced between 1806 and 1845. Massive population displacement, especially the pressure of southward migrations by Ngati Toa and allied Taranaki tribes, proved devastating around Cook Strait, in the South Island and the Chatham Islands. Entire districts were depopulated, making way for future European settlement. Tribal boundaries were redrawn. Victors enjoyed the spoils, ousting tangata whenua from their homelands less than twenty years before the Treaty of Waitangi.

The effects therefore resonate in the present, in current locations of tribes; disputes over tribal authority, and resentment about land loss just before the Treaty of Waitangi froze the distribution of power. Surveys and land sales inhibited movement and inscribed boundaries after 1840. Musket warfare had devastating effects on the mana of some iwi; new tribes enjoyed dominance, notably Ngapuhi in the north, Ngati Toa around Cook Strait, and Ngati Tuwharetoa on the volcanic plateau. Iwi who were invaded tended to form more concentrated groupings in self-defence. Large areas were depopulated or left sparsely settled because of disputes over ownership, such as around the future sites of Auckland and Wellington, where European land speculators could acquire the disputed land by purchase before 1840, to the speculators' advantage, because vulnerable groups sought a Pakeha shield.

Depopulation wrought havoc with land claims. Yet tangata whenua survived the onslaught, many returning to their former territories or intermarrying with invading tribes. Sadly, one response to seeing descendants die was to sell ancestral lands. That at least saw claims vindicated against those of rivals. With the work of the Waitangi Tribunal, however, historians have asked whether the government should recognise boundaries in 1840, based on conquests achieved through European weapons. To which others reply that many of the inter-tribal wars would have happened anyway.

For the warfare spiral to subside, a new equilibrium had to be reached that incorporated the newcomers. While missionaries claimed that they had ended the wars, the coming of peace spread Christianity rather than vice versa. Out of the debate over the extent and nature of the Maori 'conversion' a consensus has emerged about the role of former slaves, converted to Christianity during their imprisonment, who spread literacy and Maori versions of the gospel to their tribes on returning home. Christianity offered a revolutionary model of governance where laws created by the state protected peace. In the realm of ideas, Christianity proved revelatory.

Maori seized every opportunity presented by culture contact to improve their circumstances and break out of ecological constraints. Once Ngapuhi had muskets the rest of the country had to have them. At one level the wars only ended with a balance of firepower and modern pa designed for musket warfare. The wars created a large body of strategists with decades of expertise with guns and the know-how to employ European technology against Europeans. Yet the critical innovation – on the ground – was land purchase.

THE MOVE FROM MINIMUM INTERVENTION

No wonder that historians have described Colonial Office strategy as lethargic in response. Britain had wide-ranging global interests that remained centred on Europe and containing France. Empire comprised a mere fraction of strategic and commercial interests, and Australasia even less so. Not that the Colonial Office knew much about it; its mandarins relied on letters and written reports for intelligence from far-flung officials, governors, military officers, and informal agents such as missionaries and their parent societies.

Chiefs from the Bay of Islands in 1831 petitioned William IV for protection by Britain against its subjects and French ambitions. Token official intervention began in May 1833 with the arrival of James Busby as British Resident, reluctantly paid for by the Colony of New South Wales. The initiative came not from London but from Sydney, in order to be seen to be doing something about the *Elizabeth* atrocity. Sydney businessmen realised that inter-racial strife in New Zealand would hurt their profits. Busby and his wife built their home (now called the Treaty House) on a farm that they established at Waitangi. Busby was a civil official, not a military officer with access to an army. In effect the first police officer, his job was the 'maintenance of tranquillity', which included apprehending escaped convicts. Maori soon came to call him 'the watch-dog without teeth', and indigenous law prevailed. Internal dynamics in the South Pacific region were already asserting their primacy, obliging the colonial government based at Sydney to extend perfunctory policing to New Zealand.

London, meanwhile, supplied the theory of a new Christian imperialism, provided it was done on the cheap. At the Colonial Office, Sir James Stephen held evangelical Christian and humanitarian

2.5 George F. Angas, Motupoi [Motuopuhi] Pah with [Mt] Tongariro, 1844. This Ngati Tuwharetoa pa was attacked in 1828.

beliefs that became dominant in discourses of British racial superiority and imperial destiny in the 1830s. 'A clearer racial hierarchy was emerging', underlined by the notion that 'independency' – an idea from the Scottish moral philosophers – was a prerequisite of civic virtue. According to this arrangement, societies moved through 'stages' of development to high civilisation through the application of industry. As modified by evangelicalism, the Christian empire should intervene and speed up this process of development. The concept of freedom of contract leapt into fashion precisely when this transformation of empire was under way, and Australasia exemplified this global assertion of the 'rights of freeborn Englishmen'.

How would those rights apply in New Zealand? In the mid-1830s the imperial government had no motive to seize sovereignty, and in any case had to overcome the inertia imposed by lack of funds. Busby as Resident was powerless; his own property was broken into. But he featured in two episodes that have had lasting symbolic significance. First, he thought up the idea of a flag in 1834 to be flown by

New Zealand (Maori) shipping, chosen by northern chiefs, so that their ships could freely enter Australian ports. Maori had their own motives for the flag, which became a symbol of Maori sovereignty and identity. Second, he devised a Declaration of Independence in 1835, signed by 35 chiefs convened as 'The United Tribes of New Zealand' – and subsequently by another 17 chiefs – that deemed New Zealand an independent state under British protection. While this resembled petitions elsewhere in the Pacific, northern rangatira believed that it declared their sovereignty. In a case of back to the future, a reinvented United Tribes of Aotearoa, based in Northland, asserted their independent sovereignty in the 1990s, on the grounds that their ancestors had signed the declaration of 1835.

Historians agree that Busby intended the declaration to make New Zealand a British protectorate to warn off the French. For some, Busby needed a pretext to convene a meeting of chiefs, and found it in a letter from Tahiti by Charles de Thierry, announcing that he intended to establish an independent state in New Zealand, on land that he believed he had bought from the missionary Thomas Kendall. Because de Thierry styled himself 'Sovereign Chief of New Zealand', Busby had little trouble persuading local chiefs that he posed a threat. Others argue that Busby was genuinely alarmed. As he explained to Governor Bourke in Sydney, he responded by calling a meeting of chiefs

in order that they may declare the independence of this country, and assert as a collective body their entire and exclusive right to its sovereignty, and their determination to maintain that right in its integrity, and to treat as a Public Enemy any person who proposes to assume a right of sovereignty within their territories . . .

Bourke was unimpressed, given that this flouted the doctrine of *terra nullius* that operated throughout Australia by the 1830s. It is still debated whether this document amounted to a declaration of sovereignty or merely a trans-Tasman assertion of British law. It might have been designed to be both, with two different sets of readers in mind.

In England the Church Missionary Society opposed colonisation on the grounds that it led to wrongs and injuries to indigenous people. Instead the Anglicans, and their rival Wesleyans, supported cautious formal British entry. In a mounting fervour, the missionaries pressed 'fatal impact' arguments upon the Colonial Office as a reason to intervene, that New Zealand would soon be destitute of aboriginal inhabitants. Imperialism and humanitarianism 'march[ed] together' towards the annexation of New Zealand, with missionaries to the fore. Some see fatal impact as an expedient pretext for the 'fatal necessity' of extending the British Empire to New Zealand. Modern histories attach less weight to missionaries, and more to colonial government – especially its trans-Tasman functioning – and interactions with Maori. But it remains a fact critical for understanding New Zealand that the timing of the beginnings of formal British intervention coincided with the rise of the humanitarian movement and faith in Christian British imperialism. The world was a different place by 1839 from the late eighteenth century when British authorities established a convict colony at Sydney.

Sectarianism within the church influenced local factionalist politics. Roman Catholicism conveyed by priests, and later nuns, from France and Ireland provided Maori with an alternative politics, a means to compete with their Protestant neighbours and to assert an independent identity. Before the first Catholic priest, Monsignor Pompallier, arrived from France in 1838, northern chiefs had already sent two young Maori to Sydney in 1835 to learn about Catholic teachings, influenced by Irish ex-convicts. A history of New Zealand written in 1896 by Italian priest Dom Felice Vaggioli exemplified the challenge: the British censored and suppressed it. While it contained factual errors, Vaggioli's book divulged Catholicism's endorsement of the Maori right to independence. Vaggioli interpreted the flag of 1834 as a national flag whereby the British recognised Maori sovereignty. He scorned the rumour that de Thierry was a French agent, when he was a 'pathetic British citizen'; and condemned officials and Protestant missionaries as profiteers and landsharks. Conversely, de Thierry recorded the response of Wesleyan missionaries to Pompallier's arrival: he found them 'in earnest consultation as to what was to be done to get rid of the terrible intruder'.

Events began to overtake Colonial Office plans from 1837, as expansive pressures mounted, fostered by trans-Tasman links. The outbreak of another cycle of tribal warfare in the Bay of Islands prompted a petition to Sydney for armed protection. In response, Governor Bourke sent HMS *Rattlesnake* with Captain William Hobson on board. As well as being seen to impose order, this visit produced two despatches – one by Hobson and the other by Busby – that prompted London to end the policy of 'minimum intervention'. Busby wrote in his report of 'the accumulating evils of a permanent anarchy', in order to persuade the Colonial Office to intervene more strongly. Hobson exercised more influence through his suggestion that Britain acquire sovereignty over at least the parts of New Zealand that contained British settlement. Global politics continued to dominate official thinking. Preoccupied with Europe and especially French ambitions, Britain was also becoming more involved in Asia and the Pacific as eyes for profit turned to China. Belief in British racial superiority only enhanced the confidence with which officials made decisions.

The House of Commons Select Committee on Aborigines in British Settlements in 1837 identified the issues that were to preoccupy colonial officials for the rest of the century, and 'took for granted Britain's self-evident superiority'. The committee maintained that protection by imperial authorities and Christianity would lead to civilisation, including of Maori, and anticipated the Crown right of pre-emption written into the English text of the Treaty of Waitangi. By this feudal doctrine only the Crown could alienate Maori land by consent; future settlers had to purchase land from the government. In this way both humanitarianism and the need to provide a land bank for a colonial treasury were satisfied. In 1838 a House of Lords Select Committee on New Zealand endorsed the system of colonisation promoted by the 'notorious and visionary' Edward Gibbon Wakefield (see chapter 3). By 1839, British thinking had moved to advocate restricted and controlled intervention to ensure law and order in British enclaves. Letters Patent published in June 1839 extended the boundaries of New South Wales to include any ceded lands in New Zealand. Parts of the country settled by Pakeha were to be acquired from chiefs while tribes were to retain control of their own territories. Governor Gipps in Sydney now had jurisdiction over any land that might be acquired. By July the Colonial Office had come to accept the idea of full sovereignty. The imperial government appointed Hobson as consul on 30 July 1839 to exercise 'some controlling authority' over the British in New Zealand; and Lieutenant-Governor of the part of the New South Wales colony that 'extended over the New Zealand Islands'.

The New Zealand Company resolved to get there first. Formed in 1837 as the New Zealand Association, its advocates of systematic colonisation had, since the 1820s, fantasised about colonising Australasia with selected immigrants. Wakefield provided the inspiration for the utopian ideal of making South Australia and New Zealand sites of colonial experiment for a transplanted pre-industrial English class structure. In implementing this ideal, however, Wakefield was obliged to lurk in the background and work through propaganda, because of the disgrace that stuck to him following his imprisonment for the abduction of a young heiress. His brother, Colonel William Wakefield, departed as the New Zealand Company's agent on the *Tory* in May 1839, in haste to purchase land from Maori as cheaply as possible and secure a monopoly in middle New Zealand, around Cook Strait. William Wakefield sought to pre-empt the Crown right of pre-emption. Possession, after all, was nine-tenths of the law, and the New Zealand Company's proposed new town of 'Britannia' would be far from the embryonic seat of government in the Bay of Islands.

It was the voyage of the *Tory*, which anchored in the Marlborough Sounds in August 1839, and Wakefield's large and doubtful land purchases, that motivated the Colonial Office to adopt 1839, not 1840, as the date of cession of New Zealand sovereignty, on the grounds of British settlement. In September the *Tory* sailed into Wellington Harbour and was boarded by the chiefs Te Puni and Te Wharepouri of Te Ati Awa, who sought to establish their claims ahead of other relatively recent arrivals. The barque *Cuba*, carrying the Royal Artillery surveyor Captain William Mein Smith, survey cadets and labourers, followed three months later, with the first fleet of six ships close behind, containing the selected migrants. Piloted by American whalers from Kapiti, the *Cuba* entered the harbour on 5 January 1840 to be greeted by 'Warri Podi' and 'Pooni' (Te Wharepouri and Te Puni). Ever since, the story of the New Zealand Company and its first settlement at Wellington has sat uncomfortably with the history of the Treaty of Waitangi of 6 February 1840 as the foundation document of New Zealand. Because of the precipitate action of the New Zealand Company and deals done by Sydney developers, Gipps issued a proclamation on 14 January 1840 extending the New South Wales borders to include New Zealand, and by 18 January Hobson was on his way from Sydney as Lieutenant-Governor.

3

Claiming the land 1840–1860

Struggles for land have swirled around the Treaty of Waitangi of 6 February 1840, an instrument unique less in its making than in what it has become – for indigenous rights and as a mission statement for a single country – with grand goals achieved at minimal cost. Beforehand, Captain Hobson read three announcements at the Anglican Church at Kororareka (Russell) on 30 January. The first extended the boundaries of New South Wales to include New Zealand; the second declared him Lieutenant-Governor; and the third established that land titles would derive from the Crown. To secure annexation by consent Hobson next drafted a treaty, for which British humanitarianism provided precedents in North America and West Africa. Overnight, the missionary Henry Williams and his son Edward translated the text into Maori so that chiefs could discuss it, which they did all day at Busby's house on 5 February, until Hobson, several English residents and about 45 Maori chiefs signed the Maori translation of the Treaty of Waitangi on 6 February. This initial signing was done in haste; Hobson barely had time to grab his plumed hat from HMS *Herald*.

If for Hobson a treaty offered chiefs protection, for missionaries it was a covenant between Maori and the Queen as head of the English church and state. For rangatira, though, their chieftainship demanded equality in rank and power to the new Governor, as Tareha declared: 'We chiefs are the rulers and we won't be ruled over. If we were all to have a rank equal to you that might be acceptable. But if we are going to be subordinate to you, then I say get

3.1.1 Patuone, Treaty of Waitangi
signatory. With his musket and
Pakeha gentleman's dress, and the
countenance of a warrior chief,
Patuone bridged two worlds

3.1.2 Tamati Waka Nene, Treaty of
Waitangi signatory and Patuone's
brother

back to your ship and sail away'. Only a few welcomed Hobson
as a harbinger of peace and new laws to manage the impact of disease, cultural and social disturbance, and firepower. It remained for
Ngapuhi chief Tamati Waka Nene to turn debate in favour of the
treaty with his argument that it was too late to reject Hobson; settlers were already arriving; the Governor would be a friend, a judge
and a peacemaker. Even chiefs who had spoken against were swayed
by Nene.

Nene and his older brother Patuone were among the first to
sign the treaty after their relative, Hone Heke, who set the example. As his later photograph suggests, Patuone, like Nene, bridged
two worlds (3.1). At about six years of age Patuone had met Captain Cook on the *Endeavour*, and in 1814 he and Nene welcomed
Marsden from New South Wales. A great warrior, Patuone was one
of the first chiefs to be baptised by Henry Williams, and he perceived
mutual benefit in treating with the British.

This was not the case for the French Bishop Pompallier, who
queried whether the chiefs understood that the British intended

the treaty to be an instrument of cession. Pompallier, impressive in splendid robes, interceded to demand a public assurance of religious freedom before any chiefs signed with their names or moko. After the signing, Hobson tried a few words in Maori: 'Hi iwi tahi tatou', he said; 'we are one people'. This assured Christian chiefs that their people and the British would be bound as subjects of the Queen and followers of Christ. Ever since, politicians have quoted Hobson's words. As with all speech they could hold different meanings for different groups. What did unity entail? Did 'one people' mean all the same, including one law, which in British thought meant civilising and assimilating Maori? Or did it endorse the idea of a new community of Maori and Pakeha, two ethnic groups henceforth defined in relation to each other? Nopera Panakareao saw the potential for some sort of new pan-tribal governance. He signed to give the people a helmsman: 'before every one wanted to be helmsman; one said, let me steer, another, let me steer, and we never went straight'. This suggests that the treaty was as much about instilling peace in Maoridom and protecting the rights of kin groups as about how to manage engagement with Europe.

THE FOUNDING DOCUMENT

Only recently has the Treaty of Waitangi become central to national life. There are nine documents in all: the original in English and Maori, seven copies in Maori and one English reprint. After Waitangi the main Maori parchment was taken to other places in Northland. Missionaries and naval personnel carried copies of the Maori text around the country; one copy travelled to the South Island on HMS *Herald*, and some North Island chiefs signed a printed sheet of the English version, produced by the Church Missionary Society. Over 500 chiefs signed the treaty documents, and all except 39 signed a Maori version; they signed not as representatives of iwi but of hapu.

Significantly, a number of powerful non-Christian chiefs, less exposed to European influence, did not sign, notably Te Wherowhero of Waikato, Te Arawa chiefs, and Te Heuheu, paramount chief of Ngati Tuwharetoa. Wairarapa Maori were not given the opportunity. Two women signed a copy in the Cook Strait region

Victoria, the Queen of England, in her gracious remembrance of the Chiefs and Tribes of New Zealand, and through her desire to preserve to them their chieftainship and their land, and to preserve peace and quietness to them, has thought it right to send them a gentleman to be her representative to the natives of New Zealand. Let the native Chiefs in all parts of the land and in the islands consent to the Queen's Government. Now, because there are numbers of the people living in this land, and more will be coming, the Queen wishes to appoint a Government, that there may be no cause for strife between the Natives and the Pakeha, who are now without law: It has therefore pleased the Queen to appoint me, WILLIAM HOBSON, a Captain in the Royal Navy, Governor of all parts of New Zealand which shall be ceded now and at the future period to the Queen. She offers to the Chiefs of the Assembly of the Tribes of New Zealand and to the other Chiefs, the following laws:–

I. The Chiefs of (i.e. constituting) the Assembly, and all the Chiefs who are absent from the Assembly, shall cede to the Queen of England for ever the government of all their lands.

II. The Queen of England acknowledges and guarantees to the Chiefs, the Tribes, and all the people of New Zealand, the entire supremacy of their lands, of their settlements, and of all their personal property. But the Chiefs of the Assembly, and all other Chiefs, make over to the Queen the purchasing of such lands, which the man who possesses the land is willing to sell, according to prices agreed upon by him, and the purchaser appointed by the Queen to purchase for her.

III. In return for their acknowledging the Government of the Queen, the Queen of England will protect all the natives of New Zealand, and will allow them the same rights as the people of England.

(Signed) WILLIAM HOBSON
Consul, and Lieutenant-Governor

We, the Chiefs of this Assembly of the tribes of New Zealand, now assembled at Waitangi, perceiving the meaning of these words, take and consent to them all. Therefore we sign our names and our marks.

This is done at Waitangi, on the sixth day of February, in the one thousand eight hundred and fortieth year of our Lord.

3.2 The Treaty of Waitangi: English translation of Maori text, 1865 while chiefly women elsewhere were debarred. Te Heuheu, for one, would not subordinate his mana as first among chiefs to that of a woman, the English Queen.

Translations of the Treaty of Waitangi are still hotly debated. The Maori text (translated by a missionary contemporary) differs from Hobson's English original in subtle yet critical ways. Settler histories – where they referred to the treaty – relied on the English text to depict a nation founded on full and free consent. In the dominant narrative, New Zealand joined the British Empire on 6 February 1840, as part of the colony of New South Wales. New Zealand operated as a Crown colony in its own right only from 1841. In the official story of the nation, it took 150 years for the treaty to grow into a 'founding document'. Saved from a fire in 1841, the treaty sheets were put in storage in 1877, at a time when the treaty was declared to have no legal status and tribes to have no customary rights enforceable in the courts. Rediscovered in 1911, the documents – especially the parchment signed at Waitangi – were damaged by water and rats, and saved as a relic by the Dominion Museum. In the late twentieth century Maori protested that New Zealand's settler society had neglected the treaty. Not until the sesquicentennial celebrations in 1990 were its documents finally arranged on permanent public display in Wellington.

Hastily devised at the time, the treaty sheets have become a national monument: they mean different things to different groups but have had an evolving official interpretation placed upon them. Elderly New Zealanders are more familiar with a settler narrative that does not mention the treaty at all. The narrative that does – and recognises the reality that colonists depended on Maori – advances the humanitarian view of government concerned for Maori interests, which affirms that the Crown was present in New Zealand before all but a trickle of settlers and before the making of the nation state. This version is centred in the north, on the treaty ground at Waitangi and with the Governor in Auckland. In 1841 Hobson shifted the capital from Kororareka to Auckland rather than to Wellington since the site of Auckland sat on the Waitemata Harbour, between the regions of densest Maori population in Northland and the Waikato.

By contrast, the other settler story that downplayed the treaty developed from Wellington and the other five towns created by systematic colonisation. The New Zealand Company settlers who reached Wellington between January and March 1840 fully expected that their town would become the seat of government. It was this tension between Pakeha claims, between the Governor and missionaries in the north and Wellington settlers, that prompted Hobson to proclaim British sovereignty over the whole country on 21 May 1840, when the treaty documents were still circulating and southern chiefs had yet to sign. Imperial power asserted itself when challenged by its own kind.

From a Maori standpoint the treaty is the basis of the Crown's authority and legitimised European settlement in New Zealand. Maori narratives came to prominence from the 1980s, once developing treaty jurisprudence established that the Maori rather than English text of the Treaty of Waitangi had status in international law. Histories known to Maori but not taught in schools told that there was more to the treaty than the English version: the treaty had mana as the deed of their tupuna, and the Maori text was the venerated one because it contained the majority of signatures. The treaty was a living thing, a binding contract, as the missionaries had explained; invoked since the nineteenth century as a source of rights and redress, it stood as a potent symbol for Maori of their rightful constitutional place. Historians endorsed this view, which became the basis of official acceptance of the treaty as a founding document. With its legal status affirmed, the Maori text supplanted Hobson's English version, and the associated narrative grew in political power. In the process, historians began to generate 'a new myth of constitutional foundation' in which Maori had a partnership with the Crown as opposed to a vertical sovereign/ subject relationship.

The first of the treaty's three articles extended the Crown's authority over the territory of New Zealand, though there is a question mark over whether chiefs ceded sovereignty, because of the differences between the English and Maori texts. Under article 1, in the English version, the chiefs ceded the Queen 'all the rights and powers of sovereignty' over their land. In the Maori version, however, the chiefs gave the Queen 'te kawanatanga katoa', that is, 'government of all their lands' (3.2). The missionary Henry Williams coined the word 'kawanatanga' from the Maori for governor, which his audience understood in a biblical context as meaning keeping the peace, as Pontius Pilate did in Israel. Some therefore argue that for Maori to comprehend British annexation would have required use of the term 'mana', as Williams himself used in his translation of the 1835 Declaration of Independence. The implication is that the Maori text was translated in such a way as to enhance the advantages of signing.

Historians generally agree with the Waitangi Tribunal judgment that sovereignty was ceded because there never had been a national Maori sovereignty; but that chiefs and their kin groups and the people of New Zealand were nonetheless guaranteed collective and individual possession by the Queen. This is specified in article 2 which, in Hobson's English text, guaranteed

to the Chiefs and Tribes of New Zealand and to the respective individuals and families thereof the full exclusive and undisturbed possession of their Lands and Estates Forests and Fisheries and other properties which they may individually or collectively possess so long as it is their wish and desire to retain the same in their possession.

Yet the text signed by most chiefs affirmed unqualified exercise of their chieftainship, and also that of all hapu and all the people of New Zealand, over their land, homes and treasures, broadly conceived. The most debated words continue to be: 'ki nga Rangatira ki nga hapu ki nga tangata katoa o Nu Tirani te tino rangatiratanga o o ratou wenua o ratou kainga me o ratou taonga katoa' (to the Chiefs, the Tribes, and all the people of New Zealand, the entire supremacy of their lands, of their settlements, and of all their personal property). In contrast to the English text of article 2, the Maori text was also silent on the Crown right of pre-emption. It promised the Queen 'hokonga' – the buying and selling of land that Maori were willing to part with – but not exclusively, nor even as the highest priority.

Was the transition to British rule therefore dependent on devious manipulation of language or did lofty motives infuse the treaty and set an example for the world in laying down ground rules for racial harmony? The answer depends on comprehending the mindset of the missionary interpreters as well as the chiefs and Hobson. In his account of events, Henry Williams wrote that Hobson asked him to translate the treaty on 4 February, advising him 'to avoid all expressions of the English for which there was no expressive term in the Maori, preserving entire the spirit and tenor of the treaty'. This Williams thought he did. However, he was used to innovating in order to manage his everyday cross-cultural environment. Since authority was vested in the chiefly person, he created derived nouns to distinguish territorial sovereignty and rule from the person of the ruler, of rangatiratanga – chieftainship – from rangatira, and kawanatanga from kawana, the new transliteration of governor. Accordingly, language scholars have disputed that the words mana and kawanatanga 'constitute the critical issue of Maori understanding in the Treaty'. In status terms the Governor was higher than the former British Resident Busby but lower than the Queen. Moreover he was visibly present, whereas the Queen was far away in England, a difference that may explain Williams' divergent wording of the Declaration of Independence and the Treaty of Waitangi:

Busby's Declaration of Independence had declared the existence of two sovereign peoples, British and Maori, in appropriately lofty and distancing language. By contrast, the Treaty of Waitangi was describing a situation in which distance was to be collapsed, through the political union of Maori and the British in New Zealand. For Williams, the localisation of authority separated the effective and dignified functions of government; the one was present in New Zealand, the reference of the other retreated to England – to the person, and mana, of the Queen.

The word rangatiratanga was not a deceit but an innovation that 'fitted the new world better than the old'. Despite its ambiguities, the treaty signified a vote for a peaceful, Christian, Maori and Pakeha future.

The debate over how much authority Maori ceded resulted from both losses in translation and the issues of authority and race relations that the treaty left unresolved. It formally launched the process of working out those issues. The British intended to 'amalgamate' Maori into settler frameworks by civilising them and bringing them under British law. This was assumed by article 3, which promised Maori royal protection and the rights of British subjects, and has provided the grounds for one standard of citizenship ever since. From the start it was doubtful whether the policy of 'amalgamation' would allow what is now termed a bicultural approach, where Maori would share in the creation of a new nation state; the British intention was to assimilate them. Yet the chiefly signatories envisaged that the treaty would preserve their chieftainship; and their descendants continue to press this view on governments (see chapter 10).

A related controversy concerns how far Maori were embracing a new world or trying to incorporate Pakeha into their traditional world through the treaty. 'Autonomy', a common principle in late twentieth-century writing, is an inappropriate word to explain Maori behaviour in 1840. Rather the chiefs exercised a choice about a future citizenship, and in signing they chose a westernised future. They voted for a kinship model that bound Maori and Pakeha through an imagined shared genealogy that stemmed from God, by which the treaty made Maori and Pakeha 'friends' as opposed to 'enemies'.

It is credible, then, that Hobson's phrase 'Hi iwi tahi tatou' expressed not merely the British policy of amalgamation based on the Enlightenment belief in a common humanity but also the Maori policy of unity with Pakeha in order to ensure peace and order. It is likely that his words conveyed different meanings to two distinct audiences. Both the Pakeha narrative that prefers article 3 interpretations of the Treaty of Waitangi, and the Maori and official narratives that give prominence to rights under article 2, have yet to absorb this possibility that unity expressed a Maori as well as a British position. For chiefs such as Tamati Waka Nene and Patuone there was no going back. By 1840 northern chiefs had extensive contact with Europeans and their base at Sydney. In this sense the treaty denoted a response to what is now termed globalisation. But the tragedy was that Maori could not foresee the thousands of migrants from 1840 who were to tip the scales of power to the settler society.

SYSTEMATIC COLONISATION

In retrospect, struggles for land can seem straightforward. In one view, the Maori were out-gunned, as were other indigenous people. In another, settler capitalism swept everyone and everything before it. In yet another, the British colonists treated land as a commodity; the tangata whenua in contrast saw it as for the use of their descendants like their ancestors before them. Neither could grasp the other's point of view, though both understood and resented invasion and conquest. It was not only misunderstanding which provoked disputes over land and made them a pivot of New Zealand history. Europeans brought a particular moral perspective to land ownership and management, of 'use it or lose it' (see chapter 5). Backed by the biblical edict to multiply and replenish the earth, colonists believed that those who used the land most productively (their own kind) had the best moral claim to it: European 'civilisation' added value. God gave the world to 'men in Common' but not to remain 'common and uncultivated. He gave it to the use of the industrious and rational'. This belief that Europeans – in particular Englishmen – had a God-given right to the world's resources, as espoused by John Locke, spurred the colonisation of New Zealand.

All the main port towns except Auckland grew from the theory of systematic colonisation. This settler capitalist dream entailed a massive colonial experiment between 1840 and 1850 by the New Zealand Company and its offshoots. The New Zealand Company was a vast propaganda machine that set out to create towns and farms that would transplant civilisation to the New World and claim the wilderness as a garden. The theory's chief ideologue was Edward Gibbon Wakefield. From Newgate Prison in *A Letter from Sydney* (1829) he wrote his philosophy to export 'a mixture of all classes of society'. Wakefield imagined New Zealand in terms of its 'natural abundance' long before he or his siblings had set foot there. He prefabricated the very idea of New Zealand from Arcadian ideas embedded in the European imagination. In 1836, he told the House of Commons Select Committee on the disposal of lands in the colonies that near to Australia was a country that everyone described 'as the fittest country in the world for colonisation, as the most beautiful country, with the finest climate and the most productive soil . . .' New Zealand was destined to be a green and pleasant land, to borrow a phrase from the hymn 'Jerusalem' sung by generations of schoolgirls. In Wakefield's version, land was the central mechanism for the systematic creation of a colonial society that approximated a slice of a romanticised rural England, except with a thin sprinkling of friendly, assimilated natives.

Like all theories of colonisation this variant, which appeared to derive from the political economy of Adam Smith, presupposed the dispossession of indigenous people. As Wakefield explained in 1837, he proposed a 'deliberate plan and systematic efforts' to civilise a 'barbarous people'. Although he saw Maori as 'savage' he also labelled them 'superior' and, of all indigenes, the most like Europeans. Their 'peculiar aptitude' for improvement invited prospects of intermarriage with colonists so that future generations of Europeans and 'natives' would 'become one people'. In this way he incorporated the paradigm of a common humanity. Wakefield had his own performer of the role of civilised native in the form of Nahiti, a Maori visitor to London who dressed in the latest fashion. Nahiti may have assisted the Wakefield brothers' London performances in the late 1830s, but he was dumped as an interpreter in New Zealand once Edward Gibbon Wakefield's brother Colonel William Wakefield discovered that he lacked chiefly status. Wakefieldian theory imbibed a common humanity but was class bound, intended to preserve rank and distinctions, because E. G. Wakefield was a snob.

The whole basis of the theory was to sell land at a 'sufficient price' to ensure the proper balance of land, labour and capital in order to concentrate settlement and foster civilisation through clustering. The theory prescribed the sale of land at a price high enough to stop labourers from becoming landowners too soon, but not too expensive to attract worthy settlers. Profits from managed land sales were to subsidise the passages of more migrants. Young married couples were vital to the scheme because the values of motherhood and family life, fundamental to civilisation, provided a cornerstone of creating a better society. Increasingly, the rising middle classes and respectable working-class people imbibed the evangelical Christian values enshrined in marriage. These were the ideals that Wakefield invoked when he declared: 'As respects morals and manners, it is of little importance what colonial fathers are, in comparison with what the mothers are', a theory based on the support provided by his grandmother, mother and elder sister to the morally flawed men in his family. The systematic colonisation of New Zealand offered a means to redeem E. G. and W. Wakefield's reputations tarnished by imprisonment for the abduction of a teenage heiress.

As a colonial experiment, New Zealand provided a contrast with Australia. From the start New Zealand assumed an image of superiority to the Australian colonies, particularly New South Wales, which was the 'mother colony' for all the Australasian colonies except Western Australia. No matter that Kororareka was home to escaped convicts; New Zealand would develop the lessons learnt in Adelaide, the first town planned according to the Wakefieldian dream, and a non-convict settlement. New Zealand Company propaganda promoted the idea of a select type devoid of the convict stain who would set the requisite 'standard of morals and manners'.

Demonstrating the power of their European templates, the 'colonists' (cabin passengers) bound for Wellington in 1839 mentally possessed themselves of the land before they left home. The New Zealand Company held a lottery of land orders in London before its agent Colonel Wakefield had even arrived in Cook Strait on the *Tory* and drawn up a hasty deed of purchase. The ballot was for land orders rather than land because in August 1839 the company had no land to sell. Ladies were ostensibly the 'most daring speculators'. There were cheers when 'the Natives' drew a number, and the belief that their game brought good deeds enhanced the thrill of the flutter: the players believed that their lottery improved the Maori's 'chance of civilisation'. They had no inkling of how much of a lottery settling New Zealand would be in practice. Meanwhile, across the world, Te Puni and Te Wharepouri of Te Ati Awa and rival hapu around Port Nicholson of Ngati Toa and Ngati Raukawa (who named Colonel Wakefield 'Wide-awake') had no idea that Europeans had already possessed and renamed their territory. In November, still in rough seas on the *Cuba*, the company's surveyor-general Captain William Mein Smith read E. G. Wakefield's *England and America* and liked his reasoning. Realising the dream would be another matter.

The idea that Mein Smith was handed a concept plan – the 'Cobham plan' – for the town of Britannia in London is a myth constructed after the event; nowhere in his journal is there any mention of such a plan. It is more likely that designs of a town laid out in a grid pattern intersected by a wide and navigable river were used in panoramas exhibited in London to promote emigration. The planning of Wellington was left to Mein Smith by the New Zealand Company. He was a teacher and administrator with 26 years experience in the military, accustomed to following orders and presiding at courts martial. Accordingly he followed the directors' instructions to the letter. His difficulty was that the topography around Port Nicholson was more akin to the Rock of Gibraltar, where he had served with the Royal Artillery from 1829, than to the grasslands suited to the grid pattern of the British colonial town. He had experience of the latter in North America, at the British fort town of Kingston, Ontario. Somehow, at Port Nicholson he had to lay out 1100 one-acre town sections and, more absurdly, find room for parks, boulevards and 100-acre (40 ha) country sections for the investors who had paid £101 for each fictitious package of a town and country section. As he reported, he laid out Wellington 'under every species of difficulty; the incessant importunities of a large body of Settlers who had arrived by this time, a winter of unusual inclemency, no office or place of residence but a tent, and frequent hindrance from the Natives'.

William Wakefield proved another hindrance. His hostility to the surveyors charged with realising the dream captured the incongruity between the theory of colonisation and what was practicable. Mein Smith and his cadets surveyed two towns in six months because the principal agent interfered and instructed him to shift the survey from Petone to Lambton Harbour in April 1840. Smith first decided to locate the town on the flat ground at Petone, not at Pipitea where Colonel Wakefield had left stores because Pipitea, while 'a very nice site for a Town', was too small and too far from potential country sections in the Hutt Valley; Petone, on the other hand, 'afforded abundance of room' to carry out the instructions. The captain reported to the colonel: 'On your return to Port Nicholson you agreed with me in opinion, and I commenced operations'; soon settlers began to arrive. In March the Hutt River 'rose and overflowed its banks'. Smith thought the river could be made secure against future floods by clearing away driftwood and cutting channels, but Wakefield refused to provide the funds. Instead he forced a fresh start on the fragments of flat land at Pipitea and Te Aro.

At Pipitea, former Taranaki people's pa, gardens and burial grounds occupied the best land, which is now home to the New Zealand parliament. The enforced shift of site exacerbated tensions because Wakefield claimed that he had bought the land, but residents

3.3 William Mein Smith, From the Pah Pipitea, Port
Nicholson, December 1840

disagreed. Mein Smith's host Wharepouri presided over and made
over Petone for settlement, not today's downtown Wellington. Compounding the chaos, the 'tenths' reserved for Maori according to the
company's instructions were scattered by the ballot system. Some of
the 110 acres (44 ha) of Maori tenths reserves which Smith selected
were already pa sites and cultivation land, as at Pipitea, but other
occupied foreshore land was claimed for the settlers, presumably
because these sites had already been allotted to purchasers who
had priority in the London ballot. Consequently six of nine villages
disappeared.

Historians have alternately praised and denounced E. G. Wakefield and his siblings; only in 2002 did a biography accept them for
themselves and acknowledge the importance of their fantasies. But
this glossed over the unscrupulous behaviour of Colonel Wakefield
whose undermining of Mein Smith at Wellington and in reports
to London, while not unusual in the world of politics, distorted the
story of what happened on the ground. Surveyors were typical of the
pragmatic men of the outdoors whose characteristics subsequently

evolved into a national type; literally, they made a path for others. Overlooked or judged because their labours overrode indigenous genealogies, the surveyors of the Wakefieldian settlements were following orders deemed right and proper by an imperial script. They used their cross-cultural and military experience to bring the infrastructure for Pakeha New Zealand into being. It is appropriate for this descendant to acknowledge that the New Zealand Company's surveyor-general struggled to realise the colonial dream. He and his staff measured up and made it work.

Nearly 10,000 settlers migrated under company schemes in the 1840s, carrying with them hopes of a better life. Women's domestic labour as wives, mothers and workers proved critical to the whole venture, not least because there were 1.3 men for every woman. Whole families were transplanted; among these settlers were 3846 children under 13. Some of the colonial élite brought prefabricated houses with them. Hobson's house was transported to Auckland to shelter his wife and young family. This greatly disappointed the Wellington settlers who then realised that their town – conceived and advertised as the principal town – was not to be the capital. William Mein Smith shipped his Manning cottage to Port Nicholson for his migrating household, his wife Louisa and three small children. Other Manning cottages made their way to Australia in the 1830s; one became the Pegasus Arms in Christchurch. Migrants expressed pride in their possession of a piglet or a hen to feed their families. The domesticity of the venture is remarkable.

True to Arcadian myth these young people set out to colonise their new land through domesticity and husbandry, by building homes, raising families, rearing imported stock, and planting gardens. In such transplanted narratives scholars have detected the individualism in nineteenth-century Pakeha culture that recurred in a political emphasis on self-reliance. Planning of cities was envisaged from the start, with the town perceived as a symbol of civilising the wilderness. In the rural as in the urban setting, dreams of landed independence demanded immediate adaptation to the new environment. This is illustrated in William Strutt's sketches of a back settler's whare (3.4). Strutt captured the application of indigenous architecture – the whare, built from ponga logs – combined with elements of the English country cottage as resources allowed. Colonial

3.4 William Strutt, Settler putting out chimney fire, 1855 or 1856

adaptability added the canvas roof. The danger of fire was ever present, as if to confirm the thesis of historian Miles Fairburn that Arcadianism proved its own enemy when faith in 'natural abundance' failed to produce a promised land.

Strutt's image also illustrates the power of the 'pioneer legend'. New Zealand's pioneer mythology paralleled others on the frontiers of British settlement. It celebrated settlers as heroes and heroines, the men for their manly virtues of courage, enterprise, hard work and perseverance; and the women as 'colonial helpmeets' endowed with the feminine versions of these attributes. Pioneers tamed the land and, they believed, made it productive as God intended. They renamed it and made it home.

A group of French settlers had similar ideas. In 1838 the whaling captain Jean François Langlois returned to France with a deed signed by South Island chiefs that he believed gave him ownership of Banks Peninsula. This deed prompted the French equivalent of the New Zealand Company, the Nanto-Bordelaise Company, to despatch settlers to buy and occupy land in 'Southern New Zealand', because in the French view claiming the land meant occupation. Had the French not sailed into Akaroa Harbour in August to find that local Ngai Tahu had signed the Treaty of Waitangi in May 1840 the South Island might have become another Quebec. In practice a balance of power prevailed between the tiny French settlement at Akaroa and local Maori in the 1840s; but the balance shifted as the European population burgeoned as a result of organised settlement in the South Island from 1848, with the planning of the Otago settlement at Dunedin, as a Scottish Presbyterian enclave, and Christchurch as an Anglican stronghold in 1850. Ngai Tahu found that the Crown's guarantee of their land and food supplies was ignored by the Canterbury Association.

Canterbury provides a case study in settler capitalism; it represented the scheme of systematic colonisation fulfilled and the identity of its town of Christchurch grew from this precept. Unlike Auckland, which began from Sydney, the southern settlement was to be a transplanted England. It assumed as its own the goal of civilisation that had been at the heart of British colonisation overseas since the sixteenth century. Christchurch was to have a college and a cathedral.

The Canterbury Association's first four ships reached the port of Lyttelton in December 1850 after a quick passage. They may be better termed the last four ships because Canterbury was the last Wakefieldian settlement. It was also the most successful. In local history, the Canterbury scheme succeeded because of the calibre of its colonists, assisted by geography, timing, planning and pastoralism. Like other commercial cities in Australasia, Christchurch had plenty of flat ground and a separate port. Environmental obstacles did not pose an immediate hazard: the town site was bordered by a large wetland and separated from the port by hills. There was time for planning. Captain Joseph Thomas, the chief surveyor, a former Royal Engineers officer, and his assistants had completed a trigonometrical survey of the Canterbury block by the end of 1849 and laid out the port of Lyttelton and seaside suburb of Sumner as well as Christchurch in 1850 before the settlers arrived. Canterbury's pilgrims therefore enjoyed an easier start than settlers in the other colonies.

The 'forgotten forty-niners' who built roads, houses and accommodation barracks for the newcomers comprised 40 northern Maori recruited as road-builders, about 30 former Australian convicts including carpenters from Hobart, refugees from Wellington (rocked by an earthquake in 1848) and from Wellington's offshoot of Nelson, which itself lacked land for farming. Captain Thomas, who had worked on the Wanganui and Otago surveys, astutely managed scarce funds but was denied the role of leader of the settlement once the settlers arrived. That position went to J. R. Godley, whose Oxford college Christ Church provided the name for the colonial town. Ironically, the Catholic Caroline Chisholm and her family colonisation society that organised migrants to Australia saved this Church of England settlement. Chisholm ensured that the Canterbury ships were filled with 'common working people' who were 'their only chance to save the parties from ruin'.

Canterbury had an advantage over other Wakefieldian settlements in that pastoralism was allowed from the start. This was possible because Canterbury came into existence relatively late. As happened in other Australasian colonies from 1850, the port and town provided an entrepôt for metropolitan culture and at the same time for pastoral expansion in the hinterland. In fact Godley incorporated pastoralism in the scheme by issuing pasturage regulations, which guaranteed Canterbury's success. The 'advance guard of empire' in the South Island comprised hard-working pastoralists, shrewd and enterprising capitalists with lower middle-class or working-class origins whose wealth ranked far behind levels found in the United States, Britain and New South Wales. Wealthy settlers were not a 'gentry' (though they aspired to be) but part of the 'colonial capitalist class', whose assets in Canterbury were built on pastoralism and in Otago on commerce and finance. Most arrived early in the context of late settlement, before the largest immigration wave in the 1870s. It is striking how, even for the rich, the New Zealand experience was shaped from the start by shortage of money.

CROWN COLONY

Frugality was the first principle of administration by the Colonial Office. New Zealand government was established on the cheap and connoted more ideal than reality. Settlers and Maori thought the Governor possessed personal authority as a ruler 'who would protect them from each other'. The colony's viability depended on buying land cheaply from Maori and selling it at a profit to finance further immigration. This explains in part the tense relations between the government in Auckland and the New Zealand Company settlements because the Treaty of Waitangi threatened the company's land sales through the Crown right of pre-emption which decreed that the Crown alone could buy land directly from Maori. It also explains why early governments failed to act as protectors of the indigenous people, why they neglected to provide the guarantees promised in the treaty, and to intervene to check settler demands.

The Wairau dispute of 1843 became a catalyst. Shortage of land at Port Nicholson prompted a spread of New Zealand Company settlements to Wanganui, New Plymouth and Nelson by 1842, all of which created flashpoints in Maori–Pakeha relations. The dispute resulted from the Nelson settlement's demand for rural sections and especially grasslands suitable for pastoralism. Te Rauparaha and Te Rangihaeata of Ngati Toa protested to William Spain, the government commissioner appointed to investigate land sales, that they had not sold the Wairau valley to Colonel Wakefield. Their own claim to the top of the South Island was dubious and continues to be disputed. But it was foolhardy of Nelson's police magistrate Henry Thompson to decide to travel to the Wairau to arrest the chiefs for arson which had disrupted the survey. Because of this gross misjudgement Thompson and the head of the Nelson settlement, Captain Arthur Wakefield – the most honourable of the Wakefield siblings – and their party were killed. Te Rangihaeata felled them both with his greenstone mere after the Pakeha shot his wife, Te

Rongo, who was Te Rauparaha's daughter. Wairau left a legacy of embitterment for Pakeha and Maori.

To add to the shock of deaths among them, the Nelson settlers were outraged that Hobson's successor Governor Robert FitzRoy, also a naval officer, decided that the settlers were wrong to pursue the survey of the coveted pasture along the Wairau River before Commissioner Spain had investigated the contested claims to ownership. The settlers objected that appeasement of the 'savage' exacerbated conflict by encouraging Maori to believe that they owned large uncultivated tracts of land. Incensed at the bloodshed and the Governor's response, attitudes hardened. Alfred Domett, later the colony's premier, sought revenge for the Wairau episode and subsequently oversaw the confiscation of Maori land in the 1860s.

In the aftermath of the conflict Te Rauparaha and Te Rangihaeata returned to the Wellington side of Cook Strait. Hints about their relations with Pakeha can be gleaned from family histories. Charles Hartley, a young gunsmith from Cornwall who had arrived in Wellington with his parents and sister in January 1840, became a trader along the Manawatu River and later an interpreter in the Native Land Court. He and his young wife Dinah cared for Te Rangihaeata when he had serious wounds, so several times Te Rangihaeata warned them of danger in tensions between tribes and with government troops. He also advised settlers to move to Wellington. Dinah is remembered for keeping an axe behind the kitchen door not to protect herself from her Maori protectors, but from Pakeha pit sawyers who became violent when drunk. In the Manawatu, the New Zealand Company claimed to have purchased 25,000 acres but the Maori owners disputed this claim and the company was eventually allowed only 900 acres. Shady land deals were routine even in this district known for its harmonious race relations.

Clashes also erupted in the north over flagpoles and boundary markers. Hone Heke, who had led the treaty signing, clearly understood the symbolism of chopping down the British flagpole at Russell, which he did with his allies four times in 1844 and 1845; and well did the Governor understand his challenge. War resulted in the north between the British, reinforced by military aid from New South Wales and Heke's relative Tamati Waka Nene, and Heke and the elder chief Kawiti supported by 'their' Pakeha. In this war

Ngapuhi fought one another. The Anglican Church at Russell still bears the scars of gunfire while, thanks to Heke, Bishop Pompallier's house was saved. Heke considered that the Treaty of Waitangi was not being honoured. His dispute was not with Pakeha in general but with the colonial government, embodied in the Governor, over the takeover of chiefs' authority and their land. 'God made this country for us', he wrote to the new Governor George Grey, fresh in 1845 from the governorship of South Australia. Heke had agreed to be 'all as one' with the Governor, not subordinate, his chiefly authority curtailed. Conversely, other northern chiefs backed the treaty and Kawiti's son helped re-erect the flagstaff in 1858 when peace was restored.

Governor Grey failed to capture or crush Heke and Kawiti who, on balance, outwitted and refused to be intimidated or cowered by the imperial military. On the contrary, Kawiti surprised government forces by the successful conduct of trench warfare. In the wars of 1845 to 1847, Australia provided most of the military force to quell Maori resistance. Sydney and Hobart supplied arms to both sides; Australian garrisons provided soldiers as well as sailors. The resisters showed who commanded the north, however, not just through military strategy. Heke and Kawiti made peace first with Nene, their kin, before they made peace with Grey.

Around the Wellington settlement power relations tilted from the Maori world to control by the colonial government. The key moment came in 1846 when Governor Grey arrested Te Rauparaha in his own home because of rumours of an assault on Wellington, then imprisoned him without charge for ten months on a naval vessel. Te Rauparaha was not returned to his people at Otaki until 1848. The old warrior's arrest – when he professed to be neutral in local conflicts – destroyed his mana and provided the opportunity for the government to supplant the Ngati Toa chief in his realm of assumed authority by conquest around Cook Strait, an area that functioned as a highway for shipping, communication, and commerce.

The founding of a settler state followed closely on the establishment of the South Island settlements of Otago and Canterbury. In the Crown colony period from 1841 to 1853 the Governor and his executive council ruled the colony. This proved unpopular with the colonists who sought representative and responsible government.

3.5 Thomas B. Collinson, Hosey's Battle, 1847. Capt[ain]
Henderson, Capt[ain E.] Stanley, R. N., Tamati Waka Nene,
Te Wherowhero Potatau (the future Maori king). This was a
skirmish in the war at Wanganui, where Nene and Te
Wherowhero accompanied Governor Grey 'to stimulate the
missionary party to a decided course of action against the
hostiles' (James Cowan, *The New Zealand Wars*, vol. 1:
1854–64, Wellington: Government Printer, 1922, reprinted
1983, 141).

The Secretary of State for the Colonies, Earl Grey, produced a constitution in 1846 that created two provinces of New Ulster – most of
the North Island – and New Munster, comprising Wellington and
the South Island. But the newly knighted Sir George Grey denied
self-government on the grounds of injustice to Maori, who were
excluded, refusing to give power to a settler minority. As Governor
he assumed responsibility for Maori affairs. Though he too wished
to curb the power of chiefs, he appeared to involve Maori in the
provision of schools, hospitals and police, and as assessors in mag-
istrates' courts, in gifts of flour mills and equipment, and in making
settlers responsible for the trespass of stock.

New Zealand obtained representative government in the form
of a Governor and two houses of parliament on the Westminster
model under the Constitution Act 1852, proclaimed in January

1853, with a Legislative Council nominated by the Governor and an elected House of Representatives. The Act also created a system of provincial government established in six provinces: Auckland, the capital and the only non-Wakefieldian settlement, Wellington, Taranaki (centred on the town of New Plymouth), Nelson, Canterbury (Christchurch) and Otago (Dunedin). Settlers secured representative government with a male property vote in the first election in 1853. In theory there was no racial distinction concerning the franchise; propertied men included Maori men if they held individualised (European) title to land, freehold or leasehold, or lived in a European-style dwelling. In the Wairarapa for example, Te Manihera, who had invited the first pastoralists to run sheep in the 1840s, voted in 1853 and hosted the local electoral meeting at his house. Edward Gibbon Wakefield himself arrived in Wellington in 1853, cherishing the idea that with the establishment of constitutional government he could regain status as a colonial politician. Instead he found that the stigma of his convict past stuck. Responsible government for settlers followed in 1856, in tandem with the rise of early democracy in the Australasian colonies.

If the intent was to pursue amalgamation, the reality was that a mere handful of Maori were qualified to vote in the colony's first election in 1853. Not by chance, talk about a separate Maori parliament or a Maori king began simultaneously among mission-educated chiefs. Another instance of 'a show of justice' is given by clause 71 of the Constitution Act, which provided for the creation of native districts set apart from the settler provinces where Maori could live under customary law. This clause was never implemented. The onus remained with the Governor because despite – and perhaps because of – responsible government native affairs continued to be his responsibility.

By the late 1850s Maori unease deepened in response to the government track record on land purchase and militarism. The pantribal Kingitanga, centred in the Waikato, rose to the challenge, and chose Te Wherowhero Potatau as the first Maori king (standing next to Tamati Waka Nene in 3.5). A decade earlier the Waikato paramount chief had agreed to provide protection for the seat of government at Auckland, as had Patuone. Te Wherowhero did not see the kingship as opposed to Queen Victoria and sought to co-operate with the government. But escalating land disputes obliged him to oppose the Governor, stultifying Crown attempts to purchase land in the Waikato to expand settlement and link the main towns of Auckland and Wellington by road and rail.

Pastoralism signalled the future in all the Australasian colonies in the 1850s. By 1861 the government had purchased two-thirds of New Zealand, mainly in the South Island, where Grey acquired huge tracts such as by the Kemp purchase in 1848 of 20 million acres (8 million ha) for the Canterbury settlement. By contrast the government had alienated less than a quarter of the North Island by 1861, thwarting government and settler aspirations. Frustrated, in 1860 Governor Thomas Gore Browne sent in imperial troops to enforce the claim to a disputed purchase of land at Waitara in Taranaki, long coveted by settlers. The claim contravened the rights of a majority of owners – Te Ati Awa led by Wiremu Kingi, who had returned to his homeland twelve years earlier – and in doing so fired the opening round in the New Zealand wars of the 1860s. Maori were appalled because the government ignored protests that the willing sellers had no right of sale.

The wrong land purchase at Waitara and the rise of the Kingitanga combined to return the treaty to the forefront of discourse about Maori–Pakeha relations. The issue under debate became how to reconcile the exercise of Maori rights with government authority. In Gore Browne's logic, sovereignty rested neither on Maori rights nor on the rights of Englishmen, but was absolute. Perceiving Waitara and the King movement as rebellion, he sought to divide and rule by persuading the rest of Maoridom to attend a month-long conference of chiefs at Kohimarama, near Auckland, in July 1860, with the idea that the chiefs confirm their allegiance to the Crown, and to quash support for the Kingitanga. He reiterated the humanitarian view that would become a central tenet of New Zealand race relations, not for the benefit of Maori, but to assert sovereignty:

New Zealand is the only Colony where the Aborigines have been treated with unvarying kindness. It is the only Colony where they have been invited to unite with the Colonists and to become one People under one law . . . It is your adoption by Her Majesty as her subjects which makes it impossible that the Maori people should be unjustly dispossessed of their lands or property. Every Maori is a member of the British Nation . . .

The Queen saw Maori 'as a part of her especial people'. But the Governor added a threat. If they violated their 'allegiance to the Queen', they would be liable to 'forfeit [their] rights and privileges' as British subjects.

There was no such clause in the Treaty of Waitangi, though such a sub-text could be read into it. Donald McLean, who chaired the meeting at Kohimarama, personified the contradictions in the treaty and in the government's actual dealings with Maori in his combined positions as native secretary and land purchase commissioner. He sought and obtained the chiefs' endorsement of Crown allegiance, including from tribes whose leaders had not signed the treaty in 1840. Significantly for the future, he also re-presented the treaty in Maori, spelling out in the Maori language for the first time that article 2 of the Treaty of Waitangi specified rights to possession of their land, forests and fisheries.

But the chiefs disagreed with the government's policy towards Waitara and the Kingitanga. Maori believed that Maori and Pakeha should share governmental authority under the Queen and stand united but equal, walking in parallel. Such thinking at the time was expressed in religious terms, as equal and united before God. Christianity was politically empowering because it represented a higher power; and it gave Maori a new voice and a way forward in what in today's terms would be described as an increasingly cross-cultural and globalising world. What shocked Maori loyalists over Waitara was that the government had resorted to force in a civil dispute. They believed that law, not war, was the answer. In the view of Renata Tamakihikurangi of Hawkes Bay, the British government breached the treaty by resort to violence. The treaty stood for peace.

4

Remoter Australasia 1861–1890

If the Governor's decision to wage war in Taranaki over Waitara in 1860 was heavy-handed and aggressive, the invasion of the Waikato launched by Sir George Grey in July 1863 amounted to a blatant lunge for power. Indeed – as a narrow victory of numbers – it presaged the takeover by settler New Zealand that deluged Maori. From the 1860s the scales of power tipped to the settler society, and within a generation, Maori shrank from being the majority of the population to a small minority. The amount of land in Maori ownership, already much diminished, halved between 1860 and 1891. But pockets of Maori resistance nurtured a proud legacy that would rebalance relations a century and more later.

NEW ZEALAND WARS

Thanks to James Belich's scholarship, the New Zealand wars have come to be seen as the country's own civil war that played a significant part in defining Pakeha and Maori as 'us' and 'them', and created the national debt. 'New Zealand wars' can be used to include the limited northern wars as well as clashes on both sides of Cook Strait, notably at Wairau in Marlborough in the 1840s. But the wars proper raged from 1860 to 1872 across the North Island, after a decade of peace. These conflicts were begun by the government and were fought over land and sovereignty. Power, propinquity and possession decreed that war would flare in the north, because tribes still owned most of the North Island in the 1860s. Most Maori lived in the North Island, which remained under tribal control outside the isolated coastal towns. By contrast, the South Island was already in settler hands. That left Ngai Tahu the long task of fighting their claim on paper and later in parliament.

In March 1860 Governor Gore Browne ordered government troops to fire the first shots in Taranaki after Maori obstructed the survey of the Waitara block. Frightened settlers sought refuge from resisters in New Plymouth, troops burned the village at Waitara, and farms went up in smoke. For Wiremu Kingi, the offended chief, the King movement offered his only chance of support. The ensuing alliance guaranteed that the dispute would widen, but after reaching a stalemate, the parties called a truce. Irritated by Gore Browne's clumsiness, the British government replaced him by Sir George Grey, recalled in 1861 from Cape Town to Auckland to bring peace to the colony.

On the contrary, Grey brought war. Grey had changed since his first tour of duty in New Zealand; and the settler government wielded more power, while the British military retained 3000 men in the colony. Grey quietly returned the land at Waitara so that he could turn his attention to the Waikato where Potatau's successor, King Tawhiao, was gathering support. He found intolerable the challenge to the Governor's authority represented by the Kingitanga. Misadvising the British government that his preparations were defensive against an alleged Kingite plot to attack Auckland, Grey built a military road south from Auckland towards present-day Hamilton, erected the colony's first telegraph line to send military intelligence, and ordered steamboats to patrol the Waikato River. The Kingitanga warned that the military road must not cross its boundary; and its newspaper announced that the Governor's authority over Kingite territory was unacceptable. On 11 July 1863 Grey demanded that Maori up to the river declare their allegiance. In a pre-emptive strike on 12 July, he ordered Lieutenant-General Cameron to cross the Mangatawhiri stream, the line which the independence movement said that the government forces must not pass. The invasion of the Waikato had begun.

Repeatedly, the Kingite forces blocked the British military advance into the Waikato with a strategy of modern pa and raids. By February 1864 Cameron's men came up against a defensive line, built by the warrior chief Rewi Maniapoto, of earthworks that included large modern pa. It was a lopsided contest. At their peak in 1864, imperial and colonial forces numbered 18,000 against 5000 Maori. A third of the British force comprised volunteers and militia of whom half – 3000 volunteers and military settlers – came from the Australian colonies. In the most famous encounter of all, Rewi Maniapoto made his last stand – remembered as 'Rewi's last stand' – at the battle of Orakau. This episode symbolised Pakeha understanding of the wars in general, whereby Maori inevitably lost to the British after putting up a pointless but heroic resistance. When offered a chance to surrender, Rewi responded that he would fight onwards forever. When Cameron invited the women and children to leave, the reply was that they would die also. The British claimed victory at Orakau, but Rewi and his people sprang through the British cordon and escaped.

In 1864 war spread to Tauranga in the Bay of Plenty and reopened in Taranaki, where British forces faced a new foe in the form of followers of Pai Marire (goodness and peace), also known as Hauhau (the spirit of God, likened to wind). This prophet movement demonstrated the process of adjustment to colonisation in its fusion of biblical and Maori elements and by resistance to the taking of land. Its leader, Te Ua Haumene, politicised by the wrongful purchase of the Waitara block, became a Kingite supporter, and established the Hauhau church, which he believed erased missionary mistakes from Christian teaching. His was the first of several prophet movements to resist oppression and the confiscation of land.

In 1863 the colonial parliament passed the New Zealand Settlements Act, which provided for the taking of land for public purposes and enabled the Governor to establish settlements for colonisation in the North Island. Consequently the government confiscated 1.2 million acres (480,000 ha) of Kingitanga land in 1865, of which only 314,000 acres (125,600 ha) were later returned to neutrals and 'returned rebels'; and military settlers were rewarded with land grants. The confiscation fell unevenly on the government resisters, striking hard at the Waikato tribes while leaving Rewi's people, Ngati Maniapoto, relatively untouched, as if to confirm that the whole Waikato war had been engineered to secure the most fertile Auckland hinterland for settlement. But the King movement lived on, hunkered down in the King Country in the central North Island, where the Maori king effectively ruled over a state within a state.

Worse was to come. In 1865 the settler government established the Native Land Court to extinguish customary land rights, which resulted in the most serious loss of resources by all tribes. It certainly earned its contemporary title of the 'land-taking court'. The court was set up to bring land owned by Maori outside the confiscation areas 'within the reach of colonization', by making it easier to buy, and to effect the 'detribalization of the Natives', to destroy the 'principle of communism' that politicians saw as a 'barrier' to amalgamating Maori into European culture. Effectively the court sought a free market in land held by tribes through individualised property titles. In one move the court overrode the Treaty of Waitangi by ignoring the constraints of chieftainship, because, in awarding title of tribal land to individuals, it substituted its authority for chiefly authority.

In addition, Maori could only sell or lease their land once the Native Land Court had decided its title, so were forced to go to court to establish their claims; and this requirement has always bogged tribes down in lengthy legal proceedings. Court hearings ensnared people in a double bind: to ensure the rights to their land they had to secure individualised title, which dealt a blow to customary tenure and to tribal authority. Land loss followed even when tribes refused to sell, because the court limited ownership to a few named individuals. Initially it adopted a 'ten-owner' rule, registering only ten owners regardless of the number who could lay claim to the land.

In the meantime fighting continued on the east and west coasts of the North Island. The last campaign conducted by imperial troops was in 1866. Henceforth battles would be fought against Maori 'rebels' by kupapa and colonial forces, including from the Australian colonies. Kupapa could be either 'friendlies' who were Queenites rather than Kingites, or they could use the term to state their neutrality. Either way they were independent-minded.

A new warrior, Titokowaru, provoked by aggressive tactics and by confiscation of large tracts of land, took up Te Ua's cause in Taranaki in the late 1860s. Titokowaru faced seemingly impossible

odds when attacked at his stronghold in 1868 by colonial forest
rangers, a force that recruited young men with bush experience who
sought a 'free and exciting life' by striking 'terror into the marauding
natives'. Titokowaru scored a great victory, but was written out of
history because he revised the frontier adventure story's expected
ending.

Te Kooti Arikirangi Te Turuki, on the other hand, is remembered
as a prophet who defied injustice. From 1865 his iwi, Ngati Porou,
were split between a government faction of kupapa Maori and Pai
Marire supporters. Te Kooti had fought on the government's side,
but was arrested with hundreds of Pai Marire followers and imprisoned on the Chatham Islands without trial as a suspected spy. There
he founded his own religion, Ringatu, or the Upraised Hand, and
engineered a brilliant escape with 300 followers to New Zealand
in 1868. Pursued by colonial and kupapa troops, he waged guer-
rilla war, escaping into the remote Urewera district, until he finally
took refuge in 1872 in the King Country, becoming the colony's
most wanted outlaw. He was a Maori equivalent of Ned Kelly, as
famous at the time for his apparent ability to vanish. Surrounded
by ambiguities, neither chief nor tribal leader, he lived in exile yet,
unlike other outlaws, received a pardon. He became the subject of
narrative fiction, astride his white horse, even before his death. Two
of New Zealand's earliest films were *Rewi's Last Stand*, and *The Te
Kooti Trail*, shot by Rudall Hayward in 1927.

The wars changed settlement patterns across the central North
Island. Those opposed to the government often took refuge, as Te
Kooti did, in inaccessible areas inland. Confiscation after the wars
forged grievances that would simmer until the late twentieth century.
On the North Island's central plateau, the government rewarded
loyalists with confiscated land, often the territory of former enemies, which created new problems since under Maori tikanga the
newcomers could claim rights after some years in their new locations. Battles then transferred to the Native Land Court, which
after 1873 demanded even more intense individualisation of land
interests. After the wars, 'neither the treaty nor the doctrine of aboriginal title came to the rescue of Maori'. On the contrary, tolerance
dwindled. With no protection of customary title in the Native Land
Court, there would be no protection in the courts generally. An 1877
judgment by Chief Justice James Prendergast declared the treaty

a 'nullity': an outcome that followed logically from the legislative measures.

Given the futility of war, the prophet Te Whiti emerged to lead the Taranaki people in new, pacifist, methods of resistance. In 1865 the government confiscated Taranaki land as punishment under the New Zealand Settlements Act, and in 1878 began the survey of fertile plains in the province. The delay was significant because in Te Whiti's view the Governor should have occupied the confiscated land at the time of conquest. In the meantime his people reoccupied it and according to custom reaffirmed their rights of ownership. Te Whiti and his supporters – including Titokowaru – ploughed his moko across the disputed plains, obstructed newly surveyed roads, and peacefully removed the surveyors. Furious, the government passed special legislation so that it could hold hundreds of protesters without trial and imprison them with two years hard labour in South Island gaols. Then, as the prisoners returned in 1881, the government auctioned off the block at Parihaka, where Te Whiti had established a model community which attracted a following. Through spring, Taranaki people cleared, fenced and cultivated. The government responded by sending in nearly 1600 troops of the armed constabulary and volunteers, to be greeted by young girls singing and dancing. The Native Minister John Bryce ordered the arrest of Te Whiti and his colleague Tohu Kakahi; they 'walked to captivity' with great dignity and were imprisoned without trial, banished to the South Island until 1883. Bryce ordered the troops to sack Parihaka because its people refused to leave.

Parihaka and the King movement were vindicated more than a century later; both experienced expropriation to make way for small farmers from the 1880s. The government set aside native reserves within the confiscated territory but then vested the reserves in the Public Trustee, who leased them to settlers at a peppercorn rental, and in perpetuity from the 1890s. The land was sliced up but its people rebuilt Parihaka and continued to wear their symbolic headdress, of two white albatross feathers, in proud defiance. Te Whiti and Tohu, like Te Kooti, retained their following; not only did their people venerate them, but historians have since cast them as national heroes in an evolving peace tradition.

King Tawhiao finally made peace in 1881. Against his advice, however, Ngati Maniapoto – who had escaped confiscation because

4.1 P. E. jnr, 'For Diver's reasons', *Wellington Advertiser Supplement*, 19 November 1881. Bryce is carving up the protester, who wears the white feather headdress of Te Whiti's followers and lies down in passive resistance. Te Whiti's ploughmen, tents of the armed constabulary, and Mt Taranaki are in the background.

settlers did not want their rugged country – negotiated with Bryce and his successor, the Liberal John Ballance, to allow surveys for the main trunk railway through their territory. This also affected other tribes in the pan-tribal King movement because the surveys set the tribal boundaries of the five main Kingitanga iwi, including Ngati Tuwharetoa on the volcanic plateau. Before long, individuals acquired title and sold it piecemeal. The controlled opening of the King Country was soon undermined by government policies, through land agent deals with individuals that exacerbated the rivalries inherent in Maori society. Organised protest grew in the 1880s; King Tawhiao petitioned Queen Victoria, and kupapa chiefs joined the crescendo of calls to honour the treaty.

POWER IN NUMBERS

Such demands grew once Maori numbers declined and followed the pattern of population loss suffered by every indigenous society during colonisation. Some argue that this outcome was inevitable because Europeans introduced flora and fauna that subverted the ecologies that they invaded. The Pacific Islands were vulnerable because they were remote from the earth's hothouses of evolution, and New Zealand was the most isolated place of all. New infections ran amok among people with no inherited or acquired immunities, whether to tuberculosis, the biggest killer in the nineteenth century, influenza, or sexually transmitted diseases. Babies and young children were highly susceptible to gut and respiratory infections, so that among Te Arawa of the Rotorua district, for example, only half the children born by the late nineteenth century lived to adulthood. By contrast, Pakeha enjoyed high rates of child survival. The infant mortality rate declined at least from when official statistics began to be published in the 1870s, when infant mortality was already very low by world standards at about 100 deaths in the first year of life per 1000 live births, while parents saw about four of every five children grow up in settler families.

The scales of depopulation and immigration, and child survival, were such that Pakeha outnumbered Maori by 1860. Captain Cook was probably about right with his guess that there were 100,000 Maori people in 1769. By 1858 Maori numbered between 56,000 and 62,000, while Pakeha, at 59,000, were poised to tilt the balance of power. By 1878 Maori were dominated demographically by a ratio of 10 to 1, swamped by two successive immigration waves in the 1860s and 1870s. To summarise, Maori numbers fell by more than half until the 1890s, consistent with a pattern of decline in indigenous populations throughout the Pacific, while mainly British migrants arrived by the boatload.

Dispossession hit North Island tribes hard from the 1860s, and land loss led to population decline. Conversely, depopulation and displacement in the musket wars era contributed to land loss and the erosion of power; cause and effect went both ways. From the 1860s the sale of land through the Native Land Court had as radical an impact as confiscated land in rendering Maori vulnerable to disease and premature death. Most communities lost a resource base, while the land retained proved barely enough for subsistence, let alone development. Hapu who kept land suffered too because multiple owners shared blocks that were too small for everyone and were often uneconomic. Even Te Arawa – whose forces had fired the last

Table 4.1 *Population trends and Maori land ownership*

Year	Estimated Maori Population	Non-Maori Population	Land owned by Maori: ha
1800	150,000		
1820			
1840	100,000	2,000	26,709,342
1852	59,700	55,762	13,770,000
1860		79,000	8,667,000
1874	49,800	295,184	
1878	47,800	410,207	
1881	46,750	487,280	
1886	43,927	576,524	
1891	44,177	624,474	4,487,000
1896	42,113	701,101	
1901	43,143	772,719	2,890,000 (1911)

Source: Mason Durie, *Whaiora: Maori Health Development*, 36

shots in the New Zealand wars, against a retreating Te Kooti in 1872, and who did relatively well as kupapa – felt the grip of the Native Land Court. By the 1880s the effects of land purchase and prolonged land court sittings showed up in declining health status and higher mortality.

British migration, however, inundated Maori and provided the numbers to create a settler society. Given that New Zealand was so far – the furthest place – from Britain, the obstacles of distance and cost determined that migrants had to be either adventurous or given the incentive of a free or subsidised fare to journey to the opposite side of the world. Themselves a tiny fraction of the great European diaspora in the nineteenth century, Australasian migrants shipped out to the New World in four main waves. First came the convicts to eastern Australia, and second the boatloads of free migrants that included the 10,000 New Zealand Company settlers. The third and fourth waves, however, proved to be the most significant in numbers and power. The gold-seekers from 1850 to 1870 who ventured from the goldfields of California to Victoria and then New Zealand, and eventually islands in the South Pacific, brought boom times, towns and gold fever. After them followed a veritable tidal wave of planned, assisted immigration to Australasia from 1860 to 1890, and this

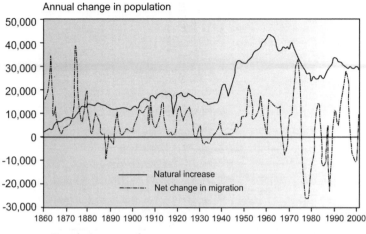

Annual change in population

4.2 Population growth

wave contained the 100,000 migrants carried to New Zealand by the vision of the business politician and Premier Julius Vogel in the 1870s.

Demographic contours illustrate how the migrants in the second half of the nineteenth century proved decisive in shaping Pakeha New Zealand, establishing a settler state and society. Natural increase (births minus deaths) rather than net migration generated most of the rate of population growth from the 1880s until the end of the twentieth century (see 4.2). Settler New Zealand was young, vigorous, and suddenly dominant.

The excess of men usual in frontier societies did not generally last long (see 4.3). Nor did the imbalance of men over women match that in the United States. Only until the 1870s did the Pakeha population bulge with men, as if the population pyramid grew a beer pot. Gold rushes around the Pacific Rim explained this temporary imbalance. Auckland merchants lured gold-seekers to the Coromandel with the offer of a reward in 1852–53, and a brief strike followed in Golden Bay – re-named for the find – in 1856–57. But the real rush to New Zealand from California and Australia began in 1861 when a Tasmanian miner, Gabriel Read, struck gold in a gully in Otago that now bears his name. Otago proved the bonanza from 1861–63, followed by the West Coast from 1864–67. While war preoccupied the North Island, gold fever consumed the south.

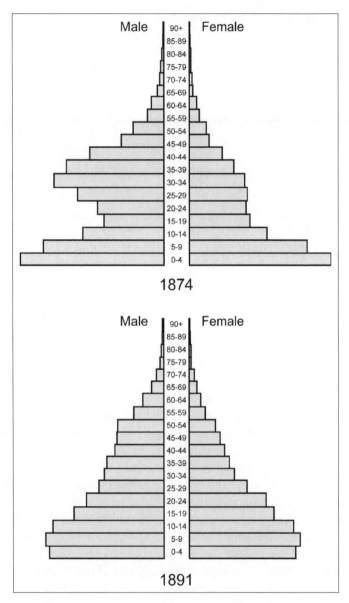

4.3 Population pyramids 1874, 1891 (European only)

Central Otago's European population soared to about 24,000 between 1861 and 1864, but halved once the swarms of gold-seekers learnt of finds on the rugged West Coast. The first and largest stream of miners, containing many Irish, came from the Australian colonies, and the second from Britain, mainly Cornwall and Devon, while the Scots sought opportunities all over New Zealand. Irish migrants also arrived by way of the Australian colonies, where they had acquired experience of life on the goldfields and retained close connections. About 37,000 reached the West Coast in 1865–67, all of them from Australia. Altogether some 195,000 gold-seekers followed the rushes to New Zealand, two-thirds from Australia and the rest from Britain. Many moved on, however, producing a net population gain from gold of 114,000 in the 1860s.

Gold's geology shaped the pattern of the rushes as diggers favoured successive types of gold deposit, from alluvial gold in the swift, ice-cold rivers of the South Island, to beach leads and coastal terraces that demanded sluicing, to gold locked in reefs of quartz, dug by deep-shaft mining. Each kind of deposit created a distinctive culture and community, from nomadic hordes under canvas who left ghost towns, to permanent towns during the underground phase, which required capital and family life. Miners dug piles of tailings and, at Ross on the West Coast and St Bathans in Otago, great holes in the ground. Culturally the rushes transformed the landscape through their impetus to early democracy. From Victoria the miners brought the concept of the miner's right and their hard-won democratic traditions, and New Zealand adopted the Victorian system of goldfields administration. In a direct response to the Eureka uprising at Ballarat, the New Zealand government extended the vote to miners, most of whom would otherwise have been excluded because they did not meet the property qualification. By 1865 the diggers' presence led to fifteen new electorates.

The gold rushes created communities that were both cosmopolitan and ethnically distinctive. Linguists have found that the New Zealand accent first appeared in mining towns in the South Island – and military towns in the North Island – because these places had English speakers from a variety of origins. Census figures for Arrowtown (near Queenstown) show people from England, Ireland, Scotland and Australia in about equal numbers. Arrowtown also had a number of people who had come from or via the Australian colonies and it is possible that this could have influenced early New Zealand English. If not to the same extent as 'Marvellous Melbourne', gold gave a fillip to Dunedin, which temporarily displaced Auckland as New Zealand's largest city and flourished into a banking and business centre, proud of its gold-rush architecture. From Victoria, too, gold lured the future premiers and colonial nationalists Julius Vogel, to start the *Otago Daily Times*, and Richard Seddon, to run a pub on the West Coast.

The gold rushes also fuelled – as in Seddon's case – racial prejudice against the Chinese. At their peak there were 4000 Chinese miners in Otago and 5000 in New Zealand, all from Guangdong province: a tiny proportion compared to the 105,000 in the United States in 1880–81 and 38,500 in Australia. Most were sojourners who experienced mixed fortunes, who remitted money and eventually returned home. Some stayed on as solitary prospectors, while others entered business and later paid for their wives to join them. Chinese in New Zealand formed part of a Pacific Rim diaspora in the 1850s and 1860s. Invited to Otago by Dunedin businessmen in 1865, when diggers flocked to the West Coast, they proved extremely efficient gold-seekers. As numbers rose, so did prejudice, heightened by anti-Chinese agitation in the Australian colonies in 1888, when Chinese refused entry to Australia were diverted to Greymouth and Dunedin. The colonial government responded with the transfer of immigration restriction policy from the Australian colonies.

Chinese have been remembered as fossickers and small-scale prospectors following behind the European diggers; but the entrepreneur Choie Sew Hoy was a prominent figure in gold dredging. It was Sew Hoy who formed the Shotover Big Beach Gold Mining Company, which initiated the first gold dredging boom of 1889–91. His dredge, which provided the prototype for the New Zealand bucket dredge, worked beaches on the Shotover River near Queenstown, where tourists now go for jet boat rides and white-water rafting.

By the 1890s the 'beer pot' in the Pakeha population pyramid had largely worked itself out. Men still outnumbered women, but the numbers of women were starting to catch up as young girls grew to adulthood (4.3). Gold fever and the associated danger of

4.4 Sew Hoy dredge gold mining

'excitement' (a condition ascribed to men), however, threatened the image of New Zealand as an ideal society because of the perceived menace posed by greed, excessive masculinity, and frontier chaos. What subversive forces would the quest for riches unleash, and what might topple the precarious maintenance of order? Miles Fairburn has argued that there was substance to such anxieties: the colony was a 'minimally organised society' between 1850 and 1880, primarily because of the tide of immigrants and the 'lightning expansion' of the frontier. High rates of loneliness, drunkenness, and interpersonal violence all suggested a society short on mutual understanding and social cohesion. The lesson was that Arcadianism was a 'fallacy'; it was 'impossible' to establish an individualistic, harmonious society 'simply on the basis of material abundance'.

Such problems, however, were not unique to the colony or to the frontiers of British settlement. Internationally, rates of violence, drunkenness and civil litigation fell and rose in broad U-curve trends from the late nineteenth to the late twentieth century. Perhaps this is why colonists were so determined to restore the yeoman ideal at the core of Arcadian imagery. They realised that their dream was fragile, at risk of failure as a result of war, gold fever, and economic downturn. Evidence of disorder merely strengthened collective resolve to experiment with new ways of doing things and to improve old ones. Contemporaries responded to imagined crises by establishing institutions such as a police force, not a paramilitary force as on the goldfields, but a combined civil and military police from 1877. Health institutions developed to counter disturbance in body and mind. Fourteen new hospitals served the goldfields in the 1860s. The first lunatic asylums appeared for the mentally ill, which, like hospitals, provided for the care of strangers, usually men without families who would have otherwise been locked in gaol.

More profoundly, colonists developed grand strategies to manage the forces of 'progress'. One such strategy was assisted immigration. The Otago provincial government responded to the gold rush by changing its immigration policy to recruit single women only, and imported 1300 in 1862. Canterbury spent almost its entire migration fund on single women in the 1860s to rectify the 'disproportion of the sexes' with the idea of protecting its myths of settlement. Again, women were seen as vital to the ideal society as wives, mothers and domestic workers, to create and raise its basis of well-behaved citizens and settled families.

CREATING A SETTLER STATE AND SOCIETY

The 1840s to the 1880s have been described as an era of 'progressive colonisation' in which the neo-British of New Zealand grew explosively. In 40 years, the settlers mined £40 million in gold, sheared £40 million of wool, and borrowed £70 million on the British market. To keep the show on the road, however – especially after the calamity of the New Zealand wars – required the establishment of what can be described as an entrepreneurial state. This model of state development entailed a close partnership between colonial government and business, and government borrowing and expenditure in the interests of business, to stimulate economic growth.

By the 1870s the spirit of colonisation needed a hand, and under Julius Vogel as colonial treasurer, government and business co-operated to attract capital and labour. Contrary to the then economic orthodoxy, Vogel determined that government enterprise could expand the economy faster than anything the private sector could achieve alone, through borrowing for public works and immigration. Vogel himself moved to London as the colony's agent-general (high commissioner) in 1876 to promote colonisation in the world centre of finance. By 1880 the government had borrowed £20 million and recruited over 100,000 extra migrants (see 4.2 and table 4.1). Isolation still ruled, however; even subsidised passages from Europe were not enough to persuade the desired number of people to take on the expense and distance of travel to New Zealand. The government offered free passages from 1873, after which agricultural labourers migrated in droves. About half of the assisted migrants of the 1870s were English; a fifth came from the west of England, including Cornwall. About a quarter were Scots. The colony also looked to Germany and Scandinavia for workers to develop North Island bush settlements.

Gradually communications began to link isolated settlements, making the connections that allowed people to think nationally. In 1876 a private telegraph cable joined New Zealand to Australia. A great earthquake lifted Wellington sufficiently to preclude building a sea wall and made room for a road to Petone in 1855, elevating the town's status. The shift of the capital south from Auckland to Wellington prepared for the centralising process a decade later. In the South Island the main trunk line increased economic and social integration, linking the port of Bluff in the far south to Christchurch. In the North Island the railway began to encroach into the King Country. Settler capitalists vied – and co-operated – with the government to purchase tribal land with title individualised through the Maori Land Court. One syndicate led by Auckland business politicians bought 86,500 acres (34,600 ha) of confiscated land in the Waikato for development and to float land deals on the London market. This vast block passed to Thomas Russell, 'as a result of clandestine negotiations with the Vogel Ministry', which justified the unlawful sale as expedient.

Although all the colonies with responsible government – the future British white Dominions – adopted the entrepreneurial model of state development, it proved strongest in Australia and New Zealand. From the earlier experience of the New Zealand Company, business politicians learnt the lesson that in order to make a profit colonial business had to obtain access to capital, for infrastructure and physical improvements, at less than full cost. The problems of distance, low institutional density and isolation encouraged government and business to get together to diminish expense, risk and distrust. In turn the colony depended on the network of finance and commercial services that together made the British Empire.

With the end of provincial government in 1876 New Zealand's political institutions resembled forms in the Australian colonies: government was unitary and centralised, with two houses, the lower house – the General Assembly – elected on the basis of one man one vote from 1879, and an appointed upper house of property owners; but in New Zealand Maori gained manhood suffrage twelve years earlier than settlers, with a view to defusing anger from the wars. From 1867 all Maori males aged 21 and over, including 'half castes', could vote for four new Maori seats in parliament. At the time the idea was to include Maori in the political process without undermining settler control. Colonial politicians made the male Maori vote conditional on no 'treason felony or infamous offence', so that 'rebels' in the wars would be denied political citizenship. Donald McLean suggested the idea of four Maori seats as a temporary measure, effectively until Maori were assimilated and tribal land was converted into individual title, whereupon Maori men could exercise the same property vote as settlers. For North Island politicians it was also convenient that the four Maori seats balanced the Pakeha electorates created by the gold rushes. The extension of the vote to all men in December 1879, following the introduction of the secret ballot in 1870, made New Zealand an early democracy. Increased popular participation and national issues began to dominate electoral politics, while class and party politics had their beginnings in the late 1880s.

Settlers committed to self-reliance (though funded by British capital) expected 'a reasonable share in the fruits of progress'. The Protestant majority saw their colony as Christian in law and ethos but without an established church where the religion of the Bible was fundamental to morality. Roman Catholics – about 12 per cent of the population – comprised a smaller minority than across the Tasman.

Education proved to be one area where religious sectarianism influenced political debate. The Sisters of St Joseph founded in South Australia began a network of schools in New Zealand from 1883, while Catholic bishops worked closely with their Australian colleagues to strengthen Roman Catholic identity. Catholicism continued to provide an alternative politics for those who sympathised with Maori grievances. In 1883 the French nun Suzanne Aubert (Mother Mary Joseph) commenced her mission to Maori on the Whanganui River. The government, however, established village primary schools for Maori a decade before it established the public schools system. Separate 'native schools' from 1867 implemented the policy of amalgamation through insistence on the use of English, and the alternative given children was stark: either 'take to the best European customs' or 'be sure to die out'. If the teachers were mainly Pakeha, assistant teachers were mainly Maori: bright teenage girls, as in mainstream primary schools. A Maori community that aspired to a school had to provide the land, half the cost of the buildings and a quarter of the teacher's salary. At the secondary level, the churches established denominational boarding schools for Maori. Schools such as the Anglican Te Aute College would prepare a Maori élite, fluent in English and Maori, who moved in both worlds.

With other English-speaking countries, New Zealand introduced free, compulsory, secular primary education in 1877, though elementary education for girls and boys was widespread in towns before the state legislated for compulsory attendance. Education gradually transformed the child's place in the family from a worker, and economic asset, to a scholar, who was precious but not contributing as much (if at all) to the family income. At first there was a high rate of non-attendance because farming families had more use for children's labour than for schoolwork. The real winners from free, state primary schooling were working-class girls whose lives changed more than boys' experiences did as girls increasingly attended school and later found employment before marriage. Girls and boys still lived by a 'gendered script'; at Taradale School out of Napier an iron fence erected in 1890 divided their playgrounds. In the main towns, in competition with church schools, the state funded separate secondary schools for girls and boys to which bright students could win scholarships. Nelson College was set up as early as 1856, while Otago and Christchurch Boys' High Schools served as preparatory schools for the new provincial university colleges, established by acts of parliament, and acquired twin schools for girls, Otago in 1869 and Christchurch Girls' High School in 1877.

The colony's first university college, Otago (1869) and the second, Canterbury (1873) became the third and fourth Australasian universities after Sydney and Melbourne. At Canterbury College women were admitted from the start on an equal basis with men because John Macmillan Brown, one of the foundation professors, insisted that 'true democracy' required that the 'best women as well as the best men' take their rightful place in arts and government. He taught and married Helen Connon, who became the first woman in the British Empire to graduate with honours when she received an MA with first-class honours in Latin and English at Canterbury College in 1881. Connon's friend, Kate Edger, was the first woman to graduate with a Bachelor's degree, from Auckland University College in 1877. These women colleagues were rediscovered in time for the centenary of women's suffrage in 1993 after decades of invisibility.

A role model for earlier generations of schoolgirls because she married her professor, Helen Macmillan Brown epitomised the new urban woman, genteel, scholarly and beautiful, who countered arguments by critics of women's higher education that too much study impaired maternity. Her greatest public achievement was as the second principal of Christchurch Girls' High School, whose academic reputation she established by preparing girls for university, while she broke with tradition by working full-time when she was a wife and mother of two small daughters.

The first female graduates proved to be path-breakers in other ways. Demographically, they led the transition in family size that transformed families across the European world: 55 per cent of Canterbury women graduates in the university's first 50 years remained unmarried, while those who did marry had small families. Such statistics appeared to confirm the stereotype that higher education made women less fit to be mothers. But graduate women thought that it better equipped them to raise superior quality children (see chapter 5).

If colonists were unexceptional in bringing such inherited ideas and cultural practices with them, in other ways they persistently broke new ground. Motivated by the principles of self-help and

4.5 Helen Connon, MA Hons 1881: University of Canterbury

family responsibility that drove the fertility decline, settler New Zealand embarked on what some scholars interpret as a colonial welfare experiment, where independence and voluntarism held sway. The government assisted families through immigration and land settlement rather than by income support. Colonists

determined not to adopt Poor Laws because they assumed such measures ought not to be necessary in a New World that would by definition be better than the old. Families should care for themselves,
and a society that aspired to be settled opted for self-help rather
than support for 'shiftless' itinerants who threatened the anticipated
respectable order of things.

Instead New Zealand borrowed concepts from the Australian
colonies; in 1884 a married women's property act allowed wives
to own property separate from their husbands, and in 1885 the
colony established a national system of hospitals and charitable aid
under local boards that created a pattern of local autonomy, mixed
funding and discretionary assistance. Widows stood at the top and
unmarried mothers at the bottom of the hierarchy of women who
had lost a male breadwinner, while unemployed men without families, judged 'undeserving', were expected to fend for themselves.
Hospitals were also 'user pays' until 1939.

Such institutional developments reflected a core belief that settlers were blessed by living in an exceptionally healthy country. The
image of a healthy outdoors life, especially for children, has consistently infused New Zealand marketing. The colony was promoted
as a health spa in the late nineteenth century, foreshadowing the
establishment of the Department of Tourist and Health Resorts –
itself a world first – in 1901. It was logical for tourism and health
to combine because good health was associated with fresh air and
a clean, unspoilt environment.

Maori were central to the health spa, and in particular Te Arawa
of the geothermal region around Rotorua. While William Fox, the
artist politician, urged the government to make the Rotorua district a national park on the Yellowstone model, Te Arawa proposed
a township to be laid out around the Rotorua hot springs, with
the idea of creating a sanatorium for tourists where visitors would
soak in hot pools and enjoy water treatments. In 1880 local Maori
agreed to lease the geyser lands rather than sell them, and to allow
the government to auction 99-year leases on their behalf. Under
the Thermal Springs District Act 1881, however, the government
obtained a monopoly on the purchase and lease of areas with hot
springs, lakes or rivers. Consequently half the Rotorua blocks were
sold by the end of the century and Native Land Court hearings lasted

a generation, leaving Te Arawa's economy in a precarious state. The core problem was that the government, not the 'native proprietors', controlled the leases. When lessees defaulted in the depression of the 1880s, government mismanagement through the difficult years compelled forced sales.

By establishing Rotorua as a tourist and health resort, however, Te Arawa became influential in shaping race relations and images of the 'exotic' Maori. As it became easier for tourists to experience the picturesque, travelling by steamship and by rail, a flurry of guidebooks to 'Boiling Water Land' appeared. By the 1880s numbers of tourists travelled from Australia to visit Rotorua and its natural wonders, including the Pink and White Terraces before they were destroyed by a volcanic eruption in 1886.

New Zealand's first national park – Tongariro – only came into being because Te Heuheu Tukino IV, paramount chief of Ngati Tuwharetoa, gifted the area that contained the three volcanic peaks of the central North Island, including Mt Ruapehu, to the people of New Zealand in 1887. The gesture was of a chief of high rank exercising his mana; the Native Land Court had made a division of the land, and awarded the tops of the mountains Tongariro and Ruapehu to Te Heuheu alone. He then gave the mountains to the people, European and Maori, for a national park, in accordance with the wish of the government. This gracious act was also expedient politically, since the volcanoes had less value for farming than for tourism. Increasingly, Pakeha as well as Maori began to appreciate New Zealand's beauty and to contemplate scenery preservation, if only in places less conducive to timber milling and sowing grass.

A FEDERAL AUSTRALASIA?

Ties of family, cultural and policy transfer, trade, travel and communications connected Australasia in the late nineteenth century. In the 1860s Charles Hursthouse, a former colonist, proposed a federation – indeed, an Australasian republic – of New Zealand and the Australian colonies, excluding Western Australia (which had reintroduced convicts). He reasoned that their 'deep natural Exchequer' of land, minerals, and agricultural resources would provide better security for loans on British money markets. By 1890

Australasia had come to mean the Australian colonies, New Zealand, Fiji, 'and any other British Colonies or possessions in Australasia'. At the Australasian Federation Conference in Melbourne in 1890 and at the federation convention in Sydney in 1891 New Zealand's representative, the pastoralist politician Captain William Russell, described the colony as a 'rather remote part of Australasia', distinguishing between the 'more remote colonies of Australasia' and the 'Australian colonies proper'. The big question for Russell was whether Australasia should federate as a British sphere in the South Pacific. Not Australia but Australasia denoted the community to which New Zealand could belong, and allowed room for the special nature of Pakeha–Maori interdependence. Ironically the New Zealand wars reinforced the faith in superior race relations. Russell repeated in 1891 that questions of 'native title' were 'of very grave moment', and Pakeha–Maori relations 'of the most serious importance'.

New Zealanders contemplated more than the 'crimson thread of kinship' (imperial blood tie) with Australians; politicians pondered the effects of the climate and environment on British racial development, imagining differently what it meant to be British. Russell told Australians that New Zealand was likely to develop a 'different national type'. Imperialism and nationalism were not mutually exclusive; often in balance, they might present as Janus-faced. Indeed, imperialism could manifest as nationalism and vice versa, blurring the boundaries of identity. In 1905 Richard Jebb gave this seeming paradox the name of 'colonial nationalism'. The 'soul of the Empire' for Jebb was 'not one, but two'; the one the awakening patriotism of the native-born in Canada, Australia, South Africa and New Zealand, and the other the British imperial 'life-task' of spreading civilisation. Many in New Zealand agreed that their country's future lay with the native-born, a name that settlers appropriated for themselves, leaving Maori for the indigenous people. Following white Australians, Pakeha were beginning to turn inward in their search for identity, to the landscape – the bush – and a future shaped by the land, even more than by the surrounding ocean. Much of the explanation for Australasia's subsequent 'dismemberment' relates to seismic shifts about 1890 in culture as well as in the economy and political institutions.

The economic bubble burst in the 1880s. Whether the colony plunged into 'long depression' from 1885 until 1895 is moot because the word 'depression' has changed its meaning and economists argue that real incomes reached a plateau rather than declined. Relative to their past experience, therefore, people felt deprived. Historians put the Long Depression in capitals because of its effects on people: unemployment, family distress, ragged children and exploited women workers, general business collapse, a crash in the property market, a ten-year banking crisis, bankruptcies and unstable ministries. They point to new class tensions and moral panic that Old World evils had appeared, such as sweating of women and children in the clothing industry, which prompted a royal commission report in 1890. In a workingman's paradise a provident husband and father would support his family. Was the ideal society tumbling down? Were migrant hopes and myths illusory?

The 1880s and 1890s in New Zealand and Australia have parallels with the 1980s and 1990s: financial institutions failed, big businessmen were bankrupted, politicians were involved in speculation, as was business in government. A 'frenzy of private borrowing' pinpointed the problem of banks lending by overdraft, where banks ran their own scheme of borrowing for development parallel to that of colonial governments. In these circumstances, a sharp drop in British capital – the drying up of loans in London – squeezed the trans-Tasman financial structure. Just as borrowing in London inflated the boom of the 1870s, shrinking British credit aggravated the downturn in the 1880s and early 1890s. Loans did not dry up only for external reasons: London financiers took fright at declining profitability in the colonies. In the 1880s New Zealand offered less attractive investment opportunities than across the Tasman, but investment there, too, rapidly dried up. The lesson was that development had to generate sufficient export income or London would tighten its grip on economic life.

Big public spending by local and central government, unpromising business ventures and excessive house building characterised all the main towns, though Auckland experienced hard times later than Dunedin and Christchurch; in the early 1880s Auckland enjoyed a suburban building boom but by 1886 had 2000 empty houses. Cheap credit and speculation in real estate brought down many in

the local business community. It probably also hurt aspiring subur-
banites burdened by mortgages and unsellable dream homes.

Hard times, combined with the British example, encouraged the
growth of 'new unionism' among unskilled workers in the trans-
Tasman labour movement, notably in export-related industries,
among seamen, watersiders, shearers, coalminers, and tailoresses.
Locally the labour movement boasted 200 unions with 63,000 members by 1890. Both unions and shipowners developed Australasian
federations, the seamen and coalminers through the Maritime Council, which affiliated to the Australian Maritime Council in 1889. The
Union Steam Ship Company, based in Dunedin, became the arch-
enemy of seamen and miners because it had a monopoly in the New
Zealand coal industry and of trans-Tasman shipping. Employers
interpreted the mere establishment of a union as an aggressive act.
For the labour movement, however, it was vital to have trade unions
recognised because unskilled men were easily replaced. New unionism asserted a form of social citizenship – the 'closed shop' – against
the market liberalism of the employers, who insisted on 'freedom
of contract'. Rising tensions in the context of depression triggered
the Maritime Strike, which spread from Sydney in September 1890,
and involved at least 50,000 workers in Australia and 8000 in New
Zealand.

The Maritime Strike did not determine the response of arbitration, although it focused attention on the idea. The crises of depression and conflict together prompted a rethink of the whole nation-
building project, giving impetus to plans to redraft the government's
role in mediating between the new settler society and global pressures. As we have seen, isolation and smallness compelled an active
role by governments, and exerted an enduring impact, shaping the
very conditions of settlement. The entrepreneurial state that emerged
foreshadowed a new model of state development. A set of social
experiments accompanied the restructuring of the economy. In finding a way out of the mire New Zealand would be rescued by the technical advance of refrigeration, as both Australia and New Zealand
responded to crisis by seeking a preferential position in the British
market.

5

Managing globalisation 1891–1913

A changed attitude to globalisation emerged out of the aura of crisis: now there was a growing trend to manage it. The Australasian colonies resolved to seize opportunities to develop new commodities for export, yet manage the social outcomes by building an edifice of progressive liberal 'state experiments'. Under Liberal governments from 1891 to 1912 reformist politicians and public servants set out to create New Zealand as a democratic social laboratory. In doing so, they enacted an Australasian model of state development.

Political scientists have shown how Australian institutions have mediated globalisation through a colonial, democratic citizenship. The 'Australian Settlement', supposedly established at federation, had as its five planks a white Australia, and associated restricted immigration; arbitration; protection; 'state paternalism' and 'imperial benevolence'. In reality it was Australasian: a distinctive Australian and New Zealand settler colonial response to guarantee 'domestic defence' against a range of shared perceived and actual external threats.

Concern about the social consequences of global forces shaped governance in all the Australasian colonies, and fostered a new liberalism. As outlined by William Pember Reeves, a newspaper editor and Liberal politician who helped fashion this regional model of state development – and as a historian, then wrote it into New Zealand history – the 'state experiments' entailed state intervention in pursuit of liberal ideals in Australia and New Zealand. The Liberals, as a party of and for the people, promoted populism. They aimed to use state intervention to make it easier to 'get on' and to create a civilised community. The Australasian 'experiments' ranged from the entrepreneurial state, women's franchise and liquor laws, and cheap land for development, to management of the effects of capitalism and competition (that is, globalisation) on labour, plus an old age pension for ageing pioneers; and the exclusion of aliens and undesirables. Political scientists have characterised the state experiments of the 1890s as social liberalism, while historians have seen them as a renewed effort to fulfil the Pakeha foundation idea of an ideal society, or to build a new, democratic world.

This era brought into sharp relief the tension between forces for exclusion, driven by imperial views of superiority, and inclusion, derived from the humanism within Enlightenment thought. The former promoted ethnic solidarity among settlers at the expense of non-Europeans; the latter benefited women; while Maori were both included and excluded.

Historians subsequently claimed the state experiments for separate national narratives, according to their own time and perspective. If New Zealand's Liberals were viewed as colonial pragmatists by 1930, radicals and humanitarians in the 1960s and, by the 1970s, technocrats determined to impose social control, late twentieth-century historians interpreted them as populists and nationalists. In their accounts, the Liberal era was one of centralisation and colonial nationalism, which saw the creation of the modern New Zealand state. Society was settling from the 1880s, as Pakeha born in New Zealand began to outnumber migrants. Pride in being a 'native-born' European manifested itself in native associations, motifs borrowed from Maoridom, and musings about New Zealand as 'Maoriland'. As this sense of national identity grew, the idea coalesced of New Zealand as a site of experiment and its people as wont to score 'firsts' and to climb to new heights.

For neo-imperial historians, on the other hand, a new system grew from the old in the Liberal era. According to Belich, from the 1880s New Zealand tightened links with Britain, rather than striving for national independence. After an era of 'progressive colonisation', technical progress in the form of refrigeration of frozen meat, butter and cheese led to 'recolonisation', joining New Zealand to

London, the centre of the British Empire, as effectively as a bridge. A closer link to Britain – then the world's largest global trader – offered a means for a remote colony to manage globalisation and conduct relations with its imperial power in an increasingly global market. One problem with this thesis, however, is that it represents the Liberal era merely as a 'transitional' phase between 'progressive colonisation' and 'recolonisation'. It does not explicitly relate either to the processes of globalisation; though implicitly New Zealanders replaced one way of relating to the world by another. Its focus on Britain and British ties is at the expense of ideas and policy transfer with Australia, and of shared Antipodean state development. Yet colonial liberals built institutions for a civil society that were shared and distinctive to Australasia for much of the twentieth century. Further, imperialism fed nationalism and nationalism fostered imperialism.

Both British and Australian dimensions are necessary to produce a balanced New Zealand history. The Australasian state experiments served to market these colonies to an imperial world. It was no accident that Reeves wrote his two-volume *State Experiments in Australia and New Zealand* in London, as New Zealand's agent-general. Britain was the only serious global power and London the centre of world finance. The British global economy grew rapidly with innovations in transport that saw a collapse in the cost of sea freight. While steamships allowed the Australasian colonies to export produce to British markets, refrigeration was the key technical advance; New Zealand made its first shipment of frozen meat in 1882. Refrigeration generated revolutionary developments not merely in the economy but in New Zealand culture.

The major change to the New Zealand political economy came when agriculture was restructured to export food as well as fibre to the British market. Assisted by British capital, the country pulled out of its economic doldrums from 1895, earlier than the eastern Australian colonies, which were also beginning to produce food for export. The Australasian colonies faced quite different conditions from Europe and North America. With a small, scattered domestic market, and the problems of vulnerability and remoteness from overseas markets and sources of technological change, Australasia would not have found it more efficient to industrialise. British investors, moreover, would not have approved: they believed in Australasia's 'natural resource benefits' as much as did the British settlers. Given the power of European mental maps, there were no credible alternative paths of development. New Zealand economic expansion was destined to be by family farms because global capital ingested Arcadian mythology.

Innovations designed to manage export economies from a distance extended beyond government to the business sector. Stock and station agents represented an Australasian response to a history and geography of isolation, by reducing the costs of marketing over long distances, transferring information about British capital, and establishing connections through settler society networks. New Zealand, being small, relied on such entrepreneurship to temper instability and shocks. Stock and station agencies became business leaders as capital and ideas traders between local farmers and the global – British – export market.

The export-led economy fostered the economic dependency of settler capitalism. The colony's increasingly bilateral, dependent trading relations with Britain reordered not only the economy, but also its physical, social and cultural landscapes. Refrigeration had dramatic ecological effects: it also raised the hopes of those for whom Arcadia meant small farming. Indeed, the way that mutton and dairy produce featured in national policies moulded forms of social and political life.

To balance the readjustment of the colony's global relations, Liberal politicians and public servants resolved to create a social laboratory. This comprised what political scientists call a social contract: an arrangement among people who recognised their mutual interests in creating a democratic society and behaved accordingly. In New Zealand, as in the Australian colonies, liberals devised a social contract between settler capitalism and the entrepreneurial state. In New Zealand, the social contract was a settler contract, encapsulated in its state experiments. The settler contract balanced the new export economy with a fresh start at consolidating the ideal society after the distress of the 1880s. To contemporaries, 'New World' and 'crisis' were contradictory terms; the very idea of

New Zealand entailed escape from Old World evils. Rather they hoped to make New Zealand a better Britain.

THE SETTLER CONTRACT

The settler contract – fundamentally a deal about land and property ownership – mediated between global forces and the colonial body politic. Intended for the 'free' settler and workingman, it was based on early democracy, although the contract was for Pakeha only. Under the Liberals, settling the land came to be viewed as a panacea to address urban ills. The new export economy based on an increasingly mechanised dairy industry revived plans for closer settlement. The idea of an independency, a block of land on which the settler and his family built a home of their own, gained momentum.

In the 1890s, Crown lands could not satisfy settler demand. Land prices rose as new land became scarce with the growing settler population and their desire to become landowners. The first Liberal government in 1891 (65 per cent migrants) aimed to make land accessible to settlers, to give them a better chance at life. This goal presumed a collective idea of an archetypal outdoors lifestyle, embodied in the settler contract: husbandry to provide for the settler family's independence and material comfort. Achieving this goal meant obtaining the best of the 11 million acres (4.4 million ha) of land still owned by Maori in the North Island, which was ideal for dairying. It also meant purchasing large estates in the South Island for subdivision into smaller farms, suited to grain and grazing sheep. Much of the land owned by Maori was timbered. The principal goal became to buy blocks from Maori as cheaply as possible, to establish bush properties for settlers in the North Island.

From 1870 to 1890 proved to be the era of major land loss for tribes in the central North Island. The government, however, bought another 2.7 million acres (1.08 million ha) between 1892 and 1899 for £775,500, or an average of 5s 9d an acre, alienated through the Native Land Court. At the same time the government paid 84s an acre for estates in the South Island owned by Europeans. Settlers acquired another 423,000 acres (169,200 ha) privately by 1907.

Accordingly, over 3 million acres (1.2 million ha) of Maori land was transferred to settlers as a result of purchases begun or completed in the 1890s. About 28 per cent of land still held by Maori in 1890 was alienated within a decade. In the process, most remaining first-class land passed into settler hands, and the state engineered this transfer extremely cheaply.

Cheap loans through advances to settlers consolidated the settler contract. The state acted as landlord for the less well-off, introducing a lease-in-perpetuity (999-year lease) in 1892 in order to provide security for settlers who could not afford to buy freehold land. Instead, landholders reserved any capital for improvements. The Liberal statute that offered the most insight into the settler contract, however, was the Advances to Settlers Act of 1894. State advances for land were for Pakeha only. They comprised another regional experiment, as Reeves observed: state loans to settlers served as a 'special reward' for 'enterprise' at the 'other end of the earth', across the Australasian colonies. With falls in commodity prices and high interest rates, a colonial farmer had to have cheaper finance to live. Advances to settlers also diminished British investors' doubts about the scope for development of New Zealand and Australian farming. The winners were small farmers, agricultural labourers and their families who had access to capital; the 'deserving', who were best able to help themselves, if the ultimate outcome can define them as winners, that is. The isolated bush settlement of Ballance is a product of state advances to settlers; named after the first Liberal Premier John Ballance, it is a dot on the map under the Tararua range, between Pahiatua and the Manawatu Gorge.

Most of all, however, the suburban house and garden came to signify the settler contract and the family ideal of land and home ownership in the New World, transporting from the Old World the idea of the country in the city. In contrast to their medieval European forebears, however, these low-density suburban houses spread outwards rather than upwards in creating the 'new urban frontier' of New Zealand towns. Descended from the rural cottage rather than the townhouse of western Europe, the standard New Zealand house was a cottage or villa of four or five rooms, and shared New World ideals, design and layout with cities in Australia and the American West. Local carpenters built houses using pattern

5.1 House in Bealey Avenue, Christchurch, possibly the
Minson family home near the Carlton Mill Bridge. This
spacious villa represented the suburban house to which most
New Zealanders aspired. Photographed *c.* 1897, flags are
flying to celebrate Queen Victoria's jubilee, and the verandah
is decorated with fashionable Chinese lanterns. Note also the
bicycle (a modern symbol), the cabbage tree (indigenous
flora), and the corrugated iron fence.

books from Australia and California. What made the ordinary New
Zealand house distinctive from its Pacific Rim cousins was that it
was built mostly in timber (with the exception of the deep south, in
Otago).

From the beginning of New Zealand townships the suburban ideal
existed, in the ideas for the Wakefieldian settlements. The ideal was
male-centred but also family-centred, built on skilled working-class
values of respectability; of separate spheres for men and women,
thrift, sobriety and security. By 1911 49 per cent of the Pakeha
population lived in urban places of over 2500 people, compared
to 55 per cent in Australia and 46 per cent in the United States.
Of this Pakeha population, 31 per cent lived in the four main centres, and 18 per cent in small towns such as Palmerston North

(home to 10,000 people). Maori, by contrast, were overwhelmingly rural. Australia and New Zealand had two of the highest home ownership rates in the world by 1911, of 50 per cent or more. Home ownership was the dominant form of tenure in settler New Zealand.

We can reconcile the argument that the Liberals espoused skilled working-class values with the idea that the farmer stood at the top of the Liberal league table of the deserving, and represented the coming man. The settler contract was realised on the dairy farm; but it also found expression in suburbia, in the ordinary small house and domestic garden.

WOMEN'S SUFFRAGE

New Zealand is proud of its history of early women's suffrage, which was granted in 1893. Yet the colony was relatively late to adopt marriage reform, introducing restricted equal rights to divorce in 1898, after Britain and the Australian colonies. There was no inconsistency in being early with one measure and late with the other, because New Zealand was a 'man's country' where women were valued as wives and mothers. On one hand, women's scarcity value offered scope for greater opportunities and potential political equality; on the other, it imposed what feminist scholars have viewed as patriarchal constraints. Historians have therefore debated whether early women's suffrage recognised women's special role in the home and family, or changes in women's status sufficient to convince politicians, and launch a women's campaign for political citizenship.

These competing arguments emphasised different images of New Zealand women, embodying the two principal themes of colonial feminism: the New Woman, who stood for freedom from women's 'disabilities', for equality and progress; and the colonial helpmeet, representing society's moral guardians and the 'mothers of the race'. Kate Sheppard of Christchurch, the national leader of the women's suffrage campaign, embodied both New Woman and colonial helpmeet. Rediscovered by women's historians for the celebration of the women's suffrage centenary in 1993, she was resurrected as a national icon with her image stamped on the New Zealand $10 note. Religious, tactful and beautiful, with a questionable private life, Kate Sheppard led a quiet campaign that won cross-spectrum support.

If we blend the arguments in the suffrage debate, it emerges that the women's movement sought equal rights on grounds of difference, that is, equality as women, for the public good. Suffragists argued that the vote would allow women to extend their maternal skills to the public world, to the greater public benefit. Among the reasons for supporting women's suffrage advanced by the Women's Christian Temperance Union in 1891, first on the list were: 'Because the enfranchisement of women is a question of public well-being', and 'Because the votes of women would add weight and power to the more settled and responsible communities'. Suffragists as helpmeets *and* New Women also wanted men to change, to stop drinking and domestic violence. As Anna Stout, wife of the chief justice Sir Robert Stout, explained: 'Our children must have pure and temperate fathers'.

For women on the urban frontier, including in New Zealand, the vote was both the ambivalent gift of men and a struggle by the colonial women's movement. Women's numbers were significant in towns, where the majority of them lived. Male settler politicians needed their support. The campaign for the vote succeeded because of co-operation between sympathetic men in parliament and the women's movement outside. While women collected the signatures on mass petitions, their conservative advocate Sir John Hall, a Canterbury pastoralist, rolled out the petitions – literally – on the floor of parliament, in a powerful public gesture.

Just as one man one vote included Maori, Pakeha and Maori women gained the vote together in 1893, just in time to vote in that year's election. In Australia, white women gained the federal vote at the same time as Indigenous Australians were denied it, under the Commonwealth Franchise Act of 1902. The contrast suggests that Maori, unlike Aboriginal Australians, were included in liberal concepts of 'the people', and of the 'British race'. But the reality was not so clear cut. Other reforms were a long time coming while gender divisions remained firmly intact. Women could join the 'women's parliament', the non-party National Council of Women, from 1896, of if they wished to participate in Liberal politics they were confined to the women's branch of the Liberal Association, established by

5.2 The Summit at Last. *New Zealand Graphic and Ladies Journal*, 1894. Amazonian womanhood assisted to the summit by the liberal man (dressed as a lawyer). Scaling new heights was already firmly embedded in the New Zealand psyche.

Maud Reeves, wife of William Pember Reeves. The first woman member of parliament, Elizabeth McCombs, was elected only in 1933, on the death of her husband, a Labour politician.

Put in an international context, women gained the vote early in places where men had also gained manhood suffrage relatively early, ushered in by gold rushes. Generally, too, women's suffrage was won early in colonial settler communities that had dispossessed indigenous people, where claiming the land was central to politics. In

these men's countries, women's rights came to the fore as reformers waged social purity campaigns against the 'demon drink' that
brought such grief to women and children, and strove to establish
new societies. Thus New Zealand became the first self-governing
country to enfranchise women to counterbalance rough men and
to promote respectability in public life. It was not the first place in
the world: that accolade went to the remote island of Pitcairn in
1838, while three mid-American states preceded New Zealand, and
the colonial parliaments in South Australia and Western Australia
voted for women's suffrage soon after New Zealand, in 1894 and
1899. In New Zealand, however, gender trumped race: humanism
included women aged 21 or more, as wives and mothers, in the
social contract.

In Australia and New Zealand, national narratives separately
claimed compulsory arbitration as a key institution, reflective of the
national psyche. The two countries were the pioneers of compulsory
industrial conciliation and arbitration, which became the pivot of
industrial relations and later their welfare states. In New Zealand,
Minister of Labour William Pember Reeves was the architect of
the 1894 Act. He gained some of his ideas from a bill drafted by
Charles Kingston, the Liberal Premier of South Australia, and some
from New South Wales and Massachusetts. New Zealand historians maintain that a Liberal–Labour alliance produced the distinctive institution. The New Zealand example, however, supports as
readily the argument that liberalism shaped compulsory arbitration
as an idea and a system. In liberal thought, arbitration operated for
a 'free, prosperous and contented people'. In addition to advances
to settlers, state arbitration in industrial disputes formed part of the
settler contract, intended for the community as a whole, not just
labour. As John Ballance explained: 'the capitalist equally with the
labourer must be identified, by residence and fulfilling all the duties
of a colonist, with the progress and destiny of New Zealand'.

Again the strategic focus was to promote export-led development
and growth, while at the same time meeting political and social
ends by striving for harmony in the workplace. The Australasian

colonies shared this strategy as another means of managing global-isation because they were too small to influence international trade cycles; instead, when times were tough they would act to avoid disputes. The system, which in New Zealand entailed local con-ciliation boards and an arbitration court, was intended to 'hold the balance' between capital and labour. In theory, it balanced the unpredictable export economy with the desire for security by work-ers, and so ensured what came to be called a 'fair go' for ordinary people.

Some historians suggest that this regional model developed from a context of financial crisis and labour unrest, combined with early democracy and ideas of bettering Britain. Long-term trends proved more significant: of settlement patterns and entrepreneurial states that allowed social engineering by middle-class professionals as politicians and public servants. Shared and parallel problems and political opportunities led to a pattern of trans-Tasman policy trans-fer. The classical Australasian form of compulsory arbitration, intro-duced in New Zealand in 1894, entered the statutes of Western Australia in 1900, although Western Australia enjoyed a gold-rush boom in the 1890s, which also made it reliant on exports. New South Wales followed in 1901, federal Australia in 1904, and South Australia and Queensland by 1912.

In turn, New Zealand adopted the original idea for its leg-islated arbitration from Australia, and later add-on policies of workers' welfare. Arbitration became a device to protect workers' living standards. Migrants travelled across the world to find a bet-ter life, and government agents promoted New Zealand as a 'work-ingman's paradise'. Following the famous Harvester judgment by the Australian arbitration court in 1907, the New Zealand arbitra-tion court adopted the principle of a 'living wage', that is, a family wage sufficient to maintain a male breadwinner, a dependent wife and three children. The family wage was gender-based, rendering women and children dependent on labour policies for male bread-winners. It expressed the principle that the workingman was entitled to marry and have a family, and earn a wage sufficient to keep his family in a small degree of comfort. The family wage supposedly acted as a bulwark against the global market because it was based not on market rates but on the cost of living.

It is ironic, then, that New Zealand wage-earners fared worse between 1890 and 1913 than workers in Australia, where common forces shaped wage movements, and with which New Zealand shared an integrated labour market. In terms of GDP per capita, New Zealand was still not far behind Australia by 1913, and Pakeha New Zealanders had the highest life expectancy in the world. Before 1890, real wage growth was stronger than productivity growth. After 1890, globalisation increased productivity and improved the terms of trade; but workers' wages declined relative to property income after 1890. The beneficiaries of the settler contract were landowners, who gained most from technical advances, notably refrigeration, because the export of frozen meat and dairy products increased the relative value of their land. This income redistribution to property might have been greater but for the state experiment with arbitration.

Unsurprisingly, labour militancy mounted as real wages failed to keep pace with workers' expectations and rising working-class respectability. West Coast coalminers, the first to use arbitration in 1896, turned against it. Miners called a 'tucker time' strike at the local coalmine at Blackball in 1908. Their action heralded the rise of independent labour in the form of the New Zealand Federation of Labour, radical, and anti-arbitration. Four of the federation's five key leaders were Australian socialists and unionists, while others had experience on British and American coalfields. Their commitment to class struggle earned them the name 'Red Feds', who led an assault from the Left on the arbitration system. Goldminers struck at Waihi in 1912. The wave of unrest, culminating in disputes in mines and at ports in 1913, reflected not merely ideological beliefs in socialism, and its call to action, but global changes in work patterns and the flow of ideas that encouraged ferment through new connections of dissent.

Proud to be 'workers', the Red Feds reinforced a competing model of manliness to the family man of artisan craft unionism whom the arbitration system served best: a 'real' man who vaunted his manly independence, evocative of mateship and sweat, and had control of his workplace and his life. The breaking away by the Red Feds, however, helped arbitration to survive. By 1912 the settler contract formed the basis of government. Small farmers successfully transformed New Zealand into the 'Empire's dairy farm', harnessing the yeoman myth in their class interests to achieve political power under Auckland farmer Bill Massey and the new, conservative Reform Party.

MAORI LAND LOSS AND PROTEST

In this structural shift, the biggest losers were Maori. Though tribes had land rights under the Treaty of Waitangi, the treaty was no longer alive in the Pakeha narrative and the settler parliament. Maori were overwhelmingly excluded from the settler contract, dispossessed, and denied capital for farming, left without a resource base to develop. They were underpaid for their land, deprived of their best land, and denied cheap loans to develop the remainder. The remnant barely provided for subsistence. The steep downward trend in Maori land holdings continued through the Liberal era, which witnessed the 'penultimate Maori land grab'. Reeves did not write about this land redistribution in his histories, and most non-Maori New Zealanders were oblivious to it. But the settler contract central to the 1890s state experiments depended on Maori land loss.

In seeking social justice for settlers, then, the Liberals created another set of injustices for Maori. They passed a series of interlocking acts of parliament between 1892 and 1896 which streamlined procedures for alienating land from hapu and largely restored the Crown right of pre-emption. Land purchases became easier, under the Department of Lands and Survey. Yet more laws added to the maze concerning tribal land, offering more scope for alternative interpretations and ambiguities, ripe for lawyers and speculators to exploit. A coercive paternalism prevailed; half the sale price went to the Public Trustee, supposedly on trust for the Maori owners. Thus hapu faced the double burden of low sale prices and money locked up in the Public Trust Office, earning low rates of interest. In 1892 the Liberal government placed the West Coast Settlement Reserves under lease-in-perpetuity at peppercorn rentals, in what amounted to a second confiscation. Settler demands prevailed over the Maori right to, and need of, income from remaining lands. Under the Native Townships Act 1895, furthermore, European townships could be built on Maori land, opening up the land for settlement by undermining native title. Potential tourist towns, and towns on the main trunk line in the central North Island (completed in 1908), were established by this method.

In 'bursting up' the great estates, sellers could retain homestead blocks; in 'bursting up' the remaining Maori estate, however, Maori were denied an equivalent status. Instead, they were confined to inadequate reserves, of at most 25 acres of their first-class land. The whole system was designed to force hapu to sell. Lands leased at trifling rates (such as halfpence an acre a year) only encouraged more sales, while the Crown monopoly of purchase depressed land prices. If Maori sold, settlers paid for the road and survey costs. If they leased land, Maori paid for the surveying. Often the only way for them to pay was by selling more land.

The assumption that only settlers could be successful farmers denied Maori access to cheap credit for development. Tribal land was perceived to be 'lying waste and unproductive'. Supporters of the Reform Party resented leases as 'intolerable' and demanded the right to freehold 'all the Native Lands which the Maoris themselves cannot use'. Where hapu held on to their land through lease, this increasingly became lease-in-perpetuity, so that their land was effectively alienated for minimal return. By the close of the nineteenth century control of most of the North Island had already transferred from Maori to Pakeha. In 1891, 2.4 million acres (960,000 ha) of Maori land were leased to Europeans and another million acres (400,000 ha) by 1911. An estimated 10.8 million acres (4.32 million ha) in the North Island (including leased blocks) remained in Maori ownership in 1911. To compound the difficulty for iwi, the most heavily populated districts were left with the least land. Around the shores of Lake Taupo, Ngati Tuwharetoa did not oppose European settlement but wished to control the process, to generate income from timber milling, and to obtain loans from the government to farm their land themselves.

Tribes fought back against the relentless assaults on their well-being. In Wellington the four Maori members of parliament argued that the settler contract breached the Treaty of Waitangi, drawing attention to landlessness and the need for resources to help Maori development. From the 1890s tribal leaders and organisations demanded that the Liberal government stop the purchase of Maori land, address the tangled problems of title, and give Maori access to capital.

The pan-tribal Kotahitanga (unity) movement spearheaded this process, and in 1895 the Kotahitanga organised a national boycott of the Native Land Court. From 1897 the movement ran its own newspaper, *Te Puke ki Hikurangi*, whose name referred to a story from Hawaiki when people survived a flood by seeking refuge on a mountain. The paper, which expressed a new pan-tribal consciousness and exemplified how Maori embraced literacy, moulded political action by venting collective problems, such as the continued alienation of land, a declining population, and government indifference to people's well-being. Kotahitanga sought a new solution: a separate Maori parliament, which it claimed as a right under the Treaty of Waitangi. The Kingitanga, too, established a rival parliament. Both presented petitions and draft bills to the settler government and sought the return of Maori chieftainship over their land. In 1897 the Kotahitanga petitioned Queen Victoria on her jubilee to stop the settler purchase of Maori land.

The Young Maori Party led by Apirana Ngata of Ngati Porou emerged from these claims to citizenship. After a secondary education at Te Aute College, Ngata became New Zealand's first Maori university graduate, of Canterbury College in 1894. Ngata's people ensured that he was educated in Pakeha knowledge to help them face the challenge of colonisation. After he entered parliament in 1905, he became indisputably the greatest Maori leader of the twentieth century, and returned to circulation posthumously as a national icon on the $50 note. Backed by the older bicultural politician James Carroll, from the late 1890s Ngata embarked on a mission to uplift the Maori people through Maori land development. He wanted Maori included in the settler contract. Both Ngata and Carroll engaged with the state and looked to the government to remedy treaty grievances.

Such efforts had some impact. In 1900 the government established Maori Land Councils to balance iwi demands to hold on to their remaining land against settler demands for land for settlement. In some areas the councils (later boards) slowed the downward trend in land loss. Even the Kingitanga became briefly reconciled to the new system, but the councils lost authority with the government once they were seen to create a block to settlement. A stocktake by a commission of inquiry conducted by Stout and Ngata in 1907 confirmed how little good land was left. After the Native Land Act 1909 removed restrictions on sales the rate of land loss speeded up: a 'Native' could 'alienate or dispose of land . . . in the same manner as a European', and Maori land could be alienated 'in the same manner as if it were European land'. That made it easier to transfer from Maori to settler.

INCLUDED AND EXCLUDED MAORI

This was a crucial period in the history of Maori health, marked by the turnaround from a decline in health and numbers in the nineteenth century to recovery in numbers, health status and hope. Colonial views of Maori as a dying race continued to colour Pakeha perceptions and to exclude them from 'the people': 'if there was any hope for a future for the Maori, it was that their blood might be perpetuated as a trace in a future strain of blended New Zealander'. The sense of mission felt by the Young Maori Party reformers spread across the country; they saw themselves as 'saviours of a race', who could see 'with the eyes of both races'. Dr Maui Pomare, Native Health Officer under the Department of Public Health established in 1901, operated a health service for Maori on a shoestring budget. In his health promotion he used the latest technology in the form of slide presentations to scare people about the water they drank. But lack of funding led to disillusionment. Maori communities suffered from typhoid, diarrhoea, respiratory diseases and relatively high infant mortality.

Ambivalently, Maori were simultaneously included in 'the people' through a post-Enlightenment stereotype of the Aryan Maori. Assembled by the public servant Edward Tregear in *The Aryan Maori* (1885), this concept offered a 'long and adventurous past for both Maori and Pakeha migrants to New Zealand, and one that linked them to a distant but common ancestry' (see chapter 1). Tregear was Cornish, steeped in classical and Arthurian legend, and imposed his mental maps on Maori in trying to understand their world. In the Antipodes, he believed, the 'Aryan of the West greet[ed the Aryan of the Eastern Seas'. This search for Maori origins was as much a search for self by Pakeha intellectuals who aspired to create a new community.

The package of Liberal state experiments required such a past for an emerging colonial nationalism, with a sub-text of shifting relations with the imperial power, Britain, from about 1900. Ever since the propaganda of the New Zealand Company settlements, New Zealanders had absorbed the myth that New Zealand's 'Better Britons' were superior to the Australian Britons. New Zealanders lacked the taint of convictism, they were moulded by a vigorous, cooler climate, and they enjoyed relations with a superior type of 'native'. Thus elevating Maori to honorary whites was a further way to render Pakeha superior to white Australians, as well as affirming the long-held belief in a hierarchy of races in which Maori were superior to Aboriginal Australians.

WHITHER AUSTRALASIA?

Such beliefs shaped New Zealand sentiment in the decision not to join the Commonwealth of Australia when the Australian colonies federated on 1 January 1901. The majority view, amid general apathy, is illustrated in 5.3. Such views underpinned Keith Sinclair's conclusion that 'most New Zealanders did not want to become Australians'.

In 1968 F. L. W. Wood (an Australian) dismissed as 'emotional fluff' the 'waffle about consummating nationhood' which choked 'sensible' economic and foreign affairs arguments against New Zealand's joining. But a dissenting view that a widespread belief in 'geographically determined racialism' explained New Zealand's decision not to federate has regained ground. On both sides of the Tasman, federation was more a matter of sentiment than a business deal. The very act of creating the Commonwealth of Australia stimulated New Zealanders to 'imagine' the distinctive and desirable features of themselves and their country.

Given that the New Zealand economy pulled out of the difficulties of the 1890s earlier than the Australian colonies, and was being restructured as Britain's farm, economics did play a part; the Australian colonies keenest to federate – Victoria, Tasmania and

HOW WE SEE IT

THE OGRE: "Come into these arms."   NEW ZEALAND: "Nay sir, those arms bear chains."

The New South Wales Premier speaking at a Federal League meeting said that as the Colonies were on the eve of federation it was proper for Great Britain to defer linking the South Sea Islands to New Zealand. He also believed that the sentiment of the people of New Zealand would force that Government into the Australian Federation.

5.3 Scatz, How we see it. *New Zealand Graphic*, 20 October 1900. Zealandia, Britannia's daughter, wearing an indigenous feather cloak, holds hands with the noble savage. She fends off the ogre of convict Australia to protect her indigenous ward (depicted as a Pacific Islander rather than Maori), and so opts for a separate destiny in the Pacific. In the background stands her imperial sister Australia. The cartoon suggests that, but for the ogre, Zealandia could have moved closer to Australia, and perhaps taught her sister something about settler–indigenous relations.

South Australia – had been the most depressed. Different mail routes across the Pacific and through Suez since the 1860s underlined the Australasian colonies' different geopolitical and strategic interests. Defence, however, was not a core issue because Britain determined their global foreign policy. Minds and markets were connected, but minds dominated over markets.

The vanity of nation-building politicians played its part in New Zealand's non-merger as in Australia's merger. R. J. Seddon (aptly nicknamed 'King Dick'), ear to the ground, shrewdly heeded the apathetic mood and determined not to let it spoil his chances of re-election by inviting discussion on the subject. Nor would he tolerate diminished prestige, as premier of a state third in importance after New South Wales and Victoria; on the contrary, he assumed the title of 'prime minister' in place of 'premier' to place himself on an equal footing with the Australian prime minister. A popular figure on both sides of the Tasman, Seddon attended the federation celebrations in Sydney on 1 January 1901 with an entourage of Maori warriors.

Australians have influenced New Zealanders' national identity more than has been historically conceded. While federation reinforced the fact that New Zealanders are not Australians, the latter also influenced New Zealand identity through common stories. The 'Tasman world' did not end in 1901. Moreover Australasia extended beyond Australia and New Zealand, and continued to function as a region even though its collective name gradually fell into disuse. The French caused a problem, by intruding into this British-dominated zone in New Caledonia and the New Hebrides. So did the Germans in Papua New Guinea and Samoa.

White Australia itself posed a problem to the perceived health and security of Australasia. As the first Australian prime minister, Edmund Barton, told New Zealand's federation commission in March 1901:

On the question of the character of the immigration which should be allowed, I take it that the ideas and sympathies of New Zealand and Australia are practically identical. If one may judge from the conversations I have had with Mr. Seddon, I should think that our objections to alien races and New Zealand's objections are practically the same, and that we have the same desire to preserve the 'European' and 'white' character of the race.

The problem as the New Zealanders saw it was which would win: the law of nature or the law of the Commonwealth? How could Australia be white when its northern third was in the tropics? Northern Australia was likely to be populated by 'Asiatic races', and Queensland used coloured – South Sea Islands – labour in its sugar industry. Miscegenation notwithstanding, would not the white race also degenerate in the tropics, so that in a few generations Queensland would become home to the 'mean white', as in the United States? Advocates of the White Australia policy insisted that Australia would show the world that the laws of nature would not limit the white man. New Zealanders, however, believed that Queensland was a blot on White Australia.

New Zealanders were also less sure as to whether the land or sea defined a community of interest. The notion of a British Australasia in the South Pacific presumed a community defined by a shared expanse of southern ocean, bound by blood, and protected by the British navy. By the time of federation, however, the bush held sway in Australian popular culture, which was already looking inward. New Zealanders were also beginning to imagine a future shaped by their islands. It was commonly believed that New Zealand would produce an island race, more British than the Australian type for being shaped by a geography similar to the British Isles. As Dunedin's Rev. William Curzon-Siggers declared, New Zealand was 'an insular nation. Australia is a continental nation. The history of all races shows that continental races and insular races diverge further and further apart'. Some cited the Tasman Sea's '1,200 miles of stormy ocean' as an impediment. But the author of this famous phrase, Sir John Hall, continued: 'That does not prevent the existence of a community of interests between us'.

The New Zealand solution was to retain the community of interest defined by sea and blood through a reciprocal treaty rather than federation. A reciprocal treaty would resolve the tension between the desire for unity of Empire – essential to combat isolation – and compelling New Zealand to sacrifice her independence. By 1901, New Zealand opinion-makers already saw a precursor of Closer Economic Relations as the best means to express and develop trans-Tasman ties (see chapter 9). Seddon established the terms for such a treaty with the Australian prime minister Alfred Deakin on his last trip to Australia in 1906, and discussed with Deakin joint Australia–New Zealand opposition to an Anglo-French deal in the New Hebrides. But he died on the way home. Then as now, New Zealand found merger with Australia acceptable, but not takeover.

Instead, New Zealand expressed its aspirations in the Pacific by annexing the Cook Islands and Niue in June 1901. Having presumed a destiny to govern Polynesia on Britain's behalf, New Zealand's dream became to acquire Samoa. Instead British strategic interests allowed Germany to secure Western Samoa in 1899 in exchange for Britain's acquisition of German New Guinea (to Australia's relief). New Zealand had to settle for the tinies: the Kermadec Islands in 1887, followed by the Cook Islands and Niue as compensation for the deal over Samoa (New Zealand had supplied the British Resident in the Cook Islands since 1891). Maori MPs supported the move because of Polynesian kinship links, while Islander chiefs favoured annexation on the understanding that land rights would be preserved, though they too lost control.

RACIAL ANXIETIES

Increasingly, the Pacific came to be seen as a buffer against Asian invasion. By the early twentieth century Asia had displaced Europe as the source of imagined military threat, heightening settler angst about remoteness and a small population. For New Zealand to be a white country, and home to a better British stock, it had to exclude 'alien races'. The discourse of Social Darwinism and a flexing eugenics movement reinforced the policy of 'domestic defence'. In the 1890s New Zealand's anti-Chinese policy hardened. The poll tax on Chinese migrants soared from £10 to £100 in 1896, and the restriction on numbers doubled from one Chinese for every 100 tons of cargo to one Chinese for every 200 tons. Fears also rose about the awakening might of Japan, which defeated China in 1895. While Chinese were the 'archetypal alien', in 1899 the Liberal government extended immigration restrictions to all non-Europeans.

This exclusiveness was not simply a matter of Aryanism; New Zealand and Australian policies were complicated by imperial policies toward China, India and Japan. In 1896 the Liberals passed an Asiatic Restriction Bill directed as much against Japanese as against Chinese, after an attempt in 1895 also to exclude Indians failed because Indians were British subjects. The bill of 1896 did not receive Royal assent because it clashed with the Anglo-Japanese Commercial Treaty that had so angered Queensland in 1894. In this context the Chinese can be viewed as scapegoats for New Zealand's failure to impose a blanket restriction on all 'Asiatics' in 1896. Faced with disapproval in London, the Australasian colonies reluctantly agreed to an imperial compromise to use the model of a dictation test to exclude aliens and 'undesirables'. Natal used such a test to restrict Indian indentured labourers, and Joseph Chamberlain of the Colonial Office suggested this device as a way for Australasia to reconcile its shared anxieties with British foreign policy.

Accordingly, New Zealand's 1899 Immigration Restriction Act prohibited migrants of non-British or Irish parentage who were unable to pass an English language test. Overtly, this alternative approach caused less offence to Japan, and to India, the jewel in the imperial crown. New Zealand did not abolish the poll tax on Chinese migrants until 1944. From 1907, Chinese migrants also had to pass a reading test of 100 words in English, assessed by customs officers. Those who were allowed to live in the country were denied citizenship from 1908 to 1952.

British global dominance bolstered beliefs in Anglo-Celtic superiority. While some aspects of Chinese and Japanese culture were admired, even fashionable (for example, the Chinese lanterns in 5.1), imperialist arrogance assumed cultural superiority as well. Settlers believed that Asians would not fit into their Christian, democratic society. On the contrary, their cleverness presented a supposed menace to democracy, ethnic solidarity and civilisation. The Chinese tradition of sojourning was interpreted negatively; the Chinese 'simply did not swim with the mainstream of colonial development'. New Zealand and Australia both shut their doors on Asia at a time when social cohesion and forming a community identity were thought crucial to building strong new young nations. Some historians consider that the 'real enemy of the Chinese was the ideal society'. But it remains true that cultivating whiteness was a central feature of creating genealogies for the new settler communities of Australasia. Whether this process is read as colonial nationalism or

5.4 John C. Blomfield, Still they come. *Free Lance*, 17 January 1905. Chinese or Japanese (to xenophobes they were
indistinguishable), depicted as coolies, pole-vaulting into New
Zealand over the barrier of immigration restrictions, aided by,
as opposed to in spite of, the poll tax to the chagrin of
Premier Richard Seddon.

'recolonisation', contemporary rhetoric trumpeted that to be pure
was to be white. To be superior was to be white. Fears and dreams
in remote New Zealand made sure that it would become as white
and British as possible.

At the same time mounting international tensions drew the
colonies into British wars. Most settlers felt bound to British kith
and kin globally; war strengthened feeling for the empire. War was
honourable, a means to test and prove virility. The Boer War 1899
to 1902 served as New Zealand's rehearsal for World War I, an
opportunity to 'prove to those of our race and those in the dear
Motherland that we were prepared, outside all questions of expense,
to help them'. Loyalties to Britain went unquestioned, and the few
dissenters, such as the pacifist Wilhelmina Sherriff Bain, were vili-
fied. Some Maori were keen to fight but were excluded on British
orders. Loyalists instead volunteered under their English names. For
the woman author of a popular history of New Zealanders and the

Boer War, this enthusiasm affirmed the warrior Maori as Pakeha brethren, moving her to ask rhetorically: 'Is there any record of white and brown of any other land being on such fraternal terms as the New Zealanders?' The colony sent ten volunteer contingents to South Africa. Volunteers and their horses were the first to leave, farewelled by a crowd of 40,000 enthusiasts; then provincial, and finally government, contingents. Twenty women schoolteachers followed to teach in the world's first concentration camps, and were nicknamed 'The Learned Eleventh'.

As on later occasions, 'imperial sentiment masked . . . a concern for New Zealand's long-term interests'. While the Boer War fed anxieties about racial degeneracy, Pacific Rim settlers were nervous about the Anglo-Japanese alliance. Japan's naval victory over Russia at Tsushima in 1905 debunked European race theory; the 'Yellow Peril' assumed a military shape. The sole consolation about the Anglo-Japanese alliance, renewed in 1905, was that it transformed the British strategic position in the Far East. Even more than Australia, New Zealand looked to Britain as protector. New Zealand acquired Dominion status in 1907, like the other three white Dominions, Canada, Australia and South Africa, granted self-government in order to prop up the British role as a Great Power. New Zealand borrowed to donate a battle cruiser to the Royal Navy, and HMS *New Zealand*, built at a cost of £1.7 million, was launched in 1911. It also co-operated more closely on defence issues with Australia.

At the same time, the undercurrent of danger posed by Japan prompted a change in attitude by Australia and New Zealand to the United States. The 1908 visit of the Great White Fleet, the popular name for the American Grand Fleet, at the invitation of Prime Ministers Alfred Deakin and Joseph Ward, saw both countries join with the United States President Roosevelt to show that 'these colonies are white men's country'.

BABY AS BEST IMMIGRANT

As war clouds gathered, population policy extended from exclusion of non-British or otherwise 'undesirable' migrants to the promotion of New Zealand-born babies. The Dominion joined in the international clamour to boost white birth rates and reduce mortality, particularly among children, who acquired a new public importance as central to the empire's and the nation's future. In the early twentieth century it was axiomatic that 'our population is best replenished and our empty spaces best filled by our own natural increase: the newborn infant, in other words, is our best immigrant'. Alarmingly, Pakeha parents joined the international trend to smaller families, irrespective of pronatalist rhetoric from the government, the churches and the medical profession. Together, declining fertility and mortality comprised a demographic and health transition that accompanied revolutions in sexuality and the family. The value of the healthy, white child rose, and with that rose the standards and status of motherhood.

The fertility decline was not simply a 'mother's mutiny'. Moralists blamed women's emancipation and higher education, and in part they were right; demographers have found that the longer girls stay at school, the fewer children they will have. But effective birth control in the absence of effective birth control methods required men's co-operation. Couples engineered the halving of the average Pakeha family from 6 children in the 1880s to 2 or 3 by the 1920s. The choices and behaviour of ordinary New Zealanders had more in common with colonial feminist beliefs, that empire and nation would benefit from fewer, higher quality children, than with official rhetoric.

Fighting back armed with the report of the birth rate inquiry in New South Wales in 1904, Seddon launched the public crusade to save the babies with a memorandum on child life preservation in the press. Grace Neill, his leading woman public servant, used this opportunity to establish the St Helens Hospitals from 1905 in the principal towns. Shrewdly, she named these state maternity hospitals after Seddon's birthplace. The St Helens Hospitals were both training schools for the new trained midwives, registered under the Midwives Act 1904, and maternity homes for the deserving, the 'respectable wives of workingmen'. Respectable working-class values, coloured by eugenics, defined the terms of inclusion. W. A. Chapple, a doctor politician, also published his *Fertility of the Unfit* in 1904, in which he expressed the anxiety that the 'unfit' – the poor and the degenerate – were outbreeding the 'fit'. Since they could do little beyond making speeches about the birth rate, however, reformers set their sights on reducing the infant mortality rate.

It was not then known that Maori infant death rates were three or four times higher than those of Pakeha, because Maori statistics were incomplete before the 1930s. Nor did reformers acknowledge that Pakeha infant mortality was already declining. When it was lowest in the world, they stressed that it was too high, as if to show how much the white baby mattered. New Zealand's voluntary infant welfare society, the Plunket Society, had its beginnings in Dunedin in 1907, and Christchurch and Auckland in 1908. It represented a response to the European health transition. While in theory Plunket was available to Maori, in practice it was not, because its principally urban focus made it inaccessible to Maori, while the government established a separate scheme of public health nurses for Maori districts. A woman's movement that had particular appeal among the well-to-do, the society took its popular name from Lady Plunket, its vice-regal patron. Its paternalist figurehead was Dr Frederic Truby King, eugenicist and superintendent of the Seacliff Mental Asylum, who embarked on a mission, supported by his wife Bella, to 'help the mothers and save the babies' in order to counter racial degeneracy. The society's first aim was 'To uphold the Sacredness of the Body and the Duty of Health; to inculcate a lofty view of the responsibilities of maternity and the duty of every mother to fit herself for the . . . natural calls of motherhood'.

The Plunket Society was a local example of an international movement, but it gained a reputation, especially among imperial devotees, for its 'systematic pioneering educational health mission' in infant welfare. Imperial women made Truby King famous after World War I: his wife, who wrote his newspaper articles, their adopted daughter Mary, who made his message Australian, Lady Plunket and her imperial sisters, his matrons, and the mothers who carried his feeding routines and mixtures along the trade routes of empire. Correspondingly, Truby King made the Plunket baby famous by taking his mission to London, so that the Truby King baby became a model among those to whom a British imperial identity mattered. The Plunket Society developed into a national icon in the twentieth century, symbolic of New Zealand as a good place to bring up children, because in the national imagination the Plunket baby came to stand for the better British type.

The 1905 All Blacks embodied the offspring to which New Zealand aspired: with 'broad hips, deep chest, square shoulders, good muscles'. In this national body-building and nation-building process, the bonny baby grew into the boy scout. The scouting movement developed rapidly, from the earlier volunteer and cadet corps. By the end of 1908, when Sir Robert Baden-Powell published *Scouting for Boys*, there were 36 scout troops in New Zealand, mostly in Canterbury. Endorsed by Baden-Powell, whom he had met in the South African War, David Cossgrove, the headmaster of Tuahiwi School, organised the New Zealand boy scout movement, which aimed to teach boys 'peaceful citizenship' through outdoor activities. It also drilled boys in martial skills. Tuahiwi is a Ngai Tahu settlement, and Cossgrove as a military officer recognised the compatibility of the Maori warrior stereotype with scouting. Mrs Cossgrove ensured that girls also had their girl peace scouts movement. With compulsory military training introduced under the Defence Act 1909, and a territorial force, New Zealand steeled its youth, and prepared to 'produce patriots capable of defending the British Empire'.

6

'All flesh is as grass' 1914–1929

'In New Zealand more than in any country in the world we find justification for the words of the Bible, "All flesh is as [sic] grass, and all the goodliness thereof is as the flower of the field."' So began the issue on pasture land of the *Making New Zealand* pictorial survey to mark New Zealand's centenary in 1940. This biblical phrase had multiple meanings for New Zealanders, in relation to 'ecological imperialism', feeding Britain, and the sacrifice of its best young men in war.

English grasses were imported to New Zealand, to be re-exported as frozen meat and dairy products, in an imperial food chain. The biblical reference suggests that New Zealand was indeed a land of milk and honey. This reference also became an anthem, sung at Anzac Day services. New Zealand not only processed imperial grass seed into flesh and blood, but the flesh of the flower of its manhood died for King and country at Gallipoli and on the Western Front in World War I.

Together, New Zealanders and Australians remembered their best and bravest young men in their distinct yet shared Anzac legends, as the 'flower of the field', in the Flanders poppy, worn on Anzac Day, 25 April. They took to heart the poem 'In Flanders Fields' composed by Canadian doctor John McCrae in 1915, which all the Allied forces in World War I made their own:

> In Flanders fields the poppies blow
> Between the crosses, row on row,
> That mark our place; and in the sky
> The larks, still bravely singing, fly
> Scarce heard amid the guns below.

For New Zealand and Australia, the battlefields of Gallipoli and the Western Front spawned a story of sacrifice and heroic archetypes of the citizen soldier. Myth-making helped to make sense of horrendous losses, whose impact at home remains almost too great to be fathomable. World War I is 'arguably the most traumatic event in New Zealand's experience', and left 'a generation of men both physically and mentally scarred'. Indeed it obliterated a chunk of the tallest and healthiest 'A1 stock', classified fit for overseas service. Approximately one in five New Zealand men were sent to defend the empire, or 10 per cent of the total population. Of about 117,000 New Zealanders who served (over 101,000 overseas), 17,000 died. A further 3300 served in the British or Australian forces. The casualty rate was high: over 59,000, or 59 per cent. Nearly all the men who enlisted early and survived were injured: the legacy of grief and trauma proved deep and lasting.

Insights into national identity can also be gained by connecting World War I with the history of food, health and development that shaped New Zealand in its aftermath. The change of name and status from a colony to the Dominion of New Zealand, in September 1907, had elevated and distinguished the country as a self-governing, British 'white Dominion', together with Australia, Canada and South Africa. People felt no contradiction between nation and empire, between New Zealand and 'Britain overseas', because theirs was a colonial nationalism. For all the siblings in this far-flung imperial family, it was a matter of course that London continued to make the decisions over war, peace and foreign policy. New Zealand's participation in World War I logically followed from a defence policy which depended on the power of Great Britain.

When Britain declared war on Germany in August 1914, conservative prime minister Bill Massey pledged the expected loyal and immediate support, and New Zealanders responded by volunteering enthusiastically. The government marshalled four expeditionary forces. The first force, assembled within three days, sailed to Samoa, landing on 29 August, and took control of German Samoa without any resistance. This prompt response reflected the degree to which settler governments had long coveted Samoa. Equally it showed how the British resumed command, because the Admiralty directed the territorial force's movements and organised its escort by the battle cruiser *Australia*. The main body of 8000 men was ready to send to Egypt on 28 August. However this expeditionary force – still the largest number of troops to leave New Zealand at one time – had to wait until October for want of a naval escort. It joined the troopships of the Australian Imperial Force off the coast of Western Australia, and arrived in Egypt by the end of the year. Imperial authorities grouped the two contingents as the New Zealand and Australian Division which, combined with the 1st Australian Division, formed the Anzacs: the Australian and New Zealand Army Corps, who landed at Gallipoli in April 1915.

Gallipoli became the pivotal episode in national mythology by marking the beginning of the Anzac tradition, parallel with, and yet separate from, the even more celebrated Australian Anzac legend. Yet the largest division – the New Zealand Division – served in France from 1916, with the heaviest losses. On the Western Front, along the Somme, and in Flanders at Messines and Passchendaele in the Ypres salient, New Zealand lost 13,250 men, nearly five times as many as the 2700 killed at Gallipoli and more than the losses in the whole of World War II.

Gallipoli became the defining moment for both New Zealand and Australia in 1915 because Gallipoli was the site where their representatives of the 'coming man' were subjected to their first – global – test and proved their manhood. The Anzacs represented the highest form of citizenship: soldiers who passed the test of war. In an age of empires, this test had to be on the ancient battlefields of Europe and, given the location of Gallipoli, the men were likened to Trojan heroes. The campaign also made Australia and New Zealand Anzac neighbours, linking them with and at the same time distinguishing them from Great Britain. The Anzacs at Gallipoli demonstrated how the best of British qualities flowered in Australasia; and at Gallipoli the men realised the hellish futility of war. In reality and in legend they hung on bravely although the campaign was a failure. On 5 May 1915 Lieutenant-Colonel Dr Percival Fenwick recorded in the diary that he wrote for his wife, 'Every day we hear more stories of the heroism of our stretcher bearers'.

Gallipoli became a sacred site because the men first spilt blood there. Most of the dead have no known graves; their bones still lie in Turkish soil. Already by the first anniversary of the landing on 25 April 1915, Anzac Day had become a focal celebration and a day of mourning. Among the men the small cove where the troops mistakenly landed soon acquired the name Anzac Beach, or Anzac Bay. To commemorate the seventieth anniversary of the campaign, Turkey officially renamed Ari Burnu beach Anzac Cove in 1985. In doing so, it acknowledged the site's sacred status to expanding numbers of Australian and New Zealand pilgrims, and reinforced Turkey's growing bonds with Australia and New Zealand as more young people retraced 'the steps of their ancestors to reclaim a part of their own heritage'.

So powerful was the tradition invented to commemorate 25 April 1915, and those who served and died in subsequent conflicts, that some would make 25 April New Zealand's national day. Anzac Day became a full public holiday and 'holy day' as if it were a Sunday in 1922, in response to a public mood. It became 'an expression of sorrow rather than an opportunity to glorify war', and at the same time reflective of the Anzac spirit in which some commentators identified the kernel of nationhood.

The main themes of the parallel Australian and New Zealand legends – courage, endurance, duty, love of country, mateship, good humour, decency in the face of dreadful odds – explain their resonances and the reverence they both command. To a loyal public World War I represented a fight for the world as they knew it; a struggle for the survival of the British Empire, and thus of civilisation. Recruiters implored the first Anzacs to fight in 'the greatest of all causes, the cause of right, of justice, and of liberty'. The Gallipoli campaign was therefore heroic even as a failure. From the start, the Gallipoli catastrophe came to denote sacrifice: by and for local communities, for the nation as well as in defence of the empire, for the British race and the entire imperial family. New Zealanders believed they had shown themselves to be superior specimens whom Britain now owed a debt. New Zealand's Roll of Honour published in 1915 softened the impact of 103 pages of photographs of the fallen with King George V's congratulations 'upon the splendid conduct and bravery displayed by the New Zealand troops at the Dardanelles, who have indeed proved themselves worthy Sons of the Empire'.

In contrast to the uniformed larrikin who became Australia's icon, the New Zealand archetype of the pioneer farmer turned soldier was a gentleman. At least he appeared to be so in the presence of Australians, encouraged by his officers to show by 'neat dress and sobriety that there was a wide difference between the two forces'. He was the quiet New Zealander, depicted by Ormond Burton in *The Silent Division*. As the smaller partner in the Anzac corps, the New Zealanders defined themselves against both the Australians and the metropolitan British. Together, the identity of Australians and New Zealanders as Anzacs distinguished them from the British Tommies and their officers in their strength, initiative and resourcefulness. In the trenches of France the Anzacs also began to describe themselves as Diggers. 'Anzac' was already a more formal, solemn, distinguished term; Digger a more informal usage, reflective of the New Zealand Pioneer Battalion's and engineers' skill in digging trenches and tunnels, as well as the collective experience of trench warfare and a colonial heritage. Diggers were 'war friends', as a soldier wrote in Flanders:

> *Digger and cobber, mate and chum –*
> *Who says there's nothing in a name?*

At the same time the New Zealand soldier who began the war as Tommy Fernleaf had become the Kiwi by 1917, conscious that he was different. As the Australian scholar Ken Inglis explained,

Anzacs together, Diggers at least in parallel, Aussies and Kiwis apart: the war had given citizens of the southern dominions two words which distinguished them from metropolitan Britons, and another pair which signalled their different nationalities.

An emphasis on distinctiveness gained ground in the 1980s in the context of conscious assertions of nationhood, when historians reinvented the Anzac legend consistent with the country's nuclear free stance and defiance of its United States ally, and difference from its other ANZUS partner, Australia (see chapter 9). Historians began to pay more attention to the experiences of the men, as a corrective to the official version of the legend which celebrated the superior British colonial type and the glory of the Great Sacrifice. The Anzac survivors told their stories only in old age, just before death; so awful was the slaughter that they had tried to block it out for their lifetimes. The 'private' narrative equally built on sacrifice, but with a new purpose, to embalm the horrors of war that the men endured. Both military historian Chris Pugsley and novelist Maurice Shadbolt determined to give the last word to the Gallipoli veterans about what actually happened. That meant installing the New Zealanders' assault on Chunuk Bair on 8 August 1915 as 'central to the New Zealand experience of Gallipoli'.

In the play *Once on Chunuk Bair*, Shadbolt created his own living memorial to the men, to enshrine the New Zealand experience in the way that Peter Weir's film *Gallipoli* told the Australian story of Lone Pine and the Nek (Shadbolt's 1982 play became a film in 1991). The effect was to highlight the 'NZ' in Anzac. In this interpretation, Anzac Day was Australia's day because the Australians landed first, before dawn on 25 April 1915, while the New Zealanders landed from 9 a.m.; 'the New Zealand role came later'. Instead Shadbolt and Pugsley proclaimed 8 August as the New Zealanders' day, when they lost their innocence. It was after Chunuk Bair that disillusionment set in with conditions and with the British, and that the Kiwi soldiers realised that they were different. Aged 88, 'Daredevil Dan' Curham of the Wellington Infantry Battalion recalled that when the Turks retook the summit of Chunuk Bair, 'It was all over. From then on we knew there was little hope of victory on the peninsula, that all the suffering had been in vain'.

Chunuk Bair had its hero in Colonel W. G. Malone, who led the August offensive. Malone inspired his men by refusing orders which he judged were suicidal, by saving lives from disease with his standards of hygiene, and from machine-gun fire by covering trenches. It was Malone who, with 760 men of the Wellington Battalion and some Maori, took and held Chunuk Bair for 36 hours. The Wellingtons could see the Dardanelles, their ultimate objective, but the British relieved them too late. Unbeknown to New Zealanders, Malone was killed by Allied shellfire, not by Turkish bullets. Worse, he became a British scapegoat. The Chunuk Bair story, then, amounted to a declaration of independence.

It is telling that the New Zealand Division adopted the Lemon Squeezer hat from 1916, which became the standard headdress in World War II. Previously the New Zealanders were instructed to wear the British peaked cap. The Lemon Squeezer, with its four distinctive dents designed so that the rain ran off, began as the headdress of the 11th Taranaki Rifles, Malone's regiment in the Wellington Battalion. Its adoption can be read as a memorial in uniform, which signifies that the emergence of a New Zealand identity among the men was indeed associated in the soldiers' minds with Malone and Chunuk Bair.

Maori warrior heroes also proved themselves on Chunuk Bair, as members of the 1st Maori Contingent, and in France, in the Pioneer Battalion. As Aryan Maori they, too, represented Britannia's warriors and the chivalric Christian soldier. But they simultaneously invoked the tradition of Tumatauenga, god of war. Maori proved to the British High Command that the 'native' could excel in war as combat troops, and to Pakeha that Maori deserved equality. The four Maori members of parliament, Dr Peter Buck (Te Rangi Hiroa), Apirana Ngata, Dr Maui Pomare and Taare Parata, with Sir James Carroll, had determined to train a Maori contingent for this very purpose, to prove Maori equality by emulating their warrior ancestry. On 3 July 1915 the Maori Contingent landed at Anzac Cove, where Buck expressed a sentiment shared with Pakeha: 'Our feet were set on a distant land where our blood was to be shed in the cause of the Empire to which we belonged'. In September 1917 the Pioneer Battalion became a full Maori unit, the New Zealand (Maori) Pioneer Battalion although, as numbers thinned, it included 200 Niueans and Cook Islanders.

IN FLANDERS FIELDS

The Western Front is the site of most deaths, but not of the legend. Here the New Zealand Division, flanked by British and Australian divisions, experienced the horrors of trench warfare, bogged in mud in France and Belgium. At the Battle of the Somme in September 1916 they made a successful attack on German trenches but some units lost over 80 per cent of their men. Reinforced with volunteers and conscripts, the New Zealand Division fought at Messines in June 1917, again successfully but with severe losses. The story of Passchendaele in 1917 is particularly significant because there

6.1 'Row on row'. Lijssenthoek Military Cemetery, the
second largest New Zealand cemetery in Belgium, 6 June
2004

on 'Black Friday', 12 October, Sergeant W. K. Wilson recorded in
his diary, 'Our boys and the Aussies went over at 5.30 and got
practically cut to pieces'. Passchendaele remains New Zealand's
worst military disaster. David Gallaher, captain of the 1905 All
Blacks, died in the assault, which the men knew was hopeless
before they started because the barbed wire was not cut and they
lacked artillery support in the rain and mud. Senior commanders
failed to learn the lessons of their earlier success, of the need to
provide artillery support to the infantry against German machine
guns.

No wonder the men of the New Zealand Division called their
magazine 'Shell-Shocks' and Tyne Cot in Belgium is the largest cemetery tended by the Commonwealth War Graves Commission. While
trauma robbed soldiers of the ability to talk about the horrors of
technological warfare, of mates shelled, gassed, and sunk in mud,
the artistically inclined drew revealing cartoons. Figure 6.2, for

6.2 A. Rule, "In Blighty!" A thing we dream about.

example, suggests that soldiers dreamed of being invalided with minor wounds to England, to be cared for by New Zealand nurses. Rather than the psychoanalytical view that it was unhealthy to repress their experience, a modern psychiatric view is that a combination of rest, alcohol or drugs, and getting on with the job – the Anzac treatment of shell shock – helps in cases of post-traumatic stress. When Captain H. S. Tremewan was shot on the Somme in September 1916, aged 23, his company commander wrote to his mother:

It will be a great comfort to you to know that the very high standard which he set himself to live up to was never diminished, and that all the roughness and hard living of active service left him unspoiled – in fact only strengthened his resolve to live a straight and honourable life.

The sub-text suggested is not repression, but resilience and living an 'honourable life' in defiance of the odds.

6.3.1 Capt. P. P. Tahiwi, Sling Camp, July 1916

6.3.2 Mrs M. Mylrea YMCA and Capt. H. S. Tremewan, Sling Camp, July 1916

THE HOME FRONT

Mary Tremewan was one of thousands of women for whom the war denoted sacrifice in the form of giving the life of her son. At his memorial service the minister comforted her that: 'His was the priceless heritage of a Christian mother'. Some mothers lost more than one son; some all their sons; the Great Sacrifice was supposed to include heroic maternal sacrifice. Supporters of the war (the majority) likened soldiers' mothers to Volumnia in Shakespeare's *Coriolanus*, who professed that had she a dozen sons, she 'would rather eleven die nobly for their country than one voluptuously surfeit out of action'. An ideal from classical myth to Mary, mother of Jesus, this fed a conviction that all mothers' sons should share the same test of manhood and all families share the burden of grief. Hence most New Zealand women supported conscription to ensure equality of sacrifice, to redistribute the pain of having all the sons in one family die or suffer dreadful injury and none in another. In fact nearly every family experienced the loss.

Unlike Australia, New Zealand introduced conscription in November 1916, to rebuild the shattered New Zealand Division after the Battle of the Somme. Henceforward its reinforcements were a mix of volunteers and conscripts. This contrast between New Zealand and Australian Anzacs, who were volunteers for the whole war, affected the tenor of their respective legends. The absence of conscripts made the Australian legend more celebratory and more militaristic. New Zealand, on the other hand, asserted a greater loyalty to empire by introducing conscription on the British model, while its legend acquired a mood more funereal and subdued, with greater emphasis on mourning the war dead. Conscription also engendered different outcomes on the home front. It spurred the formation of the New Zealand Labour Party in 1916, whereas the 'no' vote to conscription split the Labor Party in Australia.

Anti-conscription did not equate to anti-war sentiment, although these two strands of dissent overlapped. A handful of conscientious objectors refused to fight, preferring prison because they rejected the war and killing as immoral. Theirs were mainly Irish, socialist, Quaker and Christian fundamentalist loyalties. Dissent was militant among West Coast miners and the Red Feds who advanced class arguments for equality of sacrifice. These representatives of a radical, left-wing, peace tradition included unionists who played a key role in the formation of the Labour Party and leaders in Labour politics, the future prime ministers M. J. (Micky) Savage, from Victoria, and Scottish migrant Peter Fraser (chapter 7). Archibald Baxter, father of poet James K. Baxter and son-in-law of Helen Connon (chapter 4), was encouraged by his wife to write *We Will Not Cease* (1939), which only became well known on its reissue in the late 1960s, when its pacifism spoke to a generation of anti-Vietnam War protesters.

Particular iwi and hapu loyalties ensured that some Maori were pacifists. The divide had been cut in the nineteenth century by the New Zealand wars, between tribes who had fought for and against the Crown. Whereas kupapa such as Te Arawa and Ngati Porou provided volunteers for the Pioneer Battalion, the Kingitanga asserted that its men should not fight, and none did. Its leader Princess Te Puea, granddaughter of King Tawhiao, opposed the Maori MPs' support for the war. In response to recruitment calls for king and country, she retorted: 'We've got a king. But we haven't got a country', because her Tainui confederation had suffered the unjust confiscation of most of their land. Waikato people successfully resisted the government's punitive extension of conscription only to Tainui but not other iwi in 1917. In the remote Urewera, the prophet Rua Kenana, religious heir to Te Kooti, similarly opposed volunteering and was arrested, first on charges of illegally supplying liquor, and then for alleged sedition, and imprisoned until 1918 for his defiance.

Women peace activists who shared the sympathies of conscientious objectors co-opted belief in the duty of motherhood to protest that mothers did not bring lives into the world to be used as fodder for capitalists. It was their role to promote peace and arbitration; they did not raise sons to kill other mothers' sons. The Women's International League for Peace and Freedom, established in Christchurch in 1916, argued that as 'mothers of the world' they bore a global responsibility to campaign to end armed conflict.

Some women wanted to volunteer for overseas service. While two women doctors donned uniform – Agnes Bennett and Elizabeth Gunn – those who ventured closest to the front were nurses, of whom over 600 served overseas in field hospitals and on hospital ships. The nurses' memorial chapel at Christchurch Hospital is the country's only memorial to nurses from World War I, built to honour three local nurses who died when the *Marquette* sank in October 1915. Ten New Zealand nurses died in this disaster, with 19 medics and 23 Australian nurses. Confined to non-combatant, maternal roles, women joined patriotic societies to raise funds through fairs and concerts and provide 'comforts' for the soldiers. Of all their patriotic work, knitting had the greatest symbolic significance; for women, a pair of knitting needles replaced the bayonet. *Her Excellency's Knitting Book* declared: 'The men go forth to battle, the women wait – and knit'.

The Governor's wife, Lady Liverpool, led the women's war effort in her social role as leader and patron of women's philanthropic organisations. In a gesture of equality on the home front, she and Miria Pomare (later Lady Pomare), wife of Dr (Sir) Maui Pomare, who chaired the Maori recruitment committee, together set up the

Lady Liverpool and Mrs Pomare's Maori Soldiers' Fund to send parcels to the New Zealand (Maori) Pioneer Battalion.

Women as mothers played a special part in remembrance, as mourners, privately and in public. Remembering the war dead in 1925, the *New Zealand Herald* appreciated that families who laid wreaths at the newly built war memorials 'kept their own soldiers' memory green'. As the only place that named a district's dead soldiers, the local war memorial served as a site of mourning for the town's or borough's lost sons, buried so far away, many with no known graves. Given the mobility of New Zealand society, a man's name might appear on more than one monument, where he was born, and in the district's main town, aiding community remembrance. A survey counted 366 such civic memorials.

Most Anzac memorials were built in stone. About 35 per cent were simple obelisks, 17 per cent arches or gates, commonly at the entrance to rugby grounds, while the Digger emblem stood tall on 10 per cent. With the odd exception they named only the dead, unlike their Australian equivalents which honoured the dead and the living. In Oamaru, residents planted memorial oak trees from 1919 to keep their boys' memory green. An imperial symbol yet personal, associated with moral qualities and regeneration, the oaks remembered the district's sons as the 'flower of the field'. In oak and in stone, the imagined community invoked was still both empire and nation.

REPAIRING THE WAR WASTAGE

Inevitably, war heightened emphasis on the sanctity of life; premature deaths of the country's youth and universal grief renewed the value of birth, and of health, and turned more attention to the child and the mother. Invited to Australia on his way home from London by Lady Plunket's sister, Lady Munro Ferguson, wife of the Australian Governor-General, in 1919, Dr Truby King lectured that the 'great wastage of manhood, womanhood, and also infant life caused by the war must be made good'. His imperialist rhetoric intoned that women bore a public duty as mothers to 'repair the war wastage' by having more babies, and preventing infant deaths. Patriotism for women equated to motherhood. The war also gave renewed urgency to eugenic anxieties about racial degeneracy, because army medical examinations exposed a high level of unfitness. Recruits were assessed for their fitness for overseas service (A1) or otherwise (C2 or 3), and these indexes supplied eugenists with categories to classify children after the war.

World War I, then, propelled mothers and babies on to the public agenda and advanced the idea that girls and women possessed a maternal duty to the nation and empire. The Plunket Society did its bit; New Zealand's version of the international infant welfare movement developed its health mission, entering an era of expansion after the war, and Truby King and his devotees claimed the credit for the decline in infant mortality from already low levels. They helped to make New Zealand a model to the world in infant welfare on the grounds that the country with the lowest (white) infant death rate set the example for others to follow. Elsewhere I have argued that mothers deserve more credit for reduced infant mortality, and that the rise of the infant welfare movement is better understood as a response to, more than a cause of, the decline in fertility and mortality rates. Similarly Plunket's historian has reasoned that, 'With raised expectations of survival and smaller families by the 1920s, mothers invested more time and energy in child-rearing. They were "modern" women who wanted "modern" advice, and turned to the nurses for guidance, as well as for support and reassurance'.

In fact Truby King himself knew little about babies; as his rivals were quick to point out, he was a psychiatrist, not a paediatrician. His ten trips (or more) to Australia between 1919 and 1931 provoked such criticism there every time. That an elderly New Zealand doctor with a gift for the media sound bite provoked a clash of patriotisms in Australia over infant feeding methods showed how much the white baby mattered politically after World War I. New Zealand and Australia competed for the title of social laboratory in health in the 1920s, just as they competed in sport, to display the biggest, strongest, Anzac bodies. Truby King's Australian visits confirmed that his real historical significance was as a propagandist. He put mothers and babies on political agendas as much through his invective as by his broad appeal, raising political and public awareness about the value of the child to the empire and the nation. Such zealous personalities have a role in getting things done, provided they do not overstep boundaries and polarise or alienate.

For the government to be seen to be promoting the child, it had to reform public health as well as expand educational opportunities. The devastation of war served as a catalyst, but an insufficient one to jolt politicians. It took the global catastrophe of the 1918 influenza pandemic to prompt the passing of a new Health Act. The flu proved to be New Zealand's worst natural disaster. Worldwide, the pandemic killed at least 25 million, more than double the estimated 10 million war dead. Tragically, it struck hardest at young adults, men more than women, aged 25 to 45, the very cohorts most hurt by the war. At the time Pakeha did not know that the Maori death rate from the flu was one of the highest in the world, seven times the European death rate of 5.8 per 1000. It was highest of all in New Zealand-administered Western Samoa, where a fifth of the population died. By contrast American Samoa stayed free of infection by imposing a strict quarantine.

For strategic reasons, New Zealand accepted a League of Nations mandate over Samoa in 1920 where it largely continued the pre-war German system of government, as suggested by military administrators who received little help from Wellington. However, the flu unfortunately gave New Zealand rule in Samoa a reputation for incompetence, which – combined with lack of understanding and racial prejudice – fuelled distrust.

Clearly New Zealand had to reform its responses to epidemic disease, whose prevention was the primary purpose of public health. The restructured Department of Public Health, established in 1900, had its focus broadened in 1920 from the environment, sewerage and sanitation to people and personal health services, which targeted the child as the future citizen. Renamed the Department of Health, the modernised department had seven divisions, including child welfare, school, dental hygiene, and Maori hygiene. Truby King, the incoming Director of Child Welfare, advised the Minister of Health that his mission would be no less than the 'physical, mental and moral betterment of the race'.

In the 1920s 'the nation's health is the nation's wealth' became a familiar catch-cry. An irascible Truby King, already past retirement age, assumed charge of child welfare policy only briefly, before it

was returned to the Department of Education in 1925. The health
of European infants and pre-schoolers remained in the hands of the
Plunket Society. This government-subsidised voluntary organisation
enjoyed widespread influence through its class appeal to upright
middle-class people, their receptiveness often deepened by imperialist beliefs. It won the support of the wives of businessmen, of may-
oresses and prime ministers and their wives, including the Masseys
and J. G. and Marjorie Coates in the 1920s. Instead the Department
of Health turned its attention to the schoolchild, with the idea of
complete health records from the start of school to military age.

The open-air school enjoyed its heyday in New Zealand in the
1920s. The concept had originated in Germany to expose tubercular
children to sunlight and fresh air. Strong winds proved a challenge,
such as the Canterbury nor'wester, and in winter they were freezing.
This was a time when poor children walked or rode to school bare-
foot and small boys lacked socks and underpants. School medical
inspections began belatedly under the Department of Education in
1912. Transferred to the Department of Health in 1921, the school
doctors targeted defective teeth and tonsils in their search for infection. Dr Elizabeth Gunn intimidated small children in her district
by shouting: 'Show us your crockery!', war medals bristling on her
chest. Toothbrush drill epitomised the era's militarism. The concerns
were international, to educate to prevent disease, and influence the
parent through the child. But alarm mounted that there should be
poorly fed children in New Zealand, with bad teeth. Officials were
reluctant to acknowledge the existence of poverty. Faith in 'natural
abundance' demanded that children be demonstratively healthier
than in Britain. How could it be that, in this agricultural country,
children ate insufficient meat, vegetables and dairy products, and
that the milk they drank was often condensed milk? Already some
school doctors and teachers had begun to experiment with milk in
schools.

Puny children found themselves sent to health camps to gain
weight and to sunbathe on tarpaulins, to acquire a suntan. An appropriate agricultural metaphor captured the campaign objective of
'fattening human stock'. Its eugenic undertones were clear. In
December 1919 Gunn, a forthright eugenicist, organised the first
health camp for undernourished children on a farm near Wanganui,

6.4 Eat more milk, health class, 1926

under ex-army canvas. A description of a camp in 1922 illustrates contemporary attitudes: a local farm was ' . . . fattening more valuable stock than it has ever fattened before . . . for 95 boys and girls are there under canvas and enjoying wholesome living and fresh air . . . nice amiable little boys and girls with arms and legs like matches'. All were under-weight. After sunbathing at the camp, however, 'some looked more like A1 than C3. They looked rosy and sunburnt'.

That schoolchildren measured in 1927 were taller and heavier than English and especially than Australian children gave gratifying substance to the belief that New Zealand ought ideally to serve as a nursery for British stock. In the 1920s, when officials marketed the Dominion as Britain's farm, it was logical to complement advertising of primary products for export to Britain, the world's largest importer of food, with a health campaign to win the country a reputation as the best place to build strong bodies. Building the child, the empire and the nation acquired a central place in national mythology because New Zealand demonstrated prowess in producing soldiers, food and clothing, the raw material for imperial defence.

After World War I maternal deaths became central to concerns about national efficiency because deaths in childbirth undermined the core population imperative of more babies. New Zealand launched a campaign for safe maternity in the 1920s, alarmed initially by statistics published internationally that New Zealand had the second highest maternal mortality rate after the United States. This was embarrassing, to say the least, and anomalous with the proud record of the world's lowest infant mortality rate (excluding Maori). In 1923 five women died from puerperal sepsis (blood poisoning) in a private maternity hospital in Auckland. The public storm of protest compelled a commission of inquiry. Population policy, influenced by the eugenics movement, justified state involvement in maternity services.

The dispute that erupted between doctors and midwives in the 1920s over responsibility for the management of childbirth provides another case study of international trends. In New Zealand a midwife system received the backing of departmental medical advisers who were also able to demonstrate statistically that midwife deliveries were safer. But the family practitioner increasingly ministered to the family from birth. The campaign for 'safe maternity' launched by the Department of Health in 1924 prompted an institutionalised response by general practitioners, whom Dr Doris Gordon, who practised with her husband at Stratford in Taranaki, organised into the Obstetrical Society from 1927. General practitioners denied the charge that their 'meddlesome midwifery' accounted for the high maternal death rate. They asserted that, on the contrary, civilisation had made childbirth pathological, as opposed to a normal process that could be left to midwives, and a doctor service was superior precisely because it was more expensive, modern and scientific. In the 1920s the New Zealand place of birth shifted from the home to the hospital as new public maternity hospitals and wards opened. The campaign for safe maternity achieved its aim of bringing maternal mortality into line with other nations, through better care and training, strict asepsis, and the reform of the many private, mixed hospitals which practised both obstetrics and surgery. Rates of puerperal sepsis declined from 1927, before sulphonamide drugs in the 1930s and antibiotics in the 1940s. Since the quality of the carer is crucial in childbirth, improved care and cleanliness saved lives.

The New Zealand Mum came into her own from the 1920s. Politically, the women's movement achieved successes. The institution of six o'clock closing in pubs survived from 1917 to 1967. It ensured that men, whether drunk or disorderly, went home for dinner. The public bar became a men-only zone; barmaids were banned. Pressure from the revived National Council of Women won a legislative gain for women of being allowed to stand for the House of Representatives in 1919, but women could still not be appointed to the upper house, the Legislative Council. With health an aesthetic goal, for a woman to be beautiful she had to be healthy, and meet the 'fit' eugenic, racial ideal of the future wife and mother. Miss New Zealand set the standard for healthy beauty in 1926, following Miss America and Miss Australia. Significantly, a married woman could win the title.

Development priorities infused all body politics, including immigration policy. An amendment act in 1920 prescribed an undeclared white New Zealand policy; anyone not of British or Irish birth or parentage was excluded, other than at the discretion of the Minister of Customs. The white New Zealand policy was directed at the Chinese; they were the only group systematically excluded and judged a menace to the democratic ideal. That wives and children of Indians – Gujarati – already in the country were admitted indicated the importance of marriage to ideal citizenship, extending to acceptance of arranged marriages for this cheap, colonial labour. British emigrants arrived under the British 1922 Empire Settlement Act, which authorised assisted passages to the white Dominions. The target groups were single agricultural labourers, married couples, young people in their teens and domestic servants, much as in the 1840s.

New Zealanders were more urban than rural by the 1920s. Suburbs burgeoned on the outskirts of the main towns, and the number of cars on the roads doubled. The Californian bungalow replaced the villa as the desired low-cost suburban house: builders adapted designs from Californian plan books but with English Arts and Crafts embellishments. Driving the expansion of suburbia were state mortgages. Massey's Reform government continued the Liberal policy of advances to workers, providing home loans of up to 95 per cent for a suburban house and section to workingmen and returned soldiers. Electric lighting, hot water and inside toilets eased the lives of families who could afford home ownership. Electricity lit up rooms

6.5 Californian bungalow, Wakefield, Nelson

and showed the dust, inviting into the house marketing strategies of the consumer society, to target the housewife and mother. People turned on the radio and flocked to silent movies at the cinema.

EMPIRE'S DAIRY FARM

The farmer, however, became the 'backbone of the country' because of the reliance on the British economy for a large proportion of national income. The standard of living depended on the export of primary produce. So did the settler contract, which extended to the returned soldier. A rehabilitation scheme rewarded soldiers – but not Maori – with farms. Often the sections surveyed were in the backblocks, in steep, remote bush and hill country, where the soldier settlers faced environmental obstacles and financial obstacles from lack of capital.

New Zealand was the most dependent of all the Dominions on Britain, the greatest global power. On average it sent at least 75 per cent of its exports to Britain and bought 50 per cent of its imports from Britain in the 1920s. The appropriation of the Australian and

New Zealand wool clips by the imperial government from 1916 to 1920 tightened bilateral relations, but led to a stockpile not disposed of until 1924 as demand recovered after the war. Post-war dairy production continued at levels that exceeded British requirements, and the country had once again to face the problem of export income instability with prices for her produce decided overseas.

New Zealand underwent a 'grasslands revolution' from the 1920s to the 1960s that saw a three-fold increase in production based on grass. Much of this expansion depended on phosphate, crucial as fertiliser to grow grass in poor soils, mined from the tiny Pacific island of Nauru. Dairying developed in 'wet' areas with the climate and soil assumed best for cows' milk supply, in areas of forest and wetland, including the Waikato, Manawatu and Taranaki. Global consumerism transformed forest into grass for intensive agriculture, which was seen as modern and the way of the future. Dairying represented science and progress. It also imperialised the landscape, replacing native bush and fern with improved English grasses and European livestock – Friesian and Jersey cows – to feed British consumers. New Zealand supplied half of Britain's cheese and a quarter of its butter in the 1920s.

Unsurprisingly, New Zealanders internalised the image used in export marketing, of the 'The Empire's Dairy Farm'. Milk became central to images of New Zealand as 'clean and green' and a healthy place to bring up children, and the dairy farmer a masculine type in literature. Milk as a body-builder represented a form of cultural imperialism derived not from Britain but from the empire created in New Zealand. Medical arguments helped transform milk into an 'essential food', an imperial icon of health, and a medicine to counter racial degeneracy. A children's food, it was associated with health and purity. As consumerism joined science and democracy as part of the new world order, milk became the food symbolic of nourishment by the mother and the state. But dairy products also acquired masculine qualities in their association with health, strength and virility; milk had to manifest masculinity to become an empire-builder.

The Dairy Export Control Board, established in 1923, made six films to market dairy products in the 1920s, including 'New Zealand: The Empire's Dairy Farm'. All six promoted 'Fernleaf' as

6.6 Milk for muscles: drain layers, Christchurch, *c.*1920s milking the cow for morning tea

the national brand, akin to the soldiers who adopted the fernleaf as a symbol in World War I, and began with the words: 'Healthy stock – sunbathed pasture – rippling streams – assure ideal production', again projecting the vision of 'natural abundance'. All ended with a 'picturesque' sunset scene of an ocean steamer disappearing over the horizon, carrying produce to the United Kingdom. Similarly, the Anchor brand adopted by the New Zealand Co-operative Dairy Company, the country's largest dairy co-operative, signified the connection with the Royal Navy and British shipping.

In effect the films showed how British grasses were exported to New Zealand and re-imported as empire dairy products, whose quality testified to New Zealand's prosperity and successful agricultural development. The film about 'The Dairy Cow as an Empire Builder' opened with a supposedly 'romantic' reference to the transformation of Maori from warrior to worker since the New Zealand wars: 'Where Maori warriors fifty years ago held at bay English troops – to-day their descendants make a daily round gathering cream cans!' Explicitly, 'Butter for Britain wrought the change' from 'former wilderness' to 'to-day's development' of 'prosperous farm homes . . . and thriving country towns'. Civilisation of the wilderness and of Maori, then, issued from producing food accessories for British tables.

The films were part of a conscious campaign to educate the British public about New Zealand's dairy industry. Shown at trade shows in London, Glasgow and Liverpool, they were pitched at the feminine consumer because women were responsible for buying food and feeding families. With the end of the war commandeer in 1921 and the return to a free market, prices slumped. Dominion dairy farmers had to promote themselves to British consumers rather than rely on the British government. Exposed to the global marketplace, New Zealand sought a united empire with preferential trade within its borders and was disappointed by the United Kingdom's opposition to imperial preference. Instead the Dairy Board turned to a domestic imperialism, because housewives held the 'housekeeping purse': a hope that British housewives would give preference to the 'pure quality foods produced in their own Empire overseas'.

ECONOMIC INSECURITY AND POLITICAL UNCERTAINTY

Both New Zealand and Australia relied on export earnings and were therefore vulnerable to external shock, New Zealand especially so with its more open economy. 'Maximising farm income was an elusive goal' in the 1920s because British demand set limits on growth. The prosperity expected to continue after the war did not materialise. Instead policy-makers strove to manage income instability by establishing meat and dairy marketing boards and through state finance for farmers. The Meat Producers' Board of 1922 was the first export monopoly board in the world, extending the national reputation for state experiment.

While the Dominion depended on trade with Britain, it was even more dependent on its ability to borrow for development. Power concentrated in the hands of an élite who recognised the importance of the British connection and the need to satisfy London's criteria for sound financial management. Faced with this reality, New Zealand became increasingly frustrated that its banking system was tied closely to Australia's. London failed to distinguish between Australia and New Zealand; yet Australia was the biggest borrower in London, in pursuit of an ambitious programme to build 'Australia Unlimited'. Saddled with its share of debt from World War I, New Zealand found itself further beholden to London because of loans when its export market collapsed in 1929, though it escaped Australia's acute short-term debt crisis.

In such circumstances post-war hopes were dashed. A disillusioned electorate voted for a series of conservative minority governments in the 1920s, the Reform Party having lost its majority in 1922. Under the first-past-the-post voting system Reform, in government from 1912 to 1928, did not once win half the votes. The Labour Party gained traction only in the cities, deterring mainstream support until it abandoned its platform of socialisation, especially the nationalisation of land. As Michael King observed, few people 'from any background wanted to "smash" the capitalist system: most just hoped to make that system more responsive to their wants and needs'. When Massey died – the new agricultural college in Palmerston North was named after him in 1926 – J. G. Coates, a war hero, became prime minister. He too was a dairy farmer, from

Kaipara in Northland. But the election of the elderly Sir Joseph Ward as leader of a revived Liberal government, renamed United (in power from 1928 to 1931) suggested that the people had opted for nostalgia. Ostensibly they voted for Ward on the basis of a mistaken promise: with failing eyesight and subject to diabetic blackout, he famously misread his speech notes and promised to borrow £70 million instead of £7 million to cure the country's ills. Dream and reality could not have been further apart with the onset of worldwide depression.

Refuting doomsayers, from the early twentieth century, Maori health and numbers recovered despite the ravages of the 1918 influenza pandemic. As family members died from the flu, T. W. Ratana, a Maori farmer who practised Pakeha farming near Wanganui, had a vision of the Holy Ghost, which called him to unite and redeem Maori as God's chosen people. He launched a religious revival as the founder of the Ratana Church and political movement, centred on the Bible and the Treaty of Waitangi. His faith healing and his message attracted a large following among the sick and the poor, especially ex-servicemen. Ratana's son had served in Gallipoli and France, where he was badly gassed. The men of the Pioneer Battalion, who fought for equality, found themselves excluded from soldier settlement schemes to assist men to purchase homes and farms. To add to the offence, Maori had provided land for soldier settlers. Between 1910 and 1930 another 3.5 million acres (1.4 million ha) passed out of Maori hands. Ratana held special appeal for ordinary people, increasingly detribalised and landless, who eked out a subsistence living or worked as casual labourers. With a growing population there was too little left for subsistence, despite the popular prejudice about 'idle' land.

The Ratana movement presented a challenge to the tribal establishment, committed to working with the government and within what followers saw as the strait-jacket of traditional iwi leadership. The Ratana Church, registered in 1925, rivalled both the Kingitanga and Anglican tribal leaders who had organised the Pioneer Battalion. Indeed it spurred the Anglican Church to appoint its first

Maori bishop of Aotearoa, Rev. Frederick Bennett of Te Arawa, in 1928. Ratana advocated a Maori national identity. He wanted the treaty recognised in statute so that it would become operative and 'preserve the ties of brotherhood between Pakeha and Maori for all time'.

Tribal leaders such as Princess Te Puea of the Kingitanga were equally determined for their people to occupy their rightful position. To this end, Sir Apirana Ngata (knighted in 1927) campaigned in parliament on a number of fronts. He helped bring about the Native Trust Office in 1920 to oversee revenue from the lease of Maori reserves, with the long-term aim of persuading the government to agree to a policy of Maori land development that would deliver equality to Maori. When Massey's Reform government moved to open up the Urewera, the North Island's last frontier, during the war, Ngata worked to have Tuhoe, the local people, issued new consolidated titles in the 1920s to assist them in land development on their own account. Land sales continued. Undeterred, he oversaw a myriad of consolidation schemes to try to turn remnants of land held by iwi into an economic base by creating blocks large enough for dairying.

Strikingly, it was Ngata who lifted dairy farming and the idea of New Zealand as Britain's farm into another cultural context. In the 1920s he converted his own iwi Ngati Porou from sheep to dairy farming on established communal farms. He set up a training scheme to send young men, including his eldest son, to Hawkesbury Agricultural College in New South Wales to learn the latest methods. By 1926 Ngati Porou owned a co-operative dairy factory.

In sport, George Nepia dominated the rugby field with his personality and dazzling displays of kicking, tackling and fielding the ball. As 'New Zealand rugby's first superstar' he attracted large crowds in New Zealand and Australia. In addition to his talent, Nepia's success was part of a deliberate policy by Te Aute College and by Ngata to promote Maori prowess on the rugby field to counter prejudice. Nepia's popularity boosted the self-image of Maori.

Politically, Ngata's successes owed much to his friendship with J. G. Coates, Minister of Native Affairs from 1921 and Prime Minister from 1925 to 1928. Coates had grown up among Maori. Together, Ngata and Coates oversaw the first attempts to settle

Treaty of Waitangi grievances in the 1920s. The Arawa lakes agreement of 1922 provided an annuity of £6000 a year in acknowledgement of the iwi's customary rights to the lakes in the thermal districts specified in law in 1881. The Arawa Trust Board followed in 1924, which supervised the national cultural revival urged by Ngata by establishing a school of arts and crafts at Rotorua. Ngati Tuwharetoa reached their agreement with Coates in 1926, when the Tuwharetoa Trust Board was established with an annuity of £3000 from fishing licences (to fish for introduced trout) and campsite rentals at Lake Taupo. In exchange, Tuwharetoa ceded the bed of Lake Taupo for a public reserve. The Kingitanga, too, began to be heard by the government. Ever since the wars, tribes forced into poverty by confiscation had sought an inquiry, and in 1927–28 the Sim Commission found that the confiscation of three million acres (1.2 million ha) of land in Taranaki, Waikato and the Bay of Plenty under the New Zealand Settlements Act 1863 had been unjust.

But it was as Minister of Native Affairs from December 1928 in the otherwise lacklustre United government that Ngata achieved his dream of directing government policy away from alienating land from Maori for Pakeha farmers, and towards state advances for Maori to develop their own land. Legislation in 1929 authorised him as Minister of Native Affairs to advance money to settle and utilise Maori land more effectively and to encourage iwi in the practice of agriculture and self-help. At last Maori could obtain mortgages for up to 60 per cent of the value of their land, even if Pakeha settlers could borrow up to 90 per cent. The Act also empowered the minister to gazette land for development. Ngata used his powers to bring land under departmental control, survey, drain, reclaim and clear it, grass, fertilise and fence it, construct buildings, buy equipment and livestock, and hand it over to Maori farmers. Through land development schemes he strove with tribal leaders to create self-sufficient Maori communities. His quest could not have been more timely as global depression arrived.

7

Making New Zealand 1930–1949

The 1930s and 1940s was a formative era in nation-building, through the conscious 'making' of New Zealand. At the same time, New Zealanders had to 'make do' through depression and another world war, and these global onslaughts only intensified the quest for security at home and abroad. Making do and creating a nation moved in symbiosis because, as often happens with the evolution of a sense of national identity, panic, crisis, anxiety or rupture produces stories and rituals to soothe and explain. This context saw the rise to power of the first Labour government, which openly resolved to pick up where the 1890s Liberal model of state development left off. In this era politicians reinvented a tradition of a progressive, decent society that protected ordinary people from the icy winds of international competition and conflict. A geological reminder of living on the edge, the Napier earthquake of 1931, only added to the sense of fissure and fragility. New Zealand's worst environmental disaster of the twentieth century, the earthquake reinforced the urge to rebuild.

DEPRESSION

Even before the Wall Street crash in 1929, global depression and unemployment had cast a pall over the Dominion. Already the dependent economy was hit by the fall in export prices. In just two years, 1928–29 to 1930–31, export income nearly halved. Export values returned to pre-depression levels only from 1936. To maintain funds in London, New Zealand had to adopt a deflationary policy of balanced budgets. A United government led by George Forbes, a North Canterbury farmer, made the economies necessary to meet London's insistence on cost cutting. Reduced debt repayments were unthinkable because that would have impaired the ability to borrow. The government therefore slashed expenditure. The cuts were particularly severe in education, which consumed nearly half of annual public spending, and in health.

Conservatives sought solidarity to stem the crisis in a United–Reform coalition government from September 1931, which proceeded to pension off the core idea of the 'workingman's paradise'. In 1931 the Arbitration Court reduced award wage rates by 10 per cent; public service wages were also trimmed by 10 per cent then, and again in 1932. Modest family allowances (introduced in 1926) and widows and old age pensions were cut. Though offset by falling prices, the reduced pensions provoked anger at the government's seeming indifference to the needs of ordinary people. The principle of 'no pay without work' led to massive public works schemes; simultaneously the government slashed expenditure, laid off staff and re-employed them at relief rates. Arbitration in industrial disputes and union membership ceased to be compulsory in 1932, giving more power to employers. Social histories interested in ordinary people and left-wing histories view the coalition government with disdain, reflecting the bitterness of the depression era.

The depression bit deeply into community life, punishing people in debt, and those at the bottom or on the margins of society who lacked a male breadwinner. A strong work ethic offered no escape from worry and frustration. Estimates of the unemployment rate range from 12 to 15 per cent (40 per cent among Maori) yet economic research suggests that nearly 30 per cent of the workforce were not formally employed by 1933. Up to 40 per cent of the male workforce were unemployed in the worst of the crisis. Mass unemployment overwhelmed charities and charitable aid boards, etching images of the soup kitchen in popular memory. The impact of widespread insecurity varied by region; one study saw Canterbury as the most severely deprived.

Depression literature has focused on the suffering of the 'worker', the unemployed man subjected to the ignominy of relief work,

underpaid and compelled to move to rural relief camps. Distress in
the cities erupted in street riots in 1932, precipitated by relief schemes
that rotated the unemployed for a few days at a time for pitiful pay.
Unemployed men toiled with picks and shovels in harsh conditions
to build roads through the Lewis Pass and to Milford Sound in the
South Island, creating the infrastructure for future tourism, while in
the North Island workers constructed the East Coast railway. Such
extremity politicised significant sections of the community; an intel-
ligentsia fired by social injustice and inequality spawned a national
literature and art that illustrated the international genre of social
realism. John Mulgan, who served as a special constable in the 1932
riots, portrayed in his novel *Man Alone* (1939) the acute distress
in relief camps felt by the individualistic, strong-willed, egalitarian,
hard drinking, laconic male, who represented the equivalent of the
Australian 'lone hand'. Family folklore recalled the humiliation suffered by that other masculine type, the family man, demoralised by
the indignity of his failure to provide.

By the 1980s economists began to question the depression's effects
on people and whether life was as tough as claimed. Inevitably a
myth of 'The Depression' evolved because generations tend to col-
lectivise their experiences through story-telling. There was no unified experience of depression; only a unified story that smoothed
the rough edges of a national memory of hardship. In reality the
depression was a class experience, which left a gulf between the
unemployed and the employed, between workers – especially casual
labour – and the privileged. Among the better off who enjoyed relative prosperity with the rise of consumerism, the slump brought
insecurity and disappointment through defaults on mortgages, bad
investments and reduced educational prospects. The effects of the
1920s housing boom and depression showed in declining home
ownership and rising levels of renting; in Christchurch, whereas
32 per cent of houses were rented in 1926, the figure was 46 per cent
by 1936. The proportions of unskilled and semi-skilled rose and the
gap between richest and poorest widened.

In many ways women bore the brunt of hardship, of which much
evidence is hidden. One telling indicator comes from 109 married women who died from – illegal – septic abortions between

7.1 Unemployed women organise: a May Day unemployed
workers' demonstration led by a small band of women,
Christchurch, 1932

1931 and 1935. Their husbands were labourers, drivers, farmers
or farmhands, in shop work and trades vulnerable to downturn.
Official unemployment statistics excluded women, youths and
Maori employed on Native Department work schemes. Women
and youths were not entitled to relief payments, although as wage-
earners they paid unemployment tax from 1931, with the significant
exception of the large group in private domestic service. The novelist Ruth Park observed astutely: 'Women were not supposed to be
breadwinners, therefore they were not'.

Out of the gloom, however, emerged promise of change. During the worst of the slump Lyttelton voters elected New Zealand's
first woman Member of Parliament, Elizabeth McCombs, after the
death of her husband, the local Labour MP up until then. A former
suffragist, she resisted the injustice of 'unfair taxation' of low-paid
women and youths and led that campaign into parliament.

In 1933, too, New Zealand began to assert a separate financial
identity. At the Ottawa conference in 1932 Coates negotiated a system of imperial preferences that ensured the Dominions access to the
British market. To help farmers, the government devalued in 1933,
against Treasury advice. Encouraged by British experts, it also established a Reserve Bank.

Recently assessment of Coates has emerged that depicts him as a statesman faced with an impossible task of managing the global downturn at a time when New Zealand had no independent monetary policy, and borrowing was subject to the willingness of Australasian private banks answerable to the Bank of England. Indeed, Coates has been credited with creating a platform for the growth that materialised under the first Labour government. The key to recovery lay with the Reserve Bank established in 1934 to take control of credit away from the six trading banks, only one of which had its headquarters in New Zealand. The new monetary regime successfully distinguished New Zealand reserves from those of Australia, and New Zealand from the Australian banking system, establishing the desired financial separateness.

Happily, this intervention ensured that the country's recovery from depression was unusually fast; it raised real GDP per capita by a third by 1938. Often the best policy outcomes are unintended, and ironically such success was unforeseen. The policy's success also remained unrecognised until Labour entered office. In a fortunate sequence of events, the credit squeeze imposed in the period of balanced budgets created an unplanned boost to the money supply that, with devaluation, increased reserves held by the Reserve Bank, allowed lavish expenditure by the reformist Labour government, and lifted national income.

SECURITY AND RECOVERY

In the standard interpretation, the first Labour government pulled New Zealand out of the doldrums after Labour won the November 1935 election by a landslide. But it is now clear that the new monetary regime already in place by 1935 provided the mechanism for rapid recovery. With confidence and spirits buoyed, the climate of opinion changed. Social priorities were transformed as Labour made manifest Christian and humanist versions of dignity and equality. Immediately the unemployed received a Christmas bonus. The kindly Prime Minister Michael J. Savage became a legend in his lifetime; already 63 on his election, he died in 1940, his photograph framed in thousands of living rooms. Savage personified the social security scheme created by the first Labour government to raise living standards and provide security and dignity 'from the cradle to the grave'.

From Ned Kelly country in Victoria and New South Wales, an Irish Catholic with a similar background to the outlaw, Savage identified with the poor and they loved him. But he joked that he 'did not inherit [Kelly's] methods'. The Labour Party's election manifesto in 1935 proclaimed the objective: to use the 'wonderful resources of the Dominion' to restore 'a decent living standard to those who have been deprived of essentials for the past five years'. It promised to restructure the economy to secure not a minimum, but a universally comfortable standard of living for the male breadwinner and his dependants, 'with everything necessary to make a "home" and "home life" in the best sense of the meaning of those terms'. In other words, Labour resolved to restore the model of state development established during the 1890s. Only this time it partially included Maori.

For dairy farmers, the settler contract was rewritten as the right to full employment and a fair and reasonable wage in the form of guaranteed prices for primary products. Sheep farmers at the time opted to stay with the free market. The Dairy Board had already decided to assume control of marketing, but the government took over the export of all butter and cheese in 1936 in return for security for farmers in the form of a guaranteed price, based on production costs. It also provided state advances to help indebted farmers remain on the land. For workers, Labour restored the system of compulsory arbitration and unionism, and reversed depression cuts to award wages, salaries and pensions. The Industrial Conciliation and Arbitration Amendment Act of 1936 empowered the Arbitration Court to set the basic breadwinner wage at a level 'sufficient to maintain an average family, a man and his wife and three children', while continuing to assume that the working woman was single, with no children or elderly parents to support.

Nutrition surveys suggested that the young child suffered in the depression. The League of Nations urged member countries to institute nutrition inquiries and to promote the new standard of optimum child health and development, for which it prescribed milk consumption of $1\frac{1}{2}$ to 2 pints (1 litre) daily from the age of two. New Zealand responded with a national school milk scheme in 1937, followed by a dietary survey of basic wage-earners in 1939 and of Maori diets in the 1940s. School milk had political appeal because it was intended to benefit both the dairy farmer and the child as the future citizen. From 1937 the state supplied a half-pint of pasteurised bottled milk, free, to every child at primary school and kindergarten as far as practicable. For 30 years the half-pint bottle of milk a day signified, with the Plunket Society, that New Zealand was a healthy place to bring up children.

For the urban worker as for the dairy farmer, Labour believed that increasing the purchasing power of the ordinary New Zealander would boost the economy, and it did. The state took over the Reserve Bank to control credit and to finance its programme of recovery and security. This government of former Red Feds, once feared as socialists, determined to constrain the powers of bankers, and again it sought to build a civilised community, where ordinary people shared the benefits of science and education. In effect, Labour introduced a variant of 'protection all round': a controlled economy to manage the core problem of economic instability and safeguard the ideal society, this time in the form of a universal welfare state.

From 1938, then, New Zealand renewed and extended its version of the Australasian settlement, in which the family wage recovered its pivotal status in a 'workers' welfare state'. The strategy, however, did not comprise 'wage security for the worker rather than social security for the citizen'. Instead it provided worker security supplemented by non-contributory social security, the latter determined by citizenship rather than by ability to pay. New Zealand made social security a right, paid for from tax, to give the people the standard of living 'they ought to have'.

As a safeguard, Labour introduced import and exchange controls late in 1938 to manage an exchange rate crisis brought on by the flight of British capital and spiralling demand for imports as the economy recovered. Import licensing also had the intended effect of protection of industry. New Zealand lagged behind Australia in finally adopting protection of industry in 1938 to ensure security of the worker (see chapter 5). Having decided not to become an Australian state, the country grew more tied economically to Britain, which insisted on free trade and discouraged manufacturing. When

New Zealand did adopt protection, the logical consequence of the revival of worker protection in 1938, the country met strong British disapproval at the prospect of aspiring to be anything other than the empire's farm. The Australasian model of state development survived, however, because Britain soon needed all the food that New Zealand could produce to sustain its people through another world war.

The Social Security Act of 1938 restored New Zealand's status as a social laboratory. In terms of cash benefits, an improved age pension (renamed 'benefit') and an attempt to introduce universal superannuation at age 65 confirmed that removing insecurity beyond working age remained a priority. The Act introduced an unemployment benefit for men and for single women for the first time, to counter workers' loss of paid employment. The entire framework supplemented the family wage. It accepted that single women were moving into paid employment between school and marriage, but it confirmed married women and children as dependants. To ensure equal medical treatment the Act legislated for a universally free general practitioner service, free hospitals, and free maternity care, paid for by the taxpayer. The second and third eventuated, but not the first, in 1939.

Free medical care for childbirth was a notable achievement, only secured because the aims of the majority of doctors, politicians, and women overlapped. The government was obliged to listen to doctors, whom it needed to meet the ultimate objective of a free health service. Labour politicians genuinely believed that care by a doctor, traditionally available only to the wealthy, was the right of all women, and women's groups advised that 'painless maternity is every woman's right'. The Committee of Inquiry into Maternity Services of 1937–38, which included Janet Fraser, the wife of the Minister of Health, recommended that birthing mothers have access to the 'fullest degree of pain-relief consistent with safety to mother and child'. Under Labour, then, the belief in egalitarianism reinforced the trend to births managed by a doctor in hospital. Such humanitarianism was also pronatalist, since politicians hoped that financial support, 'modern' pain relief and a fortnight's rest in hospital, advocated by women's organisations, would encourage women to have more children.

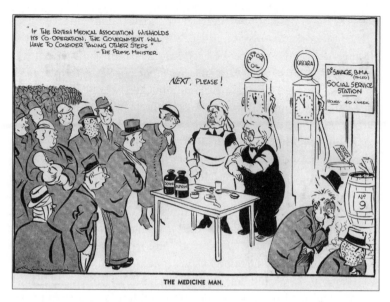

"IF THE BRITISH MEDICAL ASSOCIATION WITHHOLDS
ITS CO-OPERATION, THE GOVERNMENT WILL
HAVE TO CONSIDER TAKING OTHER STEPS"
— THE PRIME MINISTER.

THE MEDICINE MAN.

7.2 G. E. G. Minhinnick, The Medicine Man, *New Zealand
Herald*, 18 August 1938. Savage has had to resort to
distributing medicines himself.

A free general practitioner service, however, fell foul of medical
protests (see 7.2). The scheme finally introduced in 1941 acceded to
the professional demand of a fee for service; and doctors' visits were
henceforth not universally accessible in practice, nor universally free.
The doctors' top-up fee reduced the scheme to a mere state subsidy
for medical care.

Labour also made the suburban dream accessible to urbanites who
fitted the model of the nuclear family. It endorsed the ideal of home
ownership, eroded by the depression, but since low-wage families
could not afford to own a home, a refurbished entrepreneurial state
built houses for rental from 1937. State houses, compact, well built
and comfortable, and financed by Reserve Bank credit, mushroomed
in the four main cities. An enterprising builder, James Fletcher, constructed the first houses on contract. While better-off workers continued to obtain access to state finance for home ownership, the
scheme brought the ideal of a new small house on its own block
within reach of ordinary people. Typically, those families who did
not fit the model missed out.

The scheme was not intended for Maori, who remained geographically separate, second-class citizens. Land development schemes provided tribes with some new, inferior houses in rural areas. But even among iwi who had not lost so much land and resources, the majority lived in rural poverty. Chiefly families might live in bungalows on farms or in towns, but housing on marae had dirt floors and an unsafe water supply.

Labour promised Maori equality under its political alliance with the Ratana movement, on the basis of need. Maori in theory were equal citizens, but in practice they received social security benefits paid at approximately 25 per cent less than Pakeha rates, and that inequality persisted from the introduction of an old age pension in 1898 until 1945. Bureaucrats reasoned that hapu could live off the land, when in reality many were landless and had lost access to traditional food resources. Nonetheless, Maori well-being improved dramatically under Labour. Following on from Coates and Ngata, Savage expanded land development schemes; public health standards improved, the Department of Health extended health services and stepped up inquiries as to why Maori suffered higher death rates.

Social security went hand in hand with national security. New Zealand increased defence spending by 2.3 times from 1935 to 1938, when overall government expenditure expanded by 1.6 times. It established a tiny air force and recruited volunteers for home defence, which in strategic thinking included forward defence in the Pacific Islands. Internationally, the Labour government advanced the principle of collective security through the League of Nations. New Zealand alone among the Dominions criticised Britain for assuaging aggressors. It opposed Britain over Ethiopia, the Spanish civil war and the Japanese invasion of China. Above all it opposed Chamberlain's appeasement of Hitler.

There is debate about the degree of independence from British policy in New Zealand's stance. Was it moral or merely realistic? The government did show independence of interest, and 'loyal opposition' to Britain. Its security problem entailed not just home defence, but the protection of trade routes, so reliance on isolation and remoteness did not suffice. By 1938 New Zealand knew that its security depended on Britain's security in Europe. In retrospect,

Savage was vindicated in his concern for the security of the Pacific and whether a British fleet could defend Australia and New Zealand in the event of war in Europe. He was also right that because the country was small and isolated, national interests belonged with Britain and its empire.

WAR IN EUROPE

When Britain declared war on Germany on 3 September 1939 the cabinet committed New Zealand late the same day, only this time independently. From his sickbed on 5 September, the dying Savage, 'for whom war was such a disappointment', broadcast the famous sentiment:

Both with gratitude for the past, and with confidence in the future, we range ourselves without fear beside Britain. Where she goes, we go; where she stands, we stand. We are only a small and young nation, but we march . . . to a common destiny.

Truly he spoke for the country. This was a more measured response than in World War I, and from this new attitude both loyal and reluctant could gain comfort. Savage died in March 1940, replaced as wartime Prime Minister by Peter Fraser, an astute politician and a superb strategist.

Some historians highlight Labour's contrasting views of both world wars. The contrast is represented by Fraser himself and three other ministers who had been imprisoned for opposing conscription during World War I yet who were in the cabinet that introduced conscription in June 1940, copying the British regulations. The dissenters had become the establishment. In fact their thinking followed the Australian more than the New Zealand pattern: World War I, an imperial conflict, imposed a vast inequality of sacrifice by workers, as cannon fodder. World War II, on the other hand, entailed war in a just cause, between reason and Nazi force and violence. In this way of thinking, only victory could ensure peace and a democratic new order.

New Zealand made a full commitment to the war effort under Labour, who remained in power from the end of 1935 until 1949. Overall, 205,000 served, about 1 in 8 of the population, including more than 10,000 women. The Dominion mobilised over 65 per cent of all men aged 18 to 45 to provide one division – the 2nd – for Europe and subsequently a reduced 3rd Division for the Pacific, as well as sailors and aircrew. The RNZAF played an important role in training pilots as part of the empire air training scheme; in the Pacific, too, 'Air came first'. Not as many died as in World War I, and this conflict left less of a mark upon the national psyche. This time, 11,671 New Zealanders were killed, the biggest losses being among airmen, particularly in Europe. Soldiers also served in front-line combat units in Greece, Crete, the deserts of North Africa and Italy. The whole country served again as a farm, providing food first for Britain, and second for United States marines during the war in the Pacific.

Events fast overtook imperial strategy. In 1940 Hitler's blitzkrieg swept through the Low Countries, leaving Britain alone and under attack from an enemy-occupied Europe: in this context New Zealand introduced conscription, with France overrun and Italy's entry into the war. The German advance obliged the Second Echelon of 2 NZEF to be diverted for training in England from June 1940, where its troops joined the forces preparing for a German invasion. New Zealanders also fought in RAF Fighter Command and Bomber Command in Britain. The First Echelon of army volunteers, on the other hand, went to North Africa, as did the Third Echelon which arrived just as an Italian force invaded neutral Egypt. The British decision (Churchill's) to send one division each of Australians and New Zealanders to Greece in April 1941 proved disastrous. Hastily evacuated, the Anzacs suffered a serious but narrow defeat in the battle for Crete. Meanwhile Hitler repeated Napoleon's mistake of opening a second front against Russia when his armies invaded the Soviet Union in June 1941.

For New Zealand and Australia the turn of events from June 1940 in Europe bode ill for their own security in the South Pacific. Japan and China had been at war for years. New Zealand despatched men to Europe and the Mediterranean theatre on the explicit under-standing that if Japan were to strike southwards, the mighty British naval base at Singapore, which the country had helped to pay for, would serve as a bulwark. In Asia and the Pacific the entire imperial defence strategy depended on the assumption that the British fleet would defend Singapore if Japan attacked.

In June 1940, therefore, it shocked the Australian and New Zealand governments to learn that Britain could not promise a naval fleet for Singapore: they would have to rely on the United States. Diplomatic historians have described this as a 'momentous admission', of 'almost apocalyptic character'. Fraser's reply seethed with understatement; this advice was a 'departure' from 'repeated and most explicit assurances' about sending the fleet to Singapore which 'formed the basis of the whole of this Dominion's defence preparations'. He asked to send a New Zealand minister to Washington, and his deputy Walter Nash arrived in January 1942, in effect as the Dominion's first ambassador. By then Japan's offensive against the United States had transformed the war in Europe and the Mediterranean into a truly global conflict. Two issues long foreshadowed loomed from 1942: a turn to the United States as protector; and the question of whether New Zealand should bring home the 2nd Division to fight in the Pacific war.

WAR IN THE PACIFIC

The Japanese assault on Pearl Harbor on 7 December 1941 launched simultaneous stunning offensives. Japanese forces drove Americans from most of the Philippines by Christmas, and swept south to the north coast of New Guinea and the Solomon Islands. In a little over two months the Japanese invaded Southeast Asia from Burma to the Philippines, and to New Guinea in the Dutch East Indies, controlling not only the Pacific north of the Equator but intruding south from Guam to Rabaul and Bougainville, into the watery world of Australasia.

So much for the imperial strategy centred on the Singapore naval base, assumed to be impregnable: when the Japanese attacked Pearl Harbor, British ships were far from Singapore. Nor could the island withstand the assault from the north-west; its guns faced the wrong way. The fall of Singapore in February 1942 was critical for Australia and New Zealand and led them in quite separate directions. The 8th Australian Division, based at Singapore, was destroyed, almost all its men captured as prisoners of war. Australia suddenly stood on the front line with raids on Broome and Darwin and the discovery of Japanese midget submarines in Sydney Harbour.

From this point there was no Anzac rerun. Australia recalled its 6th and 7th Divisions from North Africa to meet the Japanese threat and concentrated its war effort in the Pacific, while New Zealand's 2nd Division remained in the Mediterranean. Thus the Australian war narrative centred on prisoners of war and fighting the Japanese in the islands; New Zealand's (although not exclusively) on fighting Hitler and Mussolini. This Anzac divergence had three influences on national war stories. First, it explained why the Kiwi soldier in World War II adopted the image of the 'hard man' and the 'hard case' as opposed to the gentleman, since the Australians no longer served as a reference point. New Zealanders could therefore adopt some stereotypically Australian characteristics. Second, historians have debated the extent to which Allied grand strategy, to defeat Hitler first, best met New Zealand interests, and third, whether the decision to stay in Europe reflected a colonial – or 'recolonial' – relationship.

New Zealand's smallness is a significant factor in understanding these issues. Its larger neighbour actually split its forces; 9th Australian Division stayed in the Mediterranean until the victory at El Alamein while the 6th and 7th returned. New Zealand only had one full division, which precluded a similar strategy. As far as possible, however, the country split what forces it could marshal. New Zealanders who had taken up forward positions in Pacific islands such as Fiji eventually formed two brigades of a forgotten 3rd Division in the Pacific. Moreover, the threat of invasion passed with the Battle of Midway in June 1942. New Zealand agreed to keep the 2nd Division in Europe from 1942 on the understanding that United States marines would defend New Zealand if necessary, and the first shipment of Americans arrived in June. Long-serving men also returned home on 'furlough'. Given their different geopolitics, then, both Australia and New Zealand made a realistic assessment of their respective places on the global chessboard of Anglo-American grand strategy.

Events soon proved that a Pacific war under United States command with Australia in support best met New Zealand's interests. From 1942 an accord developed, if an uneven one, between great and small white settler societies on opposite sides of the Pacific. Such agreement had been mooted during the Asian scare over

30 years before, when the American Grand Fleet sailed forth in 1908 to show that the United States planned to keep this vast region safe for white people. Given New Zealand's size and remoteness, it suited to serve as a minor player, as a rear base for the United States assault on Japanese forces in the Solomons and Papua New Guinea. Churchill's views singly were not persuasive; President Roosevelt's views understandably weighed heavily with the war cabinet because the strategy of imperial defence had failed. From 1942 New Zealand and Australia stood or fell with the United States, Britain's most important ally. The United States divided Australasia into separate military zones on the Pacific Rim (itself an American concept). The United States placed Australia and its forces in a south-west Pacific area under the command of General MacArthur of the United States army, and New Zealand and its forces in the South Pacific, under the command of Vice-Admiral Ghormley of the United States navy.

A novel consensus of farmers, business and the labour movement established that New Zealand could best serve the Allied cause by continuing its major effort in Europe alongside the British, and by leaving the Pacific to the Americans where New Zealand could help to feed United States troops. For the men of 2nd Division, it was not a case of wanting to fight for Britain, but a case of not wanting to fight in the tropics, combined with the phobia to keep out Asia. The war front was not in New Zealand but in the islands of the Pacific – Australia's 'near north' – which served as a buffer. The Japanese sweep into Australasian waters only confirmed such thinking. Anti-Japanese as well as pro-British sentiment, geography and strategy prompted New Zealand to step up her war effort from 1942, to satisfy the great power demands of Britain and the United States that on balance decided the form of national security.

WAR FRONT/HOME FRONT

At home, world war overshadowed the country's centennial in 1940, which celebrated not the Treaty of Waitangi but 'pioneers', 'progress', and the history of settlement. The first public remembrance of the treaty occurred in 1934, after Governor-General Lord Bledisloe and his wife bought and gifted Busby's house and grounds at Waitangi to the nation. The Tourist and Publicity Department hailed the 1934 celebrations while dating the 'real settlement' of New Zealand from the 'formation of the New Zealand Company . . . and the arrival of the pioneers in 1840'. It was this interpretation, giving precedence to the Wakefieldian narrative, which dominated. Wellington's *Evening Post* published its centennial issue in November 1939 to advertise the opening of the New Zealand Centennial Exhibition, and gave priority in its own coverage to the settlement of Wellington by the New Zealand Company.

The exhibition cited the dates in its title as '1939–1940', not 1940, in remembrance of the pioneers. Only at Ngata's insistence were carvings created at the Rotorua school of arts put on display; Maori in general were sidelined. Remembrance of the treaty at the centennial owed greatly to Ngata's leadership. At a re-enactment of the treaty signing at Waitangi on 6 February, Ngata led the haka. Afterwards the Governor-General opened the ceremonial carved meeting house built especially for the centenary at Waitangi. Reviewing the previous 100 years, Ngata noted that the treaty was a 'gentlemen's agreement', which had not been observed too poorly relative to the record of European colonisation elsewhere. But he warned presciently that, with lands gone, chiefly powers crumbled, and culture broken, land claims had to be settled for Maori to move forward side by side with Europeans, and made clear that 'We want to retain our individuality as a race'.

Ngata placed his hopes for equality with the 28 (Maori) Battalion, organised on a tribal basis, who were all volunteers. Ngapuhi from North Auckland served mainly in A Company; Te Arawa from the thermal district in B Company; principally Ngati Porou from Gisborne in C Company; and D Company comprised the rest. Headquarters Company became the 'Odds and Sods'. This time even Waikato supported the war effort because of Te Puea's friendship with Peter Fraser, who promised recompense for nineteenth-century land confiscation. Within boundaries set by the settler society, 28 (Maori) Battalion nudged their people closer to equality through their wartime prowess. They fought in Greece, Crete, in the desert campaigns and in Italy, and returned national heroes. Yet they were not allowed their own officers until late in the war.

At home the drive for full citizenship and Maori leadership of Maori affairs created the Maori War Effort Organisation in 1942,

7.3 'Got his man'. All soldiers were souvenir collectors. Here
men from 28 (Maori) Battalion perform for their Australian
photographer. Maori 'frightened blazes outa the Hun with
their bayonet charges . . . This one "got his man" and also a
decent souvenir, a German iron cross', Alexandria, 1 June
1941.

arranged into tribal committees, that co-ordinated recruitment, food
production and labour across the country. In some districts freezing
works and dairy factories could not have operated without the assistance of the committees. Once the officers of the Maori Battalion
returned, their experience and hopes joined with the successes of
the Maori War Effort Organisation to imagine how it could evolve
into a peacetime structure for post-war reconstruction under tribal
leadership. But Maori autonomy that operated so effectively during
the war proved to be only for the duration.

For women, too, the war offered new opportunities and adventure, but did little to change the gender script that decreed a woman's
place to be in the home. Women volunteered for patriotic duties,
as in 1914, knitting, packing parcels for servicemen, in first aid,
and as drivers. More than 75,000 enrolled in the Women's War

Service Auxiliary organised by Dr Agnes Bennett and Janet Fraser, to co-ordinate and direct 'maids of war work'. A major task entailed food production: volunteers tended rows of vegetables in home gardens, dug up lawns, in parks and around schools; 2700 worked on farms as land girls, making women's agricultural work visible. The Pacific war finally saw authorities agree to women's service in uniform. Women's auxiliaries to the armed forces numbered over 10,000 from 1942.

The war also demanded a short-term increase in the number of women in the workforce. Indeed, after the fall of Singapore, women were conscripted to meet the labour shortage. In the food and clothing industries, hospitals, the public service, banks, post and telegraph, the railways and on trams, women without young children stepped in for the duration of the war. They worked as clerical assistants and as tram girls, who daringly wore trousers. But trousers did not signal a breakdown of the segmented labour market: women's appearance in the paid workforce was temporary and subordinate.

Trousers were a wartime austerity measure in place of stockings; so were socks for schoolgirls. The depression ethos of 'making do' reached new heights with the fashion for remade, recycled clothing, and eggless cake recipes. Wartime rationing renewed the emphasis on thrift. New Zealand rationed petrol from 1939 until 1950, except for two short breaks. Paper, corrugated iron, liquor, prams and lawnmowers, china, silk stockings, canned foods and knitting wool disappeared, encouraging ingenuity with the sewing machine, in the kitchen and with self-provisioning, while the shortages vested more meaning in home preserves. The Japanese attack on Pearl Harbor led to panic buying of sugar and tea which, with butter, were rationed from 1942 as necessities; and Dr Muriel Bell, the first nutritionist in the Department of Health, advised mothers how to make rosehip syrup to feed families their Vitamin C. While meat and canned vegetables were rationed to feed the United States forces in the Pacific, butter was destined for Britain and remained restricted until 1950.

American marines transformed food habits. Their presence in large numbers from 1943 generated a new market for milk, especially milk shakes, Coca-Cola, steak, hamburgers and vegetables.

The three-fold impact of the demands of United States troops, the British market and the school milk scheme generated a milk inquiry in 1943–44 which exposed that the little milk drunk locally was not subjected to the same checks as exported dairy products and was likely to be bad. In Christchurch (unlike Auckland) most milk was unpasteurised.

The Americans also set feminine hearts aflutter, with their smart uniforms that suggested Hollywood romance. Marines had access to luxury goods, notably tobacco, silk stockings and chocolates. They proffered gifts, including flowers, and enjoyed women's company and conversation. They were also there when the most marriageable men were absent. From the viewpoint of Kiwi and male rivals wherever they were stationed, the Yanks were 'over-paid, over-sexed and over here' – usurpers and a threat to local manhood. Among young women, however, the American presence encouraged a shift in ideals of femininity from grace and refinement to sex appeal and sexual allure, as portrayed in Hollywood movies. An American boyfriend posed opportunities as well as risks in a moment of glamour and adventure.

VISIONS OF POST-WAR RECONSTRUCTION

Foreign relations were obviously tested by the American presence. The Japanese settled the question that New Zealand was 'geographically part of the Pacific', the historian F. L. W. Wood concluded in 1944. The Japanese threat spurred diplomatic representation in Washington, then Ottawa, and the establishment of the Department of External Affairs. It also provided the catalyst for frequent direct contact between Canberra and Wellington to supplement the long-standing system in both of direct ties with London, completing a Britain–Australia–New Zealand triangle. Australia and New Zealand opened high commissions in Wellington and Canberra respectively in 1943, whereas previously New Zealand had only tourist bureaus in Australia. Air travel also made it easier for policy-makers to cross the Tasman, increasing government-to-government contact.

An Australia–New Zealand Agreement (Canberra Pact) followed in January 1944. Drafted by the Australians, the agreement asserted the neighbours' long-held belief in their right to participate in all decisions about the South-west and South Pacific. Despite some sensitivity about the future of American bases and landing rights – for burgeoning air travel – in the islands, Australia and New Zealand realised that the future security of their region depended on co-operation with the United States. Most importantly, the agreement foreshadowed closer trans-Tasman ties in the post-war world. Australia and New Zealand agreed to co-operate not merely in external policy, but in the 'development of commerce'. Further, they planned to co-operate 'in achieving full employment in Australia and New Zealand and the highest standards of social security both within their borders and throughout the islands of the Pacific', and in encouraging missionary work in the Pacific islands and territories.

Fraser was deeply affected by his visit to Samoa late in 1944 to investigate the question of trusteeship for League of Nations mandated territories. Expecting to see progress under New Zealand's mandate, he was shocked by the degree of colonialism, especially in education and health, and the neglect of development. With Australia's foreign minister H. V. Evatt, he sought a new commitment to the South Pacific. To this end the South Pacific Commission, foreshadowed by the Canberra Pact, was established in 1947. Samoa changed status to a New Zealand trust territory from the end of 1946, and New Zealand adopted a plan for Samoa to prepare for self-government.

Fraser played a leading role at the San Francisco Conference that devised a charter for the United Nations in 1945. Australia and New Zealand agreed beforehand, first, that the 'territorial integrity and political independence' of members should be preserved against the threat of force and, second, on the principle of trusteeship. New Zealand's commitment to the multilateral model embodied in the United Nations in one sense represented a continuity of the Commonwealth tradition, which allowed a voice for the small and otherwise powerless. In another, it refashioned Labour's principle of collective security. Effectively New Zealand exercised its Dominion status to argue for a democratic structure to safeguard a new order in a post-war world. Having to live with great power dominance was a fact of New Zealand life. Ever mindful of the conduct of great and small power relations, all New Zealand's representatives could do was to influence the drafting of the United Nations charter to reflect humanitarian aspirations that might make global power politics operate more peacefully.

The war also added democratic principles to the goal of equal opportunity at home. From World War II, the Labour government's belief in education as a right rather than a privilege subsumed the 'new', progressive education intended to foster full development of the individual, with its focus on all-round child development from pre-school age. In 1939 Dr C. E. Beeby, a psychologist, laid down the post-war blueprint when he summarised his own idea of education for Peter Fraser, then Minister of Education, in language that he rightly judged expressed Fraser's objectives. The following statement in its call for equality of opportunity formed the 'lodestone' of education policy for a generation:

The Government's objective, broadly expressed, is that every person, whatever his level of academic ability, whether he be rich or poor, whether he live in town or country, has a right, as a citizen, to a free education of the kind for which he is best fitted and to the fullest extent of his powers.

This included the improvement of race relations by educating young Pakeha teachers about Maori culture. At Wellington Teachers' College in 1938–39, the principal, Frank Lopdell, appointed Kingi Tahiwi to teach Maori to interested students, with the goal of increasing tolerance between Maori and Pakeha. The number of kindergartens and parent-run play centres for pre-schoolers increased, influenced by international ideas. The pull-along toy to promote the toddler's motor development, painted in bright primary colours, took the form of the 'Buzzy Bee' in New Zealand, and was created from toilet roll holders in 1948. Secondary school reforms, a raised school-leaving age and revised qualifications prepared New Zealand's youth for a future of full employment. Following Australia, the government introduced a universal family benefit in 1945, of a generous 10 shillings a week for each child, payable to the mother. Teachers noticed that the allowance improved the appearance and dress of children at school.

Post-war reconstruction generally focused on the goal of full employment. Labour resolved to avoid the failures of soldier settlement after World War I with an extensive rehabilitation scheme for returned servicemen. The settler contract lived on in the development of farms for ex-servicemen, complete with houses built on state house plans, modified for their farm house function by including porches for boots and outdoor clothing. In the cities ex-servicemen enjoyed priority for state houses and for jobs, while 'pressure cooker' courses at teachers colleges and university offered men opportunities unavailable before the war.

For Maori, the 'rehab' scheme signified new opportunities. Until farms became economic, ex-servicemen were paid wages, and a Rehabilitation Department insisted on more equal housing standards. Fraser hoped that the Maori Social and Economic Advancement Act 1945 would finally bring about equality. A compromise between Maori hopes of full citizenship, raised by the war, and the resolve of the Pakeha-run Department of Native Affairs to remain in control of official policy, the Act replaced the word 'Native' with 'Maori' in official usage. But paternalism persisted because neither the government nor the general public understood the nature and size of Maori needs. The legislation subordinated the goal of development to an emphasis on welfare, where officers of 28 (Maori) Battalion, experienced leaders, returned to jobs in teaching or as welfare officers in the renamed Department of Maori Affairs. What limited authority they exercised over social, economic and welfare issues of concern to Maori was soon checked by a change of government.

The goal of equal opportunity also encouraged a series of treaty settlements between 1944 and 1946 with iwi whose grievances remained outstanding since the 1920s. Parliament passed the Waikato-Maniapoto Maori Claims Settlement Act in 1944, under which Tainui received a lump sum of £10,000 and annual payments for the next 45 years, as compensation for the vast land confiscations of the nineteenth century. Subsequent settlements allocated £5000 annually to the Taranaki Trust Board for confiscated land and compensation to Ngai Tahu of £10,000 for 30 years.

While Maori were more included in notions of 'the people' from the end of World War II, New Zealand continued to restrict entry to migrants on grounds of race. A committee on population in 1946 recommended against mass immigration, in contrast to Australian policy; the profile of the good migrant remained white and British. If immigration of 'other European types' were encouraged, the committee reported, they should be 'of such character as will, within a relatively short space of time, become completely assimilated'. That meant if other than British migrants were to be accepted, they should come from northern European countries. Non-Maori New Zealanders, 95 per cent of the people, remained 96 per cent British and proud of it. Consistent with a Commonwealth agreement on citizenship, separate New Zealand nationality came into existence in 1948, on the Canadian model. British subjects became New Zealand citizens for the first time, with New Zealand passports. But few British migrants registered for New Zealand citizenship because they remained British subjects, which suggests that ethnicity dictated who belonged. At the time no thought was given to Pacific Islanders in New Zealand-administered territories, who by default became brown New Zealanders.

Nonetheless, a sequence of symbolic moves indicated that the Dominion had become a nation by the end of the 1940s. New Zealand finally ratified the Statute of Westminster in 1947 and so attained constitutional independence five years after Australia did, in response to the fall of Singapore. The 'Dominion of New Zealand' became 'New Zealand' in 1945, and the royal coat of arms disappeared from official letterheads to be replaced by the national coat of arms, which contained a Maori warrior and Zealandia. In retrospect the era from 1930 to 1949 proved to be one of cultural nationalism, state-sponsored under a long-serving Labour government, from the introduction of public radio in 1936 to state patronage of the arts, a national museum, art gallery and orchestra.

By 1949 historians were writing books about an emerging nation state. J. B. Condliffe's *New Zealand in the Making* (1930) pursued the theme of economic development through small farming and closer settlement, from the Wakefieldian schemes of the 1840s to dairying. By World War II the popular series of pictorial survey histories, *Making New Zealand* (1939–40), used by schoolchildren for another 30 years, suggested that making the nation was very much under way (see 7.4). Published in wartime, these and other centennial publications were intended to strengthen the sense of nationhood among the Pakeha majority.

7.4 *Making New Zealand*

The assumption of the time was that making the nation and its history was a settler enterprise, achieved through their efforts. Maori belonged more to the past, serving as a preface to New Zealand history, and an occasional support act. In settler New Zealand, fourth and fifth generations meanwhile were growing up who identified with their environment. The forthright newspaper and literary magazine editor Oliver Duff co-opted the biblical imagery that the country had made its own in his idiosyncratic centennial survey, *New Zealand Now*, to explain the process of adaptation: 'There is of course a sense in which every man springs from the soil. Literally as well as figuratively all flesh is grass. A New Zealander is a man whom New Zealand earth has nourished.' The concept of flesh as grass, while definitely made in New Zealand, was no longer imperialistic. In 1930 Condliffe had pondered the effects of isolation on imperial sentiment, from his new vantage point as an expatriate in Honolulu. Disillusioned by what he later termed New Zealand's 'intellectual stagnation', he decided that imperfect knowledge lay at the basis of New Zealand's 'mother-complex'. Remoteness precluded analysis of events and encouraged resort to imperial loyalty without the necessary scholarly research.

7.5 The invincibility of the All Blacks

In the 1920s 'New Zealand's so-called mother complex reached its climax', Wood responded in the course of writing his own survey in 1943. Foreign policy was a 'drama enacted on another planet', and since New Zealand 'could do little or nothing to shape the course of events', there was 'no reason' to 'affront sentiment by any assertion for nationhood'. But that could change; and historians have debated ever since how much dependence on Britain did change after Japan's entry into the war, which propelled the adjustment to 'dual dependency' on the United States. As far as Condliffe and Wood were concerned, New Zealand's future lay with the countries that surrounded the Pacific Ocean, 'the eye of the earth'.

In a tongue in cheek sketch of late 1940s Kiwi culture and upbringing, the popular cartoonist G. E. G. Minhinnick illustrated how everyday actions contributed to the country's myths. He captured the passing on of a key myth about 'the invincibility of the All Blacks' to a small boy at his mother's knee. Mother, not father, relayed the message, illustrating the importance of nurture in the formation of identities. The national obsession with rugby could be read as continuing to play an imperial game; yet the process of telling stories about and attributing meaning to that game happened at home in New Zealand, where mothers instructed children in beliefs and values.

Politically, 1949 proved a turning point, when the principles of private enterprise and freedom as opposed to regulation and wartime controls swept Labour from office. Conservatives had rallied to form the National Party in 1936 in response to Labour's election success. Cold War clouds incited a 'yes' vote in a referendum for peacetime conscription, but with a low turnout. Once again, a small nation searched for new ways to balance internal and external security.

8

Golden weather 1950–1973

Wartime controls only ended in 1950, allowing New Zealanders to look forward to an era of post-war growth and change. The 1950s and 1960s are often recalled as a 'golden age'. In many respects they were, for the baby boomers (born from 1945 to 1961) who enjoyed a childhood unburdened by depression and war, and for the parents responsible for their upbringing. Broadly, however, the internal dynamics of the Pacific region were in flux. Bruce Mason captured the mood in *The End of the Golden Weather*, his solo dramatic performance about a summer in a boy's childhood. At adolescence, he explained,

This strange and magic light – this *golden weather* – begins to change and, for the first time, some of the troubling weathers of a man's soul are revealed to him; . . . he becomes aware of the thousand changing visages of time, touched with confusion and bewilderment, menaced by terrible depths and enigmas of experience he has never known before.

So it was for New Zealanders in the 1950s and 1960s. The unsettling of settler society had already begun, first for Maori, then for future Pacific Island migrants and lastly for Pakeha.

These were years of full employment for men – until 1967 – in an economy that increasingly needed married women in the workforce. The significant gap in life expectancy between Maori and Pakeha narrowed rapidly. A new round of culture contact began with a major movement of Maori to the cities. A generation gap opened between baby boomers and their parents, who wanted their children to better themselves through expanding educational opportunities.

Sustained growth made possible the consumer society and accompanying changes in etiquette and social norms, from hats and gloves to miniskirts and informality. Communications were transformed, linking New Zealand more strongly to the world. This was an era of social change and new interdependencies.

In art, the visionary Colin McCahon emerged as a seminal figure, treated harshly by the public for his word paintings and abstract landscapes, often done in panels. Darkness was fundamental to his artwork; in the black of McCahon's landscapes the fleeting passage of time contrasted with the land's seeming permanence. Through his painting he tried to invent a way to see 'something logical, orderly and beautiful belonging to the land and not yet to its peoples', a vision not understood and appreciated until after his death in 1987.

Politically the National Party was supreme. The government of Sidney Holland argued for 'freedom' and development, claiming the middle ground of equality of opportunity and endorsement of the settler contract. In theory National embraced the free market, which still meant dependence on Britain, now a declining world power; in practice it continued the Australasian model of state development, whose core business involved managing the economy in an increasingly uncertain and confusing post-war world dominated by the United States. The Holland government of New Zealand-born returned servicemen, loyal to Britain, contained just one woman, Hilda Ross. In 1950 the government abolished the Legislative Council, the appointed upper house, which also contained one woman, Agnes Louisa Weston, wife of the National Party's first president. (Ironically Louisa Weston was chosen when Fraser discovered that women were ineligible in the 1940s, only to become a member of the 'suicide squad' appointed on the understanding that they voted to get rid of it.) New Zealand now had a system of unicameral government, which would have unintended outcomes in terms of the untrammelled use of executive power during the ruptures of the late twentieth century.

COLD WAR AND NUCLEAR PLAYGROUND

The origins of New Zealand's late twentieth-century stance against nuclear weapons were already discernible. First, the nation faced the 'Anzac dilemma', of having to juggle the expectations of not one but two great power protectors as a result of World War II. To confound this dilemma, the less preferred protector, the United States, was now the dominant Pacific power, replacing Britain, which was in withdrawal and decline. The Antipodes were used to having a voice in British policy; strong ties, economic dependence, trust and familiarity lowered transaction costs, strategic let-downs notwithstanding. The United States, however, played by different rules, as yet unknown. 'Do as we say' appeared to be the directive.

Second, both western great powers had divergent interests from small, remote New Zealand. The country's very insignificance posed the problem of how to manage the tension between a conservative realist strategy of obediently falling in with the interests of Britain and the United States, and the idealism of seeing to its own interests by managing isolation through collective security. In the longer term, New Zealand would opt for the higher moral ground of the multilateral formula provided by the United Nations.

In retrospect the top diplomat of the time, the urbane Alister McIntosh, mused that clinging to the British connection 'paid off' as a strategy but was 'perhaps followed for too long' after the war. The war itself had demonstrated that there would be no security without the full support of the United States, who had become the essential 'great and powerful friend'. From the 1950s the external threat of the Cold War shaped defence policy. Indeed the fear of communism drove New Zealand into the Cold War – much like the fear of racial degeneracy inspired defence strategy before it – alongside Australia as a small partner in the western alliance.

Happily, the Cold War provided a new window of opportunity to keep the United States interested in a region peripheral to the main game, while maintaining traditional Commonwealth ties. Both Australia and New Zealand deplored the communist victory in China in 1949, and treated the regime in Taiwan as the Chinese government; both acquiesced in United States actions that denied West Papua to the Netherlands. With the outbreak of the Korean War in 1950 the communist threat seemed real, and the neighbours sent troops, nominally to support the United Nations, but technically as part of a Commonwealth force. In reality New Zealand and Australia supported the United States, who expected not to go in to Korea alone. At the same time, the United States sought a 'soft peace' with Japan to ensure its friendship while 'containing' the communist threat in Korea and China. This acceptance of a recent wartime enemy required a change in attitude by Australia and New Zealand. The ANZUS alliance of Australia, New Zealand and the United States proved to be their sizeable reward.

Non-military influence in South and Southeast Asia extended alongside the military through the Colombo Plan from 1950, to encourage economic development and so, it was hoped, remove the instability that nurtured the conditions for communist influence. Colombo Plan scholarships brought students from newly independent countries to study in Australia and New Zealand, idealistically to aid the Third World, and realistically to commit the United States to funding and regional security.

At bottom, any latitude sought in foreign affairs depended on the American alliance. Drafted in Canberra, the ANZUS Pact was signed in San Francisco in 1951, the first security alliance that New Zealand (or Australia) entered into without Britain. The Americans insisted on a tripartite agreement because they did not want to be subjected to British and French demands as imperial powers in the Pacific. ANZUS promised, but did not guarantee, American support in the event of threats from Asia – the old fear dressed up in new Cold War guise. The importance of ANZUS grew with time because it supplied high-level communication with Washington and easy access to the United States' superpower military intelligence and infrastructure.

Still distrustful of the 'Asian menace', New Zealand and Australia became involved in a series of small wars. New Zealand rallied to help Britain in Malaya, contributing to the Malayan Emergency in the 1950s, followed by commitments in Thailand and Malaysia in its confrontation with Indonesia in the 1960s. New Zealand participated in the Malayan Emergency as a signatory to the Southeast Asia Collective Defence Treaty of 1954, which included Britain and France with the ANZUS partners, as well as Thailand, Pakistan and the Philippines. New Zealand then followed the American lead in turning against President Sukarno in Indonesia only as he lost power in 1966. Finally, New Zealand reluctantly followed Australia into Vietnam.

Vietnam was the first war in which New Zealand participated without Britain and was the result of external pressures. To avoid any risk to ANZUS, regarded by officials as the pivot of foreign policy, a small New Zealand contingent joined the Australian taskforce. Soldiers replaced engineers already in Vietnam in 1965, followed by infantry sent as part of an Australian battalion and medics. Prime Minister Keith Holyoake, however, kept the forces' contribution to a minimum. (Alliteration bestowed on Holyoake the nickname 'Kiwi Keith' to distinguish him from an Australian cousin of the same name, which says much about Kiwi identity.) A mere 3500 New Zealanders served between 1965 and 1972, all volunteers, of whom 35 died.

Back home the Cold War permeated life. National's success at exploiting the domestic effects kept it in office throughout the 1950s and 1960s. The bitter waterfront dispute of 1951, which lasted 151 days, brought the issues to the fore, breaking the back of the powerful waterside workers' union and leaving the National Party in the ascendant. Economically, the stoush grabbed headlines because prosperity depended on the export-led economy. Before relatively cheap air travel New Zealanders relied on shipping and ports to sustain their living standards. But the organisation of work on the waterfront was the preserve of British companies concerned only with a fast turnaround and with cutting costs, which led to constant conflict with waterside workers. During the Korean War the prolonged dispute disrupted exports at a time of record prices for primary products, especially high wool prices.

In one view, the Cold War divided the labour movement between the Federation of Labour, led by F. P. Walsh, a former confidant of Fraser – and the closest the country has had to a mafia godfather – and the more militant Trade Union Congress, including the waterside workers. The militants made the critical mistake of rejecting arbitration, unwisely challenging the power of the state, which proclaimed emergency regulations and ordered armed forces on to the wharves. The refusal to accept arbitration destroyed the union and hurt public confidence in the Labour Party, while the Federation of Labour sided with the government, to their mutual advantage. In a snap election centred on the issue of law and order in 1951, National won decisively.

A more recent view of the dispute argues that Cold War rhetoric had nothing to do with the real underlying causes, which were 'structural and embedded in the labour process'. A history of low wages, insecure employment and dangerous work practices bred hostility and covert resistance, strategies used to effect against the employers when the economy improved. Management refused to recognise legitimate grievances, and governments were obliged to defer to the shipping lines' market dominance. The employers provoked the dispute and then ducked for cover, allowing the government to capitalise on Cold War hysteria and the populist platform of law and order.

Cold War jitters further spurred nuclear weapons programmes and vice versa. Throughout the bipolar contest between communism and capitalism the United States, Britain and France treated the Pacific with its sparse populations and minimal political costs as their 'nuclear playground'. In the wake of the secret Anglo-American Manhattan project during World War II, Britain sought its own nuclear deterrent. The British returned to the region to conduct nuclear tests on uninhabited islands off Western Australia and in outback South Australia in the 1950s, and hydrogen bomb tests in the Gilbert Islands (Kiribati) in 1957–58. The United States conducted atmospheric tests of atomic and hydrogen bombs in the Marshall Islands until 1958 and began a final series of tests in 1962, amid mounting public concern about nuclear fallout. Overall the Americans exploded 66 nuclear devices in the Pacific.

French bomb tests, however, provoked the strongest protest, both because they started in 1966, in violation of the Partial Test Ban Treaty of 1963, and because France used nuclear testing to assert its colonial power in Polynesia – a power long resented in New Zealand. France could not have detonated bombs above and below French Polynesia had the islands been independent. The peace movement, which formed a Campaign for Nuclear Disarmament on the British model in 1959, gathered strength as the bomb tests proliferated. New Zealanders resented experiments with nuclear bombs in what they regarded as their backyard. Concern about the effects on the Cook Islands contributed to anti-French feeling. Problematically, nuclear weapons had also become a key feature of United States military strategy. In such unintended as well as deliberate ways, Cold War tensions refracted into local policy and politics.

The development of nuclear weapons during the war created a demand for uranium, and gave rise to hopes of entering the atomic age with a find. A secret wartime search for uranium came to nothing, but in 1955 a publicly promoted search saw a Geiger counter go wild on the West Coast – in an area that is now national park – precipitating a uranium rush reminiscent of the gold rush a century earlier. Thereafter the New Zealand government, the British Atomic Energy Authority and business spent 25 years searching for uranium on the West Coast, but no viable deposits were ever found. A tantalising teaser remains; what if uranium had been discovered in economic quantities in the 1950s? Would New Zealand have developed a nuclear free policy? Had economic deposits been located the country could have followed a different path altogether.

In the 1950s the energy future, then, looked nuclear. Officials agreed on the need for nuclear power stations, but debated how to respond to competition between Britain and the United States which arose from their efforts to supply atomic equipment to the 'free world'. After signing an agreement with the United States in 1956 (as Iran did in 1957) New Zealand was able to acquire enriched uranium as fuel for research reactors and equipment, an agreement transferred in 1961 to the new International Atomic Energy Agency, and established an Institute of Nuclear Sciences. The United States 'atoms for peace' programme also donated a sub-critical reactor to the University of Canterbury, which was operating from 1961.

Nuclear power was put on the agenda because power shortages plagued post-war New Zealand. Between 1955 and 1964 electricity generation doubled yet barely kept up with soaring demand. In response, the state built infrastructure to provide electricity, just as it had done with railways. Power projects commanded the waters of the Waikato, the North Island's major river, in the 1950s, and the Waitaki River in the South Island in the 1960s. A cable across Cook Strait, envisaged in 1950 and laid in 1964, transferred energy from hydroelectric power stations in the South Island to the power-hungry North Island. Such was the scale of earthmoving required for the Benmore dam, built from 1958 to 1965, that cartoonist Nevile Lodge

"NOW WE'VE SEEN HOW EASILY EUCLIDS HANDLE THESE BIG JOBS WE'VE DECIDED TO END THE 'MAINLAND' ARGUMENT FOR GOOD - WE WANT YOU TO SHIFT THE TWO ISLANDS TOGETHER."

8.1 Nevile S. Lodge, Needmore Power Project, 1963 or 1964

suggested the argument over which island was the 'mainland' – a title claimed by the south – could be resolved by shifting the two islands together.

PEOPLING NEW ZEALAND

To the surprise of some, post-war growth did not require as many non-British migrants as expected; and this freed the country from having to compete for them. The baby boom lifted the birth rate, while enough British migrants arrived to supply two-thirds of long-term new arrivals. Assisted migration resumed in 1947 with the 'ten pound Poms', who found it cheaper to migrate than to holiday at home. Dutch comprised almost half the intake of migrants from continental Europe between 1945 and 1975; in New Zealand minds, as northern Europeans, they best approximated the British ideal. Between 1945 and 1971 almost 77,000 newcomers arrived from Britain while about 6200 migrated from the Netherlands. A mere 4500 displaced persons arrived from 1949 and

1100 Hungarian refugees, in a total of 90,000 assisted European migrants. Kin migration continued in its historical pattern until the late 1980s; Britain provided nearly half the permanent arrivals, followed by Australia with about a quarter. Post-war migration also produced a significant Dutch community, among them the de Bres and Borren families, who rose to prominence respectively in social justice issues and in hockey, and Eelco Boswijk, who set up Nelson's Chez Eelco coffee house in 1961.

With the post-war need for relationships around the Pacific Rim came the first easing of policy towards 'Asia'. As in Canada, Indians could enter as British subjects (now Commonwealth citizens). The poll tax imposed on Chinese migrants was abolished in 1944; in 1952 Chinese New Zealanders regained the right of naturalisation, denied since 1908, and only one woman qualified, followed by 20 men in the next two years. In response to the global development of restrictions at the border, the Immigration Amendment Act 1961 required non-New Zealand citizens to have an entry permit. In practice, it remained difficult for Chinese and Indians to gain entry unless they had family links. Even Britons required permits. The exception was Australians, who did not need a permit or even a passport until 1981.

Changes in migration policy accompanied changes in the economy. Whereas Europeans largely met the need for skilled labour, Pacific Islanders and Maori provided a cheap unskilled and semi-skilled workforce. In the biggest post-war shift, other parts of Australasia – brown as well as white – supplemented Britain as the leading source of migrants. With decolonisation in the Pacific Islands, the 'good migrant' came to include Islanders. Settler society illusions lasted into the 1970s that Pacific Islanders and Maori had a place in the nation as Polynesian kin and as an unskilled workforce, and that Maori were too 'integrated' to unsettle structures of power and privilege.

The numbers of Pacific Islanders were small (little more than 26,000 in 1966) but proportionally significant. The majority came from New Zealand dependencies: the Cook Islands, Niue and Tokelau, whose population largely relocated to New Zealand in 1966, and Western Samoa, a trusteeship territory subject to United Nations scrutiny until 1962. Smaller numbers from Tonga, Fiji and

Tahiti claimed real (and imagined) links. Pakeha saw Islanders as not British nor foreign, nor ethnically alien, but as another kind of Maori, a view Maori did not share. At the same time the general public remained largely oblivious to the country's legacy of subcolonialism in the Pacific. Even politicians were unaware that Pacific Islanders from New Zealand dependencies were New Zealand citizens.

New Zealand decolonised in the South Pacific earlier, but less completely, than other powers. Under New Zealand trusteeship, the Samoan constitution was modified regularly to transfer responsibility in stages to prepare for independence. Full internal self-government came in 1959 and independence in 1962, after which Western Samoans could enter the country under a quota system.

The 'free association' deal reached with the Cook Islands was a world first and a stark contrast to Australian relations with Melanesians at that time. The sequence of events paralleled the pattern in Western Samoa. In 1962 the Cook Islands was offered the choice of integration, independence, or self-government 'in free association' with New Zealand. Cook Islanders chose the last and became fully self-governing in 1965, with New Zealand responsible for foreign affairs. 'Free association' proffered the advantage to this tiny, scattered island group of the 'self-esteem of nationhood' without the 'hazards of independence'. New Zealand was well versed in how to negotiate the best of both worlds from its own experience of simultaneous dependence and independence as a British Dominion, and put this experience into practice in its Pacific territories. Niue, a single coral outcrop, followed a similar path to 'free association' by 1974, and tiny Tokelau remains a New Zealand dependency.

While New Zealand exerted an impact on Pacific Islanders, Islanders made an impact on New Zealanders' sense of themselves. Intellectuals, from economists to poets and artists, began to assert a Pacific identity. It is no accident that the Pacific-centred view of nationalist historian Keith Sinclair, who graduated with a University of New Zealand PhD, from Auckland, appeared in his classic *History of New Zealand* in 1959. Sinclair located New Zealand in the Pacific and in the New World. He opposed Britishness, which he saw as part of a South Island myth of settlement, while his rivals quipped that the Leftist Sinclair school portrayed New Zealand as 'the long pink cloud'. Pakeha–Maori relations, but not Pacific Islanders, nor Asia, nor women featured in Sinclair's history. New interdependencies between town and country brought to the forefront the place of Maori in the nation.

MAORI URBANISATION

The growth of Maori migration in search of work intensified from the 1930s, propelled by population recovery and too little land to support young people. At the same time, the long post-war boom demanded workers. World War II accelerated the 'silent migration' of Maori, raising hopes of work and a better life. Between 1945 and 1976 the Maori population transformed from predominantly rural (74 per cent) to urban (77 per cent). This was a radical change for both Maori and Pakeha, who had lived largely separate lives from the 1860s until the end of World War II. Post-war New Zealand, then, underwent another round of culture encounter.

In settler mythology the colonial town had represented the civilisation of the wilderness. The post-war move to the city and suburbs extended the process. Before the centenary of Christchurch in 1950, for example, Maori faces were rare sights in the city centre. In Auckland, tribal settlements became engulfed by suburban sprawl. Pakeha policy-makers viewed traditional pa as a blot on the landscape. 'Modern' Maori had to become urban, and suburban, by moving to the suburbs, the twentieth-century mirror image of the slum. In this context the Maori Women's Welfare League, formed in 1951, succeeded in having the booklet *Washday at the Pa* withdrawn from schools in 1964 because of its pre-modern portrayal of Maori life.

'Integration' replaced 'assimilation' as the preferred race relations policy in response to rapid demographic change. For Ngata earlier in the century, Maori belonged in rural New Zealand, within their tribal territory. His solution was to extend the settler contract to Maori, to allow them to farm and develop their own land. But World War II mobilised young Maori for the war effort, both in the services and in production; and for many this entailed a shift to the cities. After the war, this move was highly orchestrated. From a full employment perspective, the state viewed Maori youth as a

'reserve of industrial labour' who should be transferred from 'uneconomic' areas to cities and towns. At the time, there were over 20,000
job vacancies. An official relocation scheme from 1960 until 1967,
when costs were cut, provided support for families prepared to shift
centres. Young Maori women were attracted to hotel and hospital
work by cheap board and good pay, and into teaching and nursing,
all viewed as suitable training for future wives and mothers. Young
men, largely from the East Coast of the North Island, migrated to
Christchurch for trade training. Of nearly 2700 young people relocated between 1961 and 1967, 52 per cent moved to Christchurch
as apprentices.

The Hunn Report of 1960 (published in 1961) recommended
that Maori adopt a 'modern way of life'. It set out the objective of
integration: to 'combine (not fuse) the Maori and pakeha elements
to form one nation wherein Maori culture remains distinct'. This
implied 'some continuation of Maori culture'. Critics, however, dismissed this policy as assimilation by another name. It assumed state
leadership as a given, and ignored lessons of the past that Maori
problems needed to be solved by Maori themselves. In the interests of a 'one nation' policy, the government dismantled the Maori
schools system by 1969. Some Pakeha groups did take more interest
in indigenous culture. Importantly, 'integration' gave Maori room
to negotiate, for example to secure state support for building urban
marae.

The policies of integration and urbanisation transformed Maori
citizenship. Negatively, people were uprooted by land loss. Positively, the population recovery of the early twentieth century was
succeeded by a rapid improvement in life chances. Maori experienced a health transition from the 1960s that showed up in falling
fertility and death rates. Maori women's life expectancy doubled
between 1901 and 1961; the disparities with Pakeha began to close.
As the move to the cities rearranged kin networks from extended
to nuclear families, the importance of homes – represented by the
detached suburban house – grew in creating the ideal Maori as well
as European citizen. The Maori Women's Welfare League declared
its focus to be 'the mother, the child and the home', and targeted
the problem of overcrowded substandard housing, especially in
Auckland.

SUBURBAN ICONS

After the war, governments fostered a collective identity framed by domestic ideals, marriage and the family. The detached suburban house with a clipped front lawn and a more relaxed backyard where children could play, a rotary clothesline, vegetable patch, flowers for mum and a shed for dad, came to denote a national way of life supposedly accessible to all New Zealanders. Suburban houses and decentralised industrial development led to the appearance of suburban shopping centres and supermarkets in the 1960s. Woolworths spread to New Zealand from Australia in 1958 and Tom Ah Chee and partners started Foodtown in Otara the same year. In Christchurch, Hay's opened at Church Corner in 1960 and Riccarton Mall in 1965.

Suburbia spread with the (equally international) baby boom from 1945 to 1961, which resulted from a combined marriage boom of couples who delayed getting married because of the depression, and young adults who wed during or at the end of the war. Family sizes increased from little more than two to four children on average by 1960, who crowded maternity hospitals, then kindergartens and primary schools. The baby boomers buoyed demand for home appliances, especially washing machines to ease the chore of washing nappies. By the time of the late arrival of television in 1960 most homes had a washing machine and a refrigerator. Baby boomers boosted the market for children's toys and obliged fathers to build sandpits to encourage creative toddler play. The rules of child rearing had changed with the transformations in the economic and emotional value of children, as people lived longer and healthier lives. Indeed healthier children allowed the transition in child care rules from 'character' to 'personality' development, and so from Dr Truby King to Dr Spock.

New parents, having survived the depression, world war and a housing shortage, aspired avidly to a suburban house and car. But they worried about the debt incurred to own the dream. Status was increasingly derived from home ownership, and the proportion of houses owned rather than rented rose rapidly to 70 per cent. Cold War politics combined with the spirit of free enterprise to promote state endorsement of home ownership and the sale of state houses

8.2 Toddler in sandpit, Palmerston North, *c.* 1959: for the under-five set in a new house in a new subdivision, the sandpit took precedence over making a garden in an undeveloped backyard

to tenants. The National government increased the availability of state loans for house building and provided a plan service for aspiring owners. Labour – briefly in office from 1957 – added cheap home loans and a facility for parents to capitalise their children's family benefit as a house deposit. The ideal of a property-owning democracy resurfaced as a bulwark against the Cold War, a means of domestic defence in any third world war (believed imminent) and a device to contain communism and social pathology.

Ideals of womanhood came to be represented in suburbia by the pavlova, the fluffy meringue cake whose status as the national dish was also claimed by Australia. Pure, white and feminine, and a cooking hazard that required a cast-iron stove for success, the pavlova, along with the feather-light cream sponge, signified the feminine cook's cultural worth and command of the kitchen. The pavlova emerged by the 1930s out of an Australasian tradition of dainty baking using staple ingredients, in this case eggs and sugar, with cream as an accessory. An early published recipe came from the Rangiora Mothers' Union *Cookery Book of Tried and Tested Recipes*, contributed by women of the Rangiora Anglican parish at the height of depression gloom in 1933. By contrast the 1950s and early 1960s were years of eggs and produce in abundance, embellished by official marketing that 'everything tastes better with cream'.

Men's aspirations, on the other hand, came to be represented by Sir Edmund Hillary. His conquest of Mt Everest with Sherpa Tenzing Norgay in May 1953, as a member of a British expedition, and instant knighthood, forged his place as the greatest New Zealand hero. Hillary's triumph immediately before the coronation of Queen Elizabeth gave the impression that he had climbed the world's highest mountain both for the Queen and for New Zealand. Ed Hillary has encapsulated the masculine qualities celebrated in Kiwi culture, becoming the nation's favourite icon and represented on the $5 note. An imperial hero and a pioneer, the first and the best, laconic and humanitarian, a gentleman with a larrikin streak, adventurous and practical – and after Everest, a family man – Hillary strode across the landscape, conquering everything from the highest mountain to the South Pole.

By comparison the Queen (at the time of writing remembered on the $20 note) induced great excitement as the first reigning monarch to visit the Antipodes in the summer of 1953–54. The royal tour heightened patriotism, while the royal presence at Christmas 1953 comforted a community reeling from natural disaster. On Christmas Eve, at Tangiwai in the North Island, 151 people died when a lahar from the volcanic plateau washed away a rail bridge. Moments later the express train from Auckland to Wellington, packed with Christmas holiday-bound travellers, crashed into the swollen river below. The young Queen mothered the nation in her charge. At the public's insistence, busloads of school pupils turned out to greet her to put the nation of healthy children on display.

Despite and perhaps because of the favoured child-centred image, concern mounted that teenagers had not suffered wartime restraint and were growing undisciplined as a result of consumerism. Youth culture in the 1950s engendered a moral panic about teenage sexuality in the new state house suburbs. Following salacious newspaper comment, an inquiry by a special committee on moral delinquency in children and adolescents met in 1954 to investigate youth behaviour in suburban Wellington and Auckland. The committee of worthies, including a headmaster of a leading boys school and representatives of the National Council of Women and Catholic Women's League, blamed working mothers and 'oversexed' girls for hanky-panky at milk bars and on the riverbank. No matter that the rates of juvenile offending had remained unchanged for 20 years. The committee was rightly alarmed that the 1950s heralded a new era where teenagers were rebelling: 'A generation gap was emerging. The commission members and some witnesses were alarmed by Coca Cola, motorbikes and girls in jeans'. The concept of what was best in New Zealand culture came under strain as young people thought and behaved differently.

Education of the juvenile delinquents' younger siblings, the baby boomers, stretched public resources into the 1970s. Primary schools put up (and put up with) prefabricated classrooms to cope with swollen school rolls, while secondary school enrolments doubled between 1945 and 1959 as more teenagers stayed at school. Tertiary education ballooned at technical institutes and universities. The University of New Zealand, a federal institution of provincial colleges, split into separate universities in 1961. Two new universities, Massey and Waikato, opened in 1964, while the University of Canterbury moved in stages to a new suburban campus that gave more room to engineering and the sciences. Even in this small society an era awaited of youth revolution, hippie flower power and protest. Rebellion was 'in', thanks to global influences.

PROTEST MOVEMENTS

Life was transforming for mothers too. It was not the Pill (introduced in 1962) that unstitched moral codes by changing the position of women and how society viewed them: the Pill merely broke the class barrier in types of birth control use and made contraception more assured. Women married and had fewer children, at a younger age than in the past, and lived longer. This altered life course allowed married women the space to move into paid work, where the economy needed them once their children started school. By 1966 nearly 20 per cent of married Pakeha women were in the paid

workforce, compared to less than 8 per cent in 1945. They occupied a narrow range of acceptable jobs, often part-time so that they
could also remain housewives. The public service especially sought
to attract skilled women as permanent and relieving schoolteachers
of the baby boomers. A related shortage of hospital nurses persisted
throughout the 1950s and 1960s.

Ironically, the state led the way in promoting paid work for married women while simultaneously advocating domesticity. Equal pay
in the public service came into effect from 1960. The private sector
lagged for another 12 years, until the Equal Pay Act 1972. In the late
1960s the faltering of the compulsory arbitration system, which had
set the highest wage rate for skilled male workers, provided scope
for equal pay arguments to gain ground.

Barmaids were finally allowed back behind hotel bars, and six
o'clock closing ended in 1967, after half a century. The easing of
licensing laws permitted pubs to open until a respectable bedtime of
10 p.m., at last allowing hotels and restaurants to develop to international standards. But first came 'pub liberations' by an angry new
wave of young feminists in Auckland, Wellington and Christchurch
in 1971, who demanded the right of women to drink in public bars,
with their cheaper drinks than those in lounge bars that admitted
women. This demand for drinking equality stood in stark contrast
to the temperance of first wave feminism.

The Women's Liberation Movement burst on to the scene in 1970,
in protest against being sentenced to housework, which they saw as
restrictive. Typical of the hippie counter culture, women's libera-
tionists deliberately challenged the establishment and social norms.
In March 1972 the visiting celebrity feminist Germaine Greer was
arrested in Auckland for use of the word 'bullshit' in a public address
at the town hall. Through marches, theatre and public protest,
the women's libbers fought for legal change, especially concerning
illegal abortion and equal pay.

Late twentieth-century feminism grew from the international
civil rights movement and anti-Vietnam War protests, and drew in
particular on American influences. Young, urban, educated baby
boomers – anti-racist, anti-sexist and socialist – campaigned for
peace, the environment, and revolution, including in sex roles.
Young women university students were mortified to discover sexism

in the peace and civil rights movements, where young men expected
their peers to make the tea and provide sexual comforts while they
fought to free the oppressed. Such first-hand experience of second-
rate status resolved the women's libbers to free women everywhere
from a sexist, patriarchal society.

Protests against the Vietnam War revealed that the class divide in
politics was undergoing realignment as the baby boomers grew up
to join a New Left progressive middle class, keen to end the reign
of the conservative establishment. The peace protesters formed part
of a broader movement seeking liberation from the strictures of the
Cold War. Around the world a rising tide of issues-based protests
foreshadowed a new politics that rejected conservative social norms
and prejudices, and embraced new, more fluid identities. Locally,
Vietnam marked the end of consensus on foreign affairs and split
the country. Young educated professionals rallied to Labour rather
than National, attracted by Labour's anti-Vietnam stance.

Meanwhile both Britain and the United States were preparing
to pull out of Southeast Asia. The British completed their withdrawal east of Suez in the 1970s, while the United States retreated
to the Philippines and Okinawa, leaving a rump of Australian and
New Zealand military in Singapore. In the context of this great
power retreat New Zealand withdrew from Vietnam by late 1971,
leaving two training teams to be recalled by the incoming Labour
government.

Expressing a moral voice in the world became the hallmark of the
Labour government led by Norman Kirk until his premature death
in 1974. 'Big Norm', as a youthful pop song affectionately termed
him, a former engine driver and a self-educated intellectual, renewed
the Labour tradition of an independent and consciously visionary
'moral' foreign policy. With the end of the Cold War and the Vietnam
War, he opened relations with China and the USSR. By striding the
world stage he also tackled the hippie generation's *bête noire* of the
'cultural cringe', combining nationalism with internationalism. Kirk
was on the same wavelength as the protagonists of youth revolution,
who perceived themselves as global citizens. He saw the country's
smallness and isolation as an opportunity to mediate between small
countries and superpowers to whom New Zealand posed no threat,
much as had Peter Fraser at the United Nations.

8.3 Eric W. Heath, Big 3 ANZUS meeting, 'Is there some
reason we can't all support a nuclear free zone, gentlemen?'
27 February 1974

Progressive youth delighted in the Kirk government's promotion
of a nuclear-weapons-free zone in the South Pacific. In 1973 a naval
frigate set sail for Moruroa atoll with a cabinet minister and a
National Radiation Laboratory physicist on board to witness and
monitor French nuclear tests. Australia and New Zealand also took
France to the International Court of Justice.

Philosophically, the opposition to nuclear testing coalesced with
the rise of the environment movement. The South Island's world
heritage national parks were created during the baby boomers'
childhoods (Fiordland and Mt Cook in 1953). Nationalist feeling grew for the landscape as more families took car trips and
mobile holidays, staying at caravan parks or in motels. Developments in transport, such as the completion of the road through
the Haast Pass from Wanaka to Westland, encouraged the trend.
'Freedom walking' of the Milford Track without a paid guide only
began in 1964.

But how protected were these scenic wonders and holiday places where the baby boomers learnt to explore? It was simply fortuitous that much future heritage landscape survived. As families discovered their own country, concern mounted about logging, mineral exploration and rampant development without regard for scenic or conservation values. The 'Save Manapouri' campaign of the late 1960s and early 1970s marked a major shift in public attitudes away from colonising the land, towards conserving natural resources. From 1960 successive governments approved a deal by Comalco, then a British-Australian conglomerate, to provide cheap power from Lake Manapouri in Fiordland National Park for an aluminium smelter. The initial proposal entailed raising the lake level by 30 metres, which would have drowned most of the lake's islands and damaged neighbouring Lake Te Anau. The protest campaign raised critical questions of conservation versus development, domestic versus overseas capital, multinational corporations' threat to sovereignty, the role of the state, and the very values underpinning Kiwi culture. In this case public pressure resolved what a commission of inquiry could not: a petition organised by the Royal Forest and Bird Protection Society of 265,000 signatures in 1970 made a clear statement.

ECONOMIC INTERDEPENDENCIES

Environmental concerns, however, had yet to extend to questioning the impact of the third round of the grasslands revolution. Hill country hitherto off limits to pasture was sprayed from the air with phosphate dug up from Nauru without regard for the consequences in either place. Kiwi pilots conquered the last frontier of rugged hill country as pioneers of aerial top dressing. Research using radioactive cobalt had also shown up cobalt deficiencies in soil. Aerial top dressing with cobalt extended the grasslands revolution to the pumice lands of the central North Island and overcame the problem of 'bush sickness' in sheep. The new technology reflected new interdependencies once modes of travel became airborne. With the use of aircraft in hill country farming, sheep numbers rose nearly 40 per cent in the 1950s. A far-sighted teacher and author, H. C. D. Somerset, quoted the farmer who worried about the unknown effects on the land of this 'new pioneering' and 'new husbandry': 'For all we know we may be taxing it more than it will stand, even with all our manuring'. The scientific farmer was preparing to turn environmentalist.'

Aircraft accelerated the process of globalisation, which strengthened ties and forged new links throughout the world. By 1970 the cost of air travel fell to the level of sea travel, with the effect that adventurers no longer had to spend a minimum of three months away from home. Jet aircraft arrived with their deafening engines in the 1960s, after the government bought out the Qantas shareholding in Tasman Empire Airways Limited (TEAL). This company, subject to state supervision by the United Kingdom, New Zealand and Australia, had begun using British flying boats across the Tasman during the war. Both Australia and New Zealand opted for a national carrier that travelled internationally to address issues of security and remoteness. Air New Zealand emerged as the national airline, flying American Douglas aircraft, in 1965. It limited its ambitions before 1973 to the Tasman route and the Pacific, flying to Los Angeles, Hong Kong and Singapore.

Economically, the country stayed committed to the old Commonwealth club because that offered the best assurance of external stability. The Commonwealth economic network formed a tight sterling area after World War II, not always comfortable for being familial, but 'lubricated by trust', thanks to the tie of kinship. The United States was no friend in trade, unlike in defence, although it was certainly powerful, and increasingly so. Had Australia and New Zealand left the sterling area they would still have had to overcome United States agricultural protectionism, which was impossible.

Inevitably the sterling area started to unravel in the 1950s, commensurate with Britain's decline as a world power. Wartime bulk purchase agreements ended in 1954 though New Zealand retained duty free access for meat and dairy products until 1967. This shift in the power base of the world economy compelled a reordering of relationships with Britain and other countries. So did a change in tastes away from butter, cheese, and carcasses of frozen lamb and mutton. It was harder for New Zealand to adapt to changes in the international environment than it was for Australia, which could diversify by mining minerals.

Boom prices for wool during the Korean War initially masked the brewing difficulties, but also led to a drop in the proportion of exports going to Britain, as wool more readily found new markets than did butter fat. High wool prices also propelled the grasslands revolution and environmental over-reach through aerial top dressing. Economic historians argue that the post-war boom ended at the wool sales during the 1966 to 1967 season, when the wool price crashed and the Wool Commission, established in 1952, bought over 80 per cent of the wool at auction.

In many ways 1967 did herald the end of the years of prosperity. Faced with another balance of payments crisis, the National government responded in the customary 'stop-go' style with budget cuts. Not only the '6 o'clock swill' but the '10 o'clock swill' of school milk ended in 1967, at the request of education boards. That was a relief for schoolchildren who disliked warm milk. More stressful (still more for adults) was the switch from imperial weights and measures to decimals and decimal arithmetic. The beloved British system of pounds, feet, miles, and perches was bid goodbye; in came metres, hectares and kilometres. More symbolically, out went pounds, shillings and pence and in came decimal currency in 1967, reflective of the rise of the United States to global financial dominance.

Australia's decision to adopt decimal currency in 1966 proved a catalyst for the break from the British tie. Moreover the concept of the dollar was popular with the public. The democratic process produced a distinctive New Zealand coinage. All the hallmarks of populism were there: Captain Cook's *Endeavour* sailed across the 50 cent coin; the informal national emblem, the kiwi, featured on the 20 cents, with a fern backdrop, while a fernleaf furled around the 1 cent piece. A kowhai bedecked the 2 cents, a tuatara the 5 cents, and a tiki on the 10 cent coin satisfied as a replacement for the popular Maori warrior on the old shilling. With the exception of the tuatara, all of these images had a marketing pedigree: Maori motifs, the silver fern on war graves, All Blacks and sports jerseys and butter wrappers, while the tuatara made the link to ancient Gondwana. All of these symbols suggested identification with the environment.

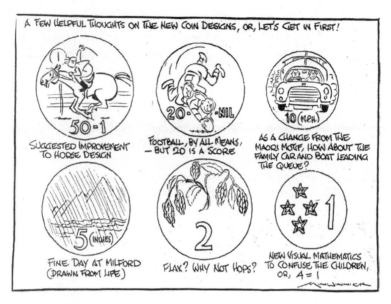

8.4 G. E. G. Minhinnick, Tails you lose! *New Zealand Herald*, 3 February 1966

Decimal currency also marked a commitment to closer ties with Australia. The New Zealand dollar was devalued, not by the British amount, but by nearly 20 per cent, which restored the parity with Australia lost in 1948. Parity with the Australian dollar increased competitiveness and made it possible for businesses to compete across the Tasman.

Britain's turning away from the Commonwealth towards Europe brought Australia and New Zealand closer together. The crunch came in 1961 when Britain announced its decision to enter the European Economic Community (EEC, now EU), and to abandon its colonial family of food producers for former enemies. But for French President Charles de Gaulle's veto against Britain's entry, New Zealand's export economy would have come unstuck. With the terms of trade in decline, the government used the breathing space from the breakdown in the British EEC negotiations to reorder its trade relations with Australia. Policy-makers began to see salvation in freer trade, and in closer relations with Asia (a future recognised by Australia first) and with each other.

New Zealand had studied the prospect of freer trade with Australia since 1956, when Sid Holland had negotiated greater access for New Zealand exports of timber and newsprint. The pulp and paper industry was one of the few industries capable of expanding exports to Australia. New Zealand also became an important market for Holden cars. After talks in 1960 the two governments resolved that they would tackle common problems by working together as closely as possible. They agreed to co-operate in dealing with the prospect of the loss of British trade privileges as Britain looked to enter the EEC. The Australia–New Zealand consultative committee on trade met in 1960 followed by a ministerial meeting in 1961, and a joint standing committee of officials to examine proposals for a free trade area. Britain tried to block any agreement, compounding the annoyance of its former colonies.

After the war the push towards forestry contributed to strengthening trans-Tasman ties. Large plantations of Radiata pine planted between the wars in the central North Island were ready for harvesting from the 1940s. The state-owned Kaingaroa forest and the Murupara project to which it gave rise were intended to diversify the export economy and to save millions of dollars by supplying Australia and New Zealand with a substitute for American newsprint. Loans from London and the United States financed the project. In another entrepreneurial state rerun, the government established a joint venture with business – Fletchers – to create the carefully branded Tasman Pulp and Paper Company, whose manufacturing plant at Kawerau was in full swing by the late 1950s. A new town, Murupara, was built to house forestry workers, while power came from geothermal resources on the volcanic plateau. A new port was built at Tauranga for the forestry hinterland. Tasman became the country's single largest manufacturing export plant, contributing 50 per cent of manufactured exports by 1965 and 45 per cent of all exports to Australia.

The growing trans-Tasman community of interest in New Zealand pine plantations and wood pulp influenced the signing of the New Zealand–Australia Free Trade Agreement (NAFTA) in 1965, which only partially espoused free trade. Two-way trade increased by over 50 per cent in the five years from 1965–66 to 1970–71. By the end of the decade Australia met all its import requirements for newsprint and pulp from New Zealand; 95 per cent of exports of newsprint were to Australia.

Australia provided a model for post-war development of an insulated kind, which manufacturers adapted and used to justify a change of direction that in turn built on the shared model of state development from the 1890s. Sir Woolf Fisher (of Fisher & Paykel whiteware) led a trade mission to Australia in 1959. The economic nationalist Bill Sutch and other officials also embraced the Australian model of development as a way of reducing imports. Sutch saw the need to broaden the narrow structure of the economy and to reduce vulnerability to fluctuations, perceiving the farm and financial sectors as wedded to colonial dependence.

Thus various trends converged to persuade Australia and New Zealand to adopt the pattern of managing a transformed position in the world by showing interest in their own region and in each other. Because of ANZUS and British withdrawal, the neighbours also behaved more as if they occupied a regional zone of defence. Trans-Tasman air travel had a big effect on popular culture, increasing the frequency of trans-Tasman sporting contests, the circulation of Australian magazines, and informal contacts.

In the end, Britain's withdrawal from empire and turn to Europe proved a nemesis. No longer could the United Kingdom's strategic interests be reconciled with the British Commonwealth as an economic community. The end of the British embrace generated a prolonged, anguished 'fight for survival'. Many older better-off Pakeha New Zealanders considered as betrayal Britain's entry in January 1973 to the EEC. That was a fair judgement, given the enigmatic prospect of compulsory decolonisation, at speed, not of Pacific Islanders, but of themselves.

9

Latest experiments 1974–1996

The final three decades of the twentieth century bore witness to the most violent ruptures since colonisation and World War I. This chapter reflects on the revolutions in economic, defence and public policy that changed how this small country related to the world, shook the political landscape into new patterns, and severely unsettled the settler society. New Zealanders found themselves gasping from the change of water in their fishbowl, their ways of life buffeted and transformed. Suddenly – but not inevitably – governments demolished institutions that had been their defining features. It was as if, overnight, everyone lived in another country.

The depression and war generation to whom British identity and attachment mattered felt the 'trauma of decolonisation'. No such trauma afflicted baby boomers provided that they were well educated and not in public service jobs, and late boomers were still at school in 1973. Apocalyptically, Britain's turn to Europe overlapped with the abandonment of the idea of the Australasian settlement. In the language of mateship that pervaded the masculine worlds of sport and politics, not only the rules of the game, but the game itself had changed. The worker and to a lesser extent the farmer, the sheep farmer especially, were no longer wanted on the team. The structure of the world economy had changed from dominance by agriculture and manufacturing to post-industrial emphasis on the service sector. Changes in technology created new jobs and rendered old unskilled ones obsolete. Traditional jobs for working-class men disappeared, spawning a new problem of low male employment levels. In this context there was no place for the settler contract.

From the 1980s New Zealand faced a restructured world economy with a brand new set of experiments devised by leaders influenced by the counter culture and student radicalism. These new, youthful leaders embraced globalisation, which may be defined as the 'process of deepening and changing links throughout the global economy' and the spread of capitalist economic relations. Here the focus is on economic integration rather than on refreshed cultural links, which are dealt with in chapter 10.

Three disturbing events marked 'the end of the golden weather' bestowed by the British embrace and foreshadowed a sequence of extreme responses to the transformed global environment. Britain's entry to the EEC in 1973 was the most symbolic for a people who had grown comfortable supplying the British dinner table. Another was the general abandonment of fixed exchange rates, after which the New Zealand dollar was 'pegged' to a basket of currencies. The first 'oil shock' supplied a third radical change as oil producers in the Middle East formed a cartel and increased prices dramatically. Though the first oil shock (followed by a second in 1979) did not prove permanent, it induced a sharp tremor in the balance of payments, depressing the national mood.

At the same time there was growing alarm that New Zealand's economic performance and standards of living had slipped below averages in the Organisation for Economic Cooperation and Development (OECD). As with health statistics earlier in the century, this ignominious placement on a global league table clashed with the national self-image of natural abundance. New Zealand slid from the top five among OECD countries to nineteenth by 1980 as global demand for its primary products ebbed. Especially galling was the fall in average real incomes relative to Australia. To add to economic woes, a rare combination of rising unemployment and high inflation, which rocketed to 18 per cent in 1976, baffled economists and policy-makers. New Zealand, like most countries, had to restructure its economy and attempt to control overseas debt. Painfully, the country metamorphosed from Britain's farm to an exporter around the Pacific Rim and beyond, especially to Australia and Asia.

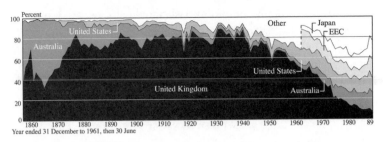

9.1 Trading partners: proportion of total exports going to different markets, 1860–1989

This process in practice was well established by the 1970s, if not yet incorporated in national types and myths. The underlying trend in the percentage of exports going to Britain, Australia and elsewhere shows that export market and product diversification had proceeded steadily since World War II (see 9.1). The evenness of the underlying trend is striking in the decline of Britain as New Zealand's major trading partner during the second half of the twentieth century. The rate of change quickened briefly around 1973 but then slowed for the remainder of the 1970s and 1980s, demonstrating that a long-run process was at work.

One argument is that 1973 marked the pivotal moment in national life, with the end of Dominionism and of revived dependence on Britain. A 'misdiagnosis' of this change, a blinkered failure to see it as the core problem facing the country, led subsequent governments down the wrong path. However the economic evidence used to promote it, illustrated in 9.1, does not support this interpretation.

Common sense suggests that 1973 and also 1984 (the year of instant globalisation under the fourth Labour government) were major turning points in New Zealand history. Both signified moments of drama when domestic politics were thrown into turmoil by global and regional pressures. Both, moreover, exposed the underlying dilemma of how to manage size and remoteness. New Zealand and Australia experienced rapid and extensive economic liberalisation in the early 1980s and 1990s, not unlike central Europe. New Zealand provided the more extreme example, because its reforms were faster and wider ranging. Further, the New Zealand reforms followed an era that is commonly associated with 'big government'. It is therefore necessary to examine the lurch from regulation to deregulation, mindful that it is not a diagnosis that leads to certain outcomes in terms of policy change but a political process of ideas, leaders and institutions.

MULDOONISM

In New Zealand culture the package of ideas, leaders and institutions under the National government from 1975 to 1984 is named 'Muldoonism' after Robert Muldoon, the Prime Minister and Minister of Finance over these years (who first rose to prominence for directing the changeover to decimal currency). An accountant, he distrusted the free market, believing in the tradition of managing the economy and society so that ordinary people could benefit from capitalism 'while being protected from its excesses'.

Short (about 5 ft 4 in, 160 cm), he intimidated people with his laser cold blue eyes, and learnt as a child to use his sharp tongue to defend himself. The first politician to use television to his advantage, he expressed his philosophy in a distinctive growl on screen, and recorded it for posterity in multiple autobiographies. 'For my part I look back to Britain', he asserted in 1981. Muldoon held to a 1950s view of the 'New Zealand way of life'. Raised by his mother and grandmother, he knew too well the stigma and hardship that accompanied the loss of a male breadwinner and held unwaveringly to the belief that social security was a right.

Muldoon's legacy is mixed, and has been disparaged by successive governments. His generous and expensive non-contributory national superannuation scheme for citizens over 60, initially at 80 per cent of the average wage, manifested 'political ageing': a shift from youth to old age as a priority of social policy. Its chief beneficiaries, Muldoon's peers, have been called the 'welfare generation', because the welfare system changed to suit them at every stage of their lives. The super scheme was affordable only because high inflation pushed income tax payers into higher tax brackets (the top rate was then 66 per cent), and broke the welfare contract between generations. New rules would operate for the baby boomers, and their children who faced student loans from the 1990s.

To many people Muldoon stood for 'divide and rule' politics, hostility to the world, and totalitarianism. The Prime Minister's closest colleagues described him as a 'genuine, combative, populist demagogue'. 'Rob's mob' – his key supporters – represented the ordinary bloke of middling New Zealand, from the returned serviceman to the Maori gang member. Groups scorned by such politics, on the other hand, protesters of all sorts including educated Maori, the women's movement, peace movement, civil rights movement and conservationists, rose up against Muldoonism as a regime of colonialism continued (see chapter 10).

In turn, Muldoon (nicknamed 'Piggy' for his looks and style) launched further attacks on the counter culture. He regulated the economy and society through the abuse of executive power. If interest rates soared too high with inflation, he regulated them downwards. A supplementary minimum price scheme to subsidise farmers encouraged unwarranted growth in sheep numbers. The second oil shock in the wake of the Iranian revolution produced a perverse short-term regime of 'car-less days', where motorists nominated a day – indicated by a sticker on the windscreen – when they would not drive. Rising unemployment mingled with a sense of oppression, divisiveness, gloom and doom stirred thousands of young people to respond by departing for Australia in search of opportunities and a brighter future. Those who left found that they had to apply to the Reserve Bank to take their savings out of the country. An across the board price and wage freeze under the eccentric Economic Stabilisation Act crowned the edifice of controls by the 1980s.

The traditional mixed economy accordingly lapsed into a 'command economy'. A series of 'Think Big' development projects to reduce dependence on imported energy sources appeared to confirm that judgement. They included methanol and ammonia-urea plants and a synthetic fuel plant, expansion of the national oil refinery and of New Zealand Steel (established in the 1960s), and a fast-tracked hydroelectric project (the Clyde Dam, completed in 1988).

In this context, it is interesting that deregulation began in the Muldoon era: Muldoon signed the Australia–New Zealand Closer Economic Relations Trade Agreement (CER) that came into effect in 1983. Doug Anthony, the Australian Deputy Prime Minister, recalled that his hardest job was handling the respective prime

9.2 Robert Muldoon and Malcolm Fraser

ministers because Muldoon and Australia's Malcolm Fraser disliked each other. Figure 9.2 suggests why, from Muldoon's perspective. His attitude to Australia generally is captured in the joke coined by a columnist, that the exodus of New Zealanders to Australia raised the IQ of both countries. Importantly, Muldoon had a rapport with Anthony. Conversely, Fraser related well to Brian Talboys, the diplomatic New Zealand Deputy Prime Minister. Together, Fraser and Talboys issued the landmark Nareen statement in 1978 which affirmed that Australia and New Zealand were linked by 'deep ties of common origin and shared ideas and institutions', which logically suggested that they face new global circumstances together and encouraged closer relations with each other. Their prime ministers had met annually since the 1960s and numerous links had developed under NAFTA, helped by improved communications. But this heavily regulated trade agreement had become bogged in detail. Anthony's proposal for a 'closer economic association' to take advantage of new opportunities, especially in Asia, followed Talboys' initiatives to work together internationally and in the region, and set in train the process that led from NAFTA to CER.

Twenty years later CER shone as the major positive legacy of the conservative Muldoon government. Two-way trade had expanded 500 per cent. The agreement, initiated quietly, proved a big success, helped by a historically integrated labour market. The same was true of capital markets. Australia became New Zealand's biggest trading partner, while New Zealand was Australia's fifth largest market and, importantly, often the first export market for Australian business. Economically the countries rapidly integrated in ways that would astound the political leaders of the 1890s. Any shopping trip demonstrated this; whether to buy clothing, furniture or food, in both countries, using Australian banking facilities. The two economies integrated and moved so closely together by the beginning of the twenty-first century that the New Zealand and New South Wales economies marched in lock step.

Consequently CER is celebrated as the most comprehensive, effective and mutually compatible free trade agreement in the world. This confounds any analysis of the Muldoon era as solely associated with big government. CER is routinely not associated with Muldoonism, which is synonymous with regulation, cynical abuse of democracy and dictatorship; yet it shares that lineage.

The package of ideas, leaders and institutions associated with the economic liberalisation experiment that followed on from Muldoonism came to be known as 'Rogernomics'. The reforms were named for Roger Douglas, the Minister of Finance in the fourth Labour government, which swept into office in a snap election in July 1984. A new generation of policy-makers keen to end the reign of the conservative establishment formed 'arguably the most radical government in New Zealand's history'; it was also the best educated, and dominated by lawyers. A number of ministers were still in their thirties and the leadership in their early forties. The new Prime Minister David Lange, a 'complicated and gifted man' who loved India and fun parks, delighted the public with his witty intelligence, his quips, and his humanism. While Lange operated among the many, his henchman Douglas, who grew up in a state house, was ideologically enthusiastic and uncompromising. Free of Muldoon, an atmosphere of energy surrounded the new government, in whom the people placed great expectations.

An aura of crisis created the opportunity for Lange's cabinet to launch a swathe of economic reforms. Broadly, Rogernomics reformers believed that the 'jerry-built economic structure' required 'drastic restructuring' as a 'matter of urgency'. More immediately, New Zealand suffered a costly run on the dollar before and after the snap election. The enduring image of crisis was of Muldoon himself, announcing the election on television with slurred speech as if drunk, and refusing after the election to devalue the dollar, against the advice of the incoming government. This violated constitutional conventions. A currency crisis therefore bred a constitutional crisis, cementing convictions that he had pitched the country headlong into economic chaos.

The devaluation crisis and its threat to the country's reputation for political stability justified, but did not determine, the shape of the reforms to follow. Long-run justifications for the Rogernomics revolution included the decline in economic performance relative to the OECD average, the massive balance of payments deficit, rampaging inflation, the expensive super scheme, excessive regulation, the 'Think Big' projects, and the general failure to adjust to changing realities. Allegedly the body politic had become infected with all the problems said to be poisoning capitalism, such as import and capital controls, strong trade unions, a large state sector, and a redistributive welfare state. New Zealand, the neoliberal reformers argued, had still not adjusted to Britain's abandonment of its empire thanks to Muldoon's intransigence, and had immediately to catch up with the rest of the world. Salvation lay with the free market.

Rogernomics has been likened to a 'blitzkrieg' because the reforms proceeded so fast and extensively, with all the zeal of a crusade. Lange's cabinet intoned the motto: 'we will do the right thing', bonded by a sense of crisis and the 'audacity' of their policy directions. Twenty years later, ministers in that cabinet insisted they did do 'the right thing'. This raises a philosophical problem, because to assume that you know what the right thing is indicates a conviction of rightness, that there is a right way and a wrong way, and that people who disagree with you are wrong: 'there is no alternative', in the contemporary catch-phrase. There is always an alternative, as the Australian case shows.

In pursuit of change an inner circle of reformers in cabinet, Treasury and the Reserve Bank demolished the Australasian model of state development that their forebears had created in response to equivalent global forces 90 years earlier, and supplanted it with an Anglo-American neoliberal orthodoxy. The speed and extent of reforms depended much on thinking that Treasury and Reserve Bank advisers had already done. Reformers resolved to return the country to this orthodoxy after a 'long period of deviancy', citing absurdities that ranged from the Margarine Act 1908, designed to protect butter, to Muldoon's use of the Economic Stabilisation Act. Moreover, the reformers intended that their revolution be irreversible. This rejection of the past marked the 'end of history' in its local manifestations. The ideology of the free market would brook no competition from a historical set of 'state experiments'. Rather a new set would take their place, in true pioneering spirit, and the workingman's paradise would be pensioned off, the old compromise of social protection against vicissitudes of the market abandoned. A pioneering heritage demanded no less.

While the Labour Party membership and the public knew that change was necessary, the proposed means of change provoked an ideological struggle between the parliamentary Labour Party and the cabinet. Some argue that 'change became the end not the means'. For his part, Douglas did not wait to consult beyond his inner circle because he believed that consultation would thwart his goals. His Treasury advisers shared this mindset because the government lacked a consensus over whether the proposed economic reforms represented the appropriate way forward.

The comprehensive reform package embraced globalisation. Disciples could market Rogernomics as another 'New Zealand experiment' and even the 'great experiment' precisely because the lurch to neoliberalism was so extreme and abrupt. New Zealand presented the ideal field trial for structural reform because it was small and isolated. In the late twentieth century, furthermore, a single house of parliament that could push through reforms added gloss to the laboratory conditions. Continuities were not merely rhetorical; the democratic social laboratory in Australasia again created an edifice of progressive liberal 'state experiments' to manage global forces. Only the new set eagerly accepted globalisation without cushioning it, and threw out the old set. Traditional icons and the collective memory associated with them (however short) were relegated to the rubbish tip as deviant and obsolete.

The market's icon was not the worker but the consumer, presented with an alluring choice of things to buy, from clothing made in China to cars made in Japan. The worker became a tradeable commodity. Finance capital outstripped industrial capital and power transferred to people and institutions with access to international finance. That debt should bestow power, not shame, illustrated the shift in values. Restructuring related directly to transformed global links. Unemployment and structural change in the economy from industry to services and information technology also helped unravel old accommodations. Henceforth neoliberals strove to expose the economy to external shocks to make it more adaptable and resilient.

From 1984, therefore, New Zealand underwent 'a theory driven revolution' derived from neo-classical economics and New Right philosophies, including (but not confined to) the monetarism of Milton Friedman and the Chicago School, public choice and agency theory and the new institutional economics. A small élite of strategically placed individuals in cabinet, Treasury, and the Reserve Bank introduced the changes, supported by the Business Roundtable comprised of CEOs from the 200 largest companies. Within this circle, Douglas worked with Treasury before running ideas past his associate finance ministers, lawyers Richard Prebble and David Caygill, followed by Lange and his deputy Geoffrey Palmer. This group then persuaded cabinet. Leaders of the inner circle and their friends had been graduate students in the United States. Embarrassed by the smallness and parochialism of their quaint country, they returned home yearning to drag New Zealand into the global village.

Local circumstances, however, made the changes that New Zealanders experienced faster, more extensive and closer to theoretical purity than elsewhere. The first economic reforms introduced financial deregulation. Following Australia, the Labour government floated the exchange rate, deregulated banking and abolished exchange and price controls. It dismantled trade barriers, removing import licensing, while farmers faced the sudden removal of agricultural subsidies. It targeted inflation and held the Reserve Bank responsible for maintaining the inflation rate between 0 and 2 per cent, which became a requirement under the Reserve Bank Act 1989 (the upper bound was 3 per cent from 1996). Tax reform followed to broaden the tax base: within two years (in 1986) Labour introduced a goods and services tax of 10 per cent on all domestic spending (except financial services), before raising it to 12.5 per cent in 1989. Marginal income tax rates flattened; the top tax rate slid from 66 per cent to 33 per cent by 1988. The government also introduced a tax surcharge on national superannuation.

Public sector reforms made familiar institutions unrecognisable. Service arms of government had business mores imposed on them, damaging the values and quality of the core public service through the use of language that expressed the ethos of cost cutting and competition. Policy split from delivery functions and funders from providers. Consequently the number of departments doubled. New Zealand became the only country to have two defence departments: one to reflect on strategy and one to fight. Only at the last moment was the principal task of policy advice added to the State Sector Act, which perceived the restructured public sector's role as management.

The Department of Labour and the State Services Commission fared better because they restructured themselves. Labour market reform proved to be the only instance where interest groups were consulted. While the ripple effect of wage adjustments under the old arbitration system ceased in 1984, under the Labour Relations Act 1987 a labour court and voluntary arbitration commission replaced the historic system of compulsory arbitration. Capital and labour ceased to be at the core of state development.

Reforms to government trading arms achieved the most success in efficiency terms. From 1987 state-owned enterprises (SOEs) were legislatively required to act as businesses and pursue the profit motive. The SOE Act, passed in October 1986, established nine state-owned corporations, including three split from the dismembered Post Office: NZ Post, Postbank (previously the Post Office Savings Bank) and Telecom. State sector unions that opposed restructuring, suspicious that it would lead to state asset sales, were assured that the reforms represented the 'answer' not the 'road to privatisation', and that no one would lose their job.

For the unions, deception comprised the Rogernomics means of change since, from one obscurantist word and process to another, corporatisation did lead rapidly to privatisation. Public asset sales extended from Telecom, Postbank and State Insurance to the 'Think Big' projects. Government mortgages, the Rural Bank, cutting rights in state forests, Air New Zealand and the railways were all sold. Thus the public infrastructure created over the previous century was outfitted in corporate clothing and put up for tender. Big business did well out of the sales of public assets while the merchant bankers who brokered the sales did best of all. Fletcher Challenge acquired 'Think Big' projects and Business Roundtable members enjoyed appointments as chairmen of SOEs. In this sense the tradition of the entrepreneurial state continued despite Rogernomics. Scandal attached to the fate of the Bank of New Zealand, which had to be rescued in a story that paralleled the 1890s. Saved by the taxpayer after it had been partly privatised by merchant bankers, the flagship bank was sold to the National Australia Bank.

Social costs were high. Rather than slashing short-term costs, the reforms maximised them for those affected. Transaction costs were huge. A career public service disappeared. The cabinet overlooked the effects of multiple restructuring on small communities: small towns lost their local post offices (432 in total), defining institutions since the nineteenth century that eased remoteness. More importantly every step in the restructuring programme produced a wave of redundancies. Former post office employees and workers in the forestry industry in the central North Island – often Maori – were particularly hard hit.

Despite public resistance to Rogernomics by the late 1980s, a National government from 1990 picked up the reform policies and pursued yet more change. The Employment Contracts Act 1991 radically deregulated the labour market and adopted individual contracts in employment. For the union movement the cycle had returned to the nineteenth century. Ironically, individuals such as Jim Bolger, the National Prime Minister from 1990 and previously associated with the Muldoon era, extended the market reforms to social policy.

This agenda dictated severe welfare cuts in 1991. Ruth Richardson, representative of the 'new broom' New Right as the first woman Minister of Finance, set out to shift responsibility for family welfare from the state to the individual under a regime that equated self-reliance with personal responsibility and paid work. Policy-makers lodged their faith in the belief that economic growth would 'deliver jobs and reduce welfare dependency'. Thus successive governments embraced orthodox, neoliberal approaches to globalisation.

CONTINUITIES

Striking continuities exist between Muldoonism and Rogernomics because the streamlined Westminster system in the second half of the twentieth century allowed a concentration of power in cabinet that was 'enormous' and 'intolerable'. Both Muldoonism and Rogernomics illustrated extremes in the use and misuse of executive power by an inner circle of strong personalities who dominated policy-making in a small society. If Muldoon's attempt to manage the post-modern dilemmas of the late twentieth century was short-term and ad hoc, while the approach pursued by Rogernomics was long-term and coherent, the country's small scale made possible both swings of the pendulum.

Each could exploit the absence of the checks and balances found in larger democracies. New Zealand's unicameral political system was simple: without an upper house, there were no parliamentary checks on executive power; the first-past-the-post voting system ensured that cabinet controlled the legislature. No written constitution stood silently sentinel to collective values. In a perceived crisis, it was easy for missionary reformers to pursue their beliefs, while a village culture reinforced the dearth of debate.

In such circumstances the fourth Labour government 'changed the processes and identity of public policy'. A case study of continuities is given by the 1990s health reforms. Statistics showed that the health system before the reforms performed well by OECD standards; ideology, however, judged that public hospitals, which consumed about 70 per cent of the health budget, were inefficient. In 1988 a hospital taskforce, chaired by businessman and forestry SOE head Alan Gibbs, concentrated on restructuring as the panacea for the public hospital system's alleged woes. The Gibbs report asserted that the triumvirate of matron, medical superintendent and administrator stifled leadership and led to weak hospital management by allowing professionals undue influence. Instead nurses, doctors and administrators should be responsible to a CEO, and hospitals should be run competitively as businesses.

The Bolger National government duly introduced wide-ranging market-oriented health reforms based on the Gibbs report that transformed the culture of health care delivery. No other country with a public health system introduced such unfettered market reforms. Neither the health sector nor the public was consulted, on the assumption that health professionals would capture the process; collective memory and expertise were pilloried. The forcing of a managerial model on health destroyed the hospital career path for nurses so that many of the most experienced health workers left. Events soon disproved the theories.

Scholars have since confirmed what practitioners in public hospitals knew, that market approaches to the delivery of health care have 'major limitations'. The health experiments were unsustainable.

From 1993 the theory that funders should be split from providers divided the country into four different health systems, each with its own contractual arrangements and standards of care. Imposing a competitive model on the public health system polarised clinicians and managers, and had to be abandoned in 1996 as untenable. The greatest lesson was in learning what not to do. Structural change itself – four times in a decade – was demonstrated to be 'an impediment for the health sector'.

Through the politics of experiment, therefore, New Zealand transformed from one of the most regulated to one of the freest economies in the world. Old institutions vanished. New identities emerged, many informally and some forcefully. Few lamented the abandonment of the historic compromise shared with Australia, because of its rigidities. The speed and mode of change was the problem, as well as the neglect of a replacement for the settler contract. If the rush to deregulate seemed headlong in Australia, when compared with New Zealand, there at least the federal political system ensured a more selective and gradual approach to reform.

Arguably the greatest benefits of free trade derived not from Rogernomics but from CER, which prepared New Zealand to be internationally competitive and developed business confidence. CER was extended from goods to services in 1988 and remaining barriers were removed by 1990, five years ahead of schedule, although areas of cultural sensitivity such as television broadcasting remained exempt. The economy grew more resilient from embracing globalisation, but many of the gains moved offshore.

Socially, the prosperity promised to 'trickle down' to the nation as a whole failed to eventuate. Income inequality grew more rapidly than in any other country in the OECD as real incomes of low-income households fell between 1984 and 1996. Inevitably the winners were the educated and affluent whose lives were enriched by choice and opportunities. The language of class itself became a casualty as global capitalism triumphed over labour.

From the 1990s, however, GNP per capita began to recover, prompting Treasury to infer from long-term trends that the institutional and policy reforms of the 1980s were responsible. The shopper benefited from the open economy, not the worker, for the farmer and the worker were no longer the focus and rationale of state development. From the 1980s café culture arrived. Rusty cars vanished from the roads to be replaced by late-model imports. Trans-Tasman retail chains graced rebuilt shopping malls. Food, wine and the hospitality industry grew more cosmopolitan and life more interesting and varied for those with purchasing power.

Underneath the technicolour consumerism, however, lurked a problem evident from the early twentieth century: that technological advances were crucial to economic growth. Technological innovation was not the focus of this experiment, which centred in practice on abandonment of the past and on cutting costs. For this reason Rogernomics could not deliver to low-income and ordinary people what its apostles promised.

Globalisation, on the other hand, demanded new approaches to issues at the heart of how people identify with place and community. Despite the pain of constant experiment, New Zealanders generally embraced the process with alacrity as a way of adjusting to their country's size, remoteness from the rest of the world and slim resources. Globalisation encouraged a broader outlook. Many options lie between the poles of parochialism and globalism, and nowhere are these more evident than in defence policy.

NUCLEAR FREE NEW ZEALAND

The transformed face of the country extended to foreign affairs. Assertion of a nuclear free identity coincided with the last stage of the Cold War and spelled the end of dependence on the United States. For many the pronouncement of a nuclear free nation amounted to a declaration of independence – if it also 'made explicit the role of power in New Zealand's foreign relations' by pitting New Zealand as a metaphorical David against the Goliath of the United States. In contrast to its economic reforms, the fourth Labour government possessed a mandate to oppose nuclear weapons, and nuclear power as well by the mid-1980s; but it did not have a mandate to scuttle ANZUS.

Anti-nuclear sentiment triggered the snap election in July 1984, in the context of campaigns to promote world peace through disarmament stirred by mounting Cold War tensions between the United

States and the Soviet Union. Locally, United States navy visits invited protest and publicity. In June 1984 Labour MP Richard Prebble introduced a nuclear free New Zealand bill (one of a series since the 1970s) to ban not only nuclear armed and nuclear powered ships but also nuclear reactors and waste. Since the National government had a majority of one, Muldoon warned that he saw the vote as a matter of confidence; and called an early election on the pretext that National MP Marilyn Waring crossed the floor to support the nuclear free principle. He claimed that Waring's feminist anti-nuclear stance undermined his ability to govern, when in all likelihood he could not create a credible budget.

The critical moment in New Zealand–United States relations came early in 1985, when New Zealand refused a request for a visit from the elderly destroyer USS *Buchanan* on the grounds that it could carry nuclear weapons. Controversy still exists as to how New Zealand defied its major ally and was ejected from the American alliance. Labour entered office intent on declaring New Zealand nuclear free but campaigned on a compromise policy of a nuclear free nation within an updated ANZUS alliance, which it proposed to renegotiate to accommodate the nuclear free concept. This compromise acknowledged that the public supported the non-nuclear policy but also wanted continued membership of ANZUS. In practice the hope to update the alliance was unrealistic.

In practice, too, the policies of New Zealand and the United States were irreconcilable. The United States stuck rigidly to its principle of neither confirming nor denying whether its vessels were nuclear armed or powered, while New Zealand stated that ships were welcome provided that they were not nuclear powered and did not carry nuclear weapons. New Zealand decided to make its own assessment while the United States remained adamant that New Zealand must not cite American evidence.

Responsibility for the critical decision to refuse a visit by the USS *Buchanan* is still disputed in detail because processes were in train on many different fronts after the 1984 election and the separate initiatives did not develop in concert. Lange liaised privately with American officials. He did not undertake to allow a naval visit but asked for time to talk to his party. The officials in turn heard what they wanted to hear. In the meantime a select group of New Zealand officials headed by the chief of defence staff obtained approval to negotiate with the United States admiral in charge of the Pacific to ensure that the ship proposed was a 'clapped out old destroyer' on which no one would put nuclear weapons. The officials cited evidence that showed 'beyond reasonable doubt' that the USS *Buchanan* was neither nuclear propelled nor nuclear armed, couching their advice in understated diplomatic language. Lange, however, did not send the prepared papers to cabinet, who knew nothing about this course of events. In addition, peace protests supported by the party faithful were mounting against naval visits and for declaring New Zealand nuclear free.

By the time that the American request to send the USS *Buchanan* came through in January 1985, Lange was away in the Pacific and Geoffrey Palmer was Acting Prime Minister. In Palmer's legal (as opposed to political) interpretation, the officials' report contained insufficient proof to satisfy cabinet that the destroyer was not nuclear armed. He judged that he could not make a decision within the terms of the test proposed for Labour's future legislation to declare New Zealand nuclear free. Irrespective of the intention to avoid this impasse, cabinet could not escape it in a politically acceptable way. Palmer sent for Lange, who plainly objected to nuclear weapons and nuclear propulsion.

A former Labour minister has since claimed that Lange was outmanoeuvred by 'in-house critics' over the nuclear ships issue. The alleged 'atom splitters' were the Labour Party executive, specifically Helen Clark, the future prime minister, and Margaret Wilson, the future attorney-general (then the party president), both peace activists and opponents of Rogernomics. In this critique Clark and Wilson wielded influence through tightening the language of party policy, removing the ambiguity desired by diplomats and the United States that allowed room to negotiate visits.

Within the party executive, Wilson saw the non-nuclear policy as 'a test of principle'. The party opposed visits by 'nuclear-weaponed and nuclear-powered ships' even if the cabinet might be prepared to shift ground to conserve the ANZUS alliance. Wilson believed most party members also wanted New Zealand to withdraw from ANZUS as part of a more independent foreign policy appropriate for a small nation in the South Pacific. The party executive saw the episode as a test of the democratic process and of sovereignty in the face of opposition by the United States as the global superpower. Wilson, as party president, reminded Palmer in January 1985 that

> unless there was clear proof that the ship was neither nuclear powered nor nuclear armed, its visit would be in breach of the policy. He said the ship was not nuclear powered but that the United States would not break its policy of neither confirming nor denying the presence of nuclear weapons. I then established that the ship was capable of carrying nuclear weapons.

This posed the problem. The party executive therefore reaffirmed its 'strong support' for the nuclear free policy and urged the government to refuse entry. On his return from the Pacific, Lange took the issue to caucus as the executive requested. By this account, then, the Labour caucus made the critical decision, not the executive, nor Lange, although Wilson and the party's executive demonstrated clear leadership. So did Palmer by his own account. If we piece together the strands of evidence, then, we see that a failure of process created a space for women's politics.

Labour women hailed the non-nuclear policy's implementation as a 'triumph for democracy'. This was a principled view consistent with the party's lineage, updated by feminist counter culture politics designed to challenge centres of power. Such politics advocated not isolationism but the agency of the global citizen, active in the international peace and women's movements, determined to conserve New Zealand's advantages in being small and isolated and to make a stand for peace.

Lange subsequently claimed the nuclear free mantle as his own. It was he who publicised the nuclear free policy on the world stage and stirred nationalism at home by making headlines a month later with a debate at the Oxford Union. 'There is no moral case for nuclear weapons', Lange told his Oxford audience in March 1985: 'Rejecting nuclear weapons is to assert what is human over the evil nature of the weapon; it is to restore to humanity the power of decision; it is to allow true moral force to reign supreme'.

The effect on ANZUS of the *Buchanan* incident is illustrated in 9.3. Note the paddle power of the New Zealand waka in contrast to the space age technology of the United States vessel. The New Zealand decision stunned the United States, who retaliated strongly,

9.3 Eric W. Heath, ANZUS, 5 February 1985

declared ANZUS 'inoperative' in relation to New Zealand and severed ties, imposing a freeze on high-level contacts. In August 1986 the United States took the formal step of suspending its security commitment under the alliance, demoting New Zealand from 'ally' to 'friend'. The cartoon elucidates a further theme in this small country's relations with its allies: New Zealand's absence, but not presence, attracts comment.

In addition to a clash of principles, the row highlighted differences in perception of nuclear deterrence and in attitudes to security among the alliance partners. In the United States view, New Zealand had to choose between ANZUS and its nuclear free policy. From a New Zealand perspective, nuclear weapons were irrelevant to the defence of the South Pacific. Australia took the contrasting view that membership of ANZUS implied that Australia should not contest the 'neither confirm nor deny' policy. After the rift, Australia worked hard to preserve its relations first with the United States and second with New Zealand. Australian diplomats were especially concerned that a bilateral alliance with the United States would be a less advantageous deal than ANZUS.

While New Zealand sought to limit the damage already done, *realpolitik* – American power – prevailed. If, for the United States, the moment of breach came when the USS *Buchanan* was rejected, locally 'the breach came when the United States took measures against New Zealand'. The suspension by the United States of its security obligations when the alliance did not provide for suspension of a member only increased popular support for Lange and the Labour government.

Thus the idea of a nuclear free nation came to feature in collective identity, prompted by resistance to American demands that conflicted with perceived national interests. Ironically, the USS *Buchanan* incident and the nuclear free policy's popularity created room to advance the divisive economic reforms. A second defining incident, involving France, assured public celebration of the nuclear free policy. Three French secret agents bombed the Greenpeace flagship the *Rainbow Warrior* in Auckland Harbour in July 1985, killing a photographer. In classic 'whodunnit' style, Auckland police exposed two of the agents with assistance from an army of sleuths supplied by the public, who were shocked as the French operation was unveiled. The French government attempted a cover-up before admitting responsibility, and provoked further outrage when it broke an agreement reached on the detention of the perpetrators. The French factor affirmed ancient Anglo-French prejudices and exacerbated tensions with the United States over a nuclear free Pacific. New Zealanders, raised on warrior stereotypes, would not tolerate being bullied and bombed in an act of 'state terrorism' executed not by enemies, but by a 'great and powerful friend' and an ally whom New Zealanders had defended in two world wars.

Together the USS *Buchanan* and *Rainbow Warrior* incidents assured the passage of the Nuclear-Free Zone, Disarmament and Arms Control Act in 1987 that declared New Zealand nuclear free. It also assured the revival of plans for a nuclear free zone in the South Pacific proposed by Kirk in the early 1970s. The Treaty of Rarotonga in August 1985 created a zone that stretched from the Equator to the Antarctic and west of Papua New Guinea to Easter Island. No nuclear weapons were to be tested in this vast area, although the protocol did not affect the passage of nuclear vessels because of rights under international law to 'freedom of the seas'. This sequence of

9.4 The stricken *Rainbow Warrior* in Auckland Harbour,
July 1985

events encouraged an enhanced focus on and identification with the
South Pacific, and faith in the idea that a small, isolated nation set a
moral example to the world. As we have seen, both these elements of
a new nationalism that imagined the country to be a moral, Pacific
paradise had precedents. So did the image of the alien ship in the
harbour as a threat to the body politic.

The report of the Corner Committee (named for chairman Frank
Corner, a retired diplomat) in July 1986 illumined popular attitudes. Its other members comprised a left-wing academic, a woman
scientist and a retired Maori army general, who surprised Lange
with their unanimous conclusions. The inquiry's poll results are
summarised in Table 9.1.

As the table shows, New Zealanders were evenly divided between
the desire 'to be in an alliance with larger countries' and the desire to
be nuclear free. The majority wanted the impossible: to be nuclear
free and remain in ANZUS. Further, 92 per cent (identical to the
proportion who opposed nuclear weapons) thought Australia was
important to New Zealand's defence and security. Strengthening ties
with Australia, the committee concluded, was 'the most promising
option left open to New Zealand'. Not only did closer relations with

Table 9.1 *What did New Zealanders want?*

per cent	vote	
92	no nuclear weapons	
73	(often the same people)	pro nuclear free New Zealand
72	pro alliances with larger countries	
71	pro ANZUS	
80	**prefer nuclear free New Zealand**	**within ANZUS**
44	stay in ANZUS	and ban nuclear ships
37	stay in ANZUS	and allow nuclear ships
	If nuclear free in ANZUS	**impossible:**
52	stay in ANZUS	and allow nuclear ships which may or may not be nuclear armed or powered
44	withdraw from ANZUS	and ban nuclear ships

Source: Compiled from *Defence and Security: What New Zealanders Want.* Wellington: Defence Committee of Enquiry, 1986

Australia stand in the 'mainstream tradition' of policy-making but it would focus on 'New Zealand's own region, the South Pacific' and leave open the possibility of a return to ANZUS in the future.

Thus the nuclear free idea, while it annoyed Australia, propelled New Zealand closer to its neighbour. The defence imbroglio boosted the success of the CER agreement, while affirming New Zealand identity as not Australian. Correspondingly Canberra decided after lively debate that Australia's interests would be best served by strengthening the defence relationship with New Zealand. Both Australia and New Zealand therefore resolved to strengthen ties in the second half of the 1980s. Despite deep differences over the nuclear issue, the Anzac defence relationship grew closer, culminating in a joint project to build a series of new Anzac frigates to enable the two neighbours to act alone and in tandem in the South Pacific.

But the ANZUS crisis left a legacy of unresolved tension in the trans-Tasman relationship. Defence had been a key motive for Australia to support CER, and it resurfaced as the bugbear in otherwise warm relations in the late twentieth century because of simmering resentment that New Zealand was not pulling its weight in defence. After 1985 New Zealand tried to fit into an Australian model of strategic interests; but it failed to meet neighbourly expectations, both because it lacked resources and because New Zealanders had a distinctive strategic outlook. While they shared solidarity of kinship and purpose, New Zealanders had a different idea of what constituted the Pacific, and historically felt less exposed to threats that, real and imagined, appeared from Southeast Asia.

Overall the most important outcome of the ruptures in economic and defence policy from the 1970s proved to be the transformed relationship with Australia. Australasia had been forgotten in the twentieth century, but it re-emerged with globalisation. At the same time the ANZUS issue lurked as a potential confounder of multiple Tasman connections and harmonies. Anzac Day, the shared sacred day, acquired new layers of meaning: the funereal Anzac tradition, and late discoveries of the men's actual experiences of war, accommodated the concept of a nuclear free nation – and vice versa – from the 1980s in a dual tradition of remembrance of war and peace that could hold meaning for everyone.

Nuclear free New Zealand was a woman's as well as a man's country. A new generation, men and women born in the 1940s and 1950s and raised in New Zealand, entered positions of power and influence. This new generation also formed a new class of professionals determined to attack the 'cultural cringe'. Importantly, their counter culture convictions could be accommodated by existing myths. This urban, educated, post-war generation, reared to question standards and norms, embraced the youth revolution that made them global citizens. Simultaneously, they donned a 'made in New Zealand' identity in their passage to adulthood.

A transfer of political power between generations thus helps explain the lurch from Muldoonism to Rogernomics. It also resolves the apparent paradox of nuclear free New Zealand and enthusiasm for an Anglo-American neoliberal orthodoxy. Both the nuclear free principle and Rogernomics were crusades that made the country a model for the world and aspired to set a moral example. Both proceeded along a historical path that claimed state experiments as expressions of identity and marketing exercises. The nuclear free experiment enjoyed majority support, if complicated by regret over the demise of ANZUS, and sought and found meaning in the geographic facts of smallness and isolation. The economic experiment, on the other hand, undermined the Labour government's credibility.

The neoliberal crusade split Labour because of a fundamental philosophical dispute over the nature of fairness, especially to those least able to cope, the people without personal wealth or power. Jim Anderton left to form the NewLabour Party in 1989. The 'crash through' or 'blitzkrieg' approach also undermined the legitimacy of the political system because it was fundamentally undemocratic. In order to impose some control on executive power, New Zealanders therefore turned to electoral reform. By referendum in 1993 the people changed the method of voting from first-past-the-post (FPP) to mixed-member-proportional (MMP) in the hope that this would ensure fairness and introduce checks and balances in the system through more consensual policy-making. A coalition government assumed power in 1996, in a new parliament based on proportional representation. Not only would this constrain the executive, people hoped, but a more representative parliament could better speak for multiple identities and an expanding citizenship.

10

Treaty revival 1974–2003

Expanding citizenship composed the second part of the greatest rupture in New Zealand history since colonisation, the New Zealand wars, and World War I. Rupture in the very meaning of New Zealandness obliged people to adapt to new ideas about who belonged. The country reshaped its political institutions to reflect that its people and culture had grown more diverse and connected to the world, and to accommodate the concept of biculturalism.

THE TREATY COMES ALIVE

Internally the Treaty of Waitangi's return to public life drove these changes. The wairua (spirit) of the treaty makes it unique in the world, determined its place in history and, in turn, shaped national myth-making in the late twentieth century. Gradually the Maori narrative of the treaty began to seep into public awareness. Maori had consistently called for the Crown to honour the treaty; pronounced a 'simple nullity' by the courts in 1877, its spirit stirred 100 years later not just in Maoridom but in the body politic, changing assumptions entrenched since 1840 about the importance of land to Maori and decision-making about paths ahead.

Lobbied by the Ratana movement to make 6 February a national day, the Labour government declared Waitangi Day a day of thanksgiving and commemoration in 1960. In 1974 it became a public holiday, briefly known as New Zealand Day until the name reverted to Waitangi Day in 1976. The Kirk government hoped that the

Waitangi anniversary would become a national day distinctive for its remembrance not of a revolution or war, but of a peaceful agreement between two peoples. But Muldoon reverted to the name Waitangi Day because he disliked the motive behind the invention of a New Zealand day, to prepare for a multicultural future. Muldoon refused to exchange the virtues of sameness for those of difference, and to substitute pluralism for assimilationist policies of 'one law for all', or integration, their replacement from the 1960s. Conversely, some Maori opposed having Waitangi Day whitewashed.

From the 1960s, population recovery and urbanisation spurred debate about the place of Maori in modern society. Renewed culture contact and a high rate of intermarriage (half of Maori marriages were with Pakeha) made indigenous disadvantage more obvious. Internationally, there was emphasis on equal rights to citizenship. Young, educated, urban Maori, alert to the American civil rights movement and United Nations advocacy of human rights, demanded a fairer share of resources, and to have their status as tangata whenua acknowledged. Schooled in counter culture values, they called for the decolonisation of New Zealand.

Maori youth also lost patience with their conservative elders. But Maori leadership itself was shifting ground. The Maori Council, appointed by a National government in 1963 from tribal notables, to balance the Ratana movement's influence on the four Maori seats (held by Labour), provided advice to the government which strongly expressed conservative Maori views. By the late 1960s Maori concerns to retain the last vestiges of tribal land rose alongside youth protest, magnified by migration to the cities.

In Auckland, youthful activists joined progressive movements such as the Maori Organisation on Human Rights in 1968 and the Maori Students' Association, and embraced Marxist beliefs that indigenous rights went hand in hand with class struggle. Radicals and university students seeking mana motuhake joined the 'young warriors' of Nga Tamatoa, modelled on the American Black Power movement who, dressed in black, staged protests at Waitangi Day ceremonies from 1971 – the United Nations year for the elimination of racial discrimination – declaring it a day of mourning. They drew attention to the loss of the Maori language and to the treaty as a fraud, calling for a boycott of the annual celebrations.

Increasingly, tensions erupted every 6 February due to a clash of treaty narratives.

Struggles for land resurfaced in the 1960s as National governments befuddled by the political effects of urbanisation persisted with the settler concern that tribal land was not effectively used and that this hindered economic development. Rather the assumption was that now Maori were urbanised, tribes no longer needed their ancestral land, which had lost its central cultural importance. On the contrary, as university students asserted in 1966, Maori lands were for Maori use: misguided moves by the government to 'Europeanise' tribal land as part of the drive to integrate Maori incited protests rather than promoting racial harmony as intended.

A series of statutes in 1967 provided the catalyst for rising waves of protest. Land policy had changed little since the 1840s, and 1967 marked the height of official attempts to force Maori land into European law. An amendment to the Maori Affairs Act did nothing new in extending the dictum of 'use it or lose it' (chapter 5). Yet it was universally condemned by Maori. The settler narrative had not changed; but ideas about the meaning and place of Maori land and the emergence of a new language of protest had altered. Campaigners against the legislation frequently referred to the Treaty of Waitangi. Supposed equality had not allowed Maori collectively or as tribes to engage with the modern economy and the state as their ancestors had expected when they signed the treaty: 'Maori people were fed up', not merely with 'the sense of being left on the margins of a Pakeha-dominated economy' but with being ignored and patronised.

As a result, Maori, Nga Tamatoa, radicals and kaumatua together, took to the road on the Maori Land March in 1975 to alert Pakeha and the government to the issues, and to fight the 'last land grab' represented by the 1967 Act, as well as others passed soon after concerning rates, public works and local government schemes, all of which allowed the taking of tribal land. The protesters' slogan echoed the Kingitanga call: 'not one more acre of Maori land'. Led by 80-year-old Whina Cooper, the foundation president of the Maori Women's Welfare League, the protesters walked from the far north to Wellington. On the last day they marched to parliament powerfully and silently in the rain, to deliver their message not merely about grievances over the loss of ancestral land – which had grown more, not less, important to urban people – but that the government should finally acknowledge property rights under the Treaty of Waitangi.

Recourse to the treaty required Maori to educate Pakeha, since the latter either did not know about the treaty's history or dismissed the document as a historic relic, or assumed that – in the English version – its tenets had been upheld. In response to the land march, the Kirk Labour government passed the Treaty of Waitangi Act 1975. Matiu Rata, Minister of Maori Affairs, who strongly opposed the measures of 1967, proposed a tribunal that would be empowered to deal with modern treaty grievances, as a corollary to the concept of 6 February as a national day. The tribunal proved to be a milestone: while it could only make recommendations, it marked the 'observance' and 'confirmation' of the 'principles of the Treaty of Waitangi', leaving the principles to be interpreted in the future.

More than the land march, however, the Bastion Point protest in Auckland in 1977–78 aroused public consciousness through the medium of television. By this time about 1.3 million hectares of land remained with tribes. Orakei, Bastion Point's original name, was the home of Ngati Whatua, who sold Auckland in 1840. The 1977 protest, though the first to gain publicity because it broke the law, followed ten court actions. Dispute had simmered ever since 1869 when the Native Land Court vested the Orakei block of 280 hectares in three hapu and in 1873 issued a certificate of title in the name of 13 members of Ngati Whatua, disinheriting the rest of the tribe. The title had a rider that the land should be inalienable, but in 1886 the state took land under the Public Works Act for defence purposes, on the pretext of a Russian naval scare. In 1898 the trustees were declared 'owners' with power to alienate the remaining land, although the Stout-Ngata commission of 1907 declared this partition illegal. Between 1914 and 1928 the state purchased the entire remaining block except for one hectare which contained the marae, ignoring a legal decision to declare 15.6 hectares 'inalienable'. In 1951 the National government compulsorily acquired the last sliver of land except for the cemetery, removed the residents to state houses nearby, and burned the marae in an exercise of 'slum clearance' to remove this blot on modern Auckland.

For Ngati Whatua who had watched the burning of their ancestral place and grown up poor in state housing, the final insult was the Muldoon government's decision to sell the remaining land at Bastion Point, with its harbour views, to developers. Led by Joe Hawke, later an MP, the tribe challenged the Crown's ownership. Bastion Point symbolised the social aspects of Muldoonism since, after a 506-day occupation, Muldoon sent in police and the army to remove the protesters. Television viewers were shocked to watch the Riot Act read and 222 people arrested. Through the prolonged dispute the public learnt about this case study of creeping dispossession, and plain unfairness: local people had been forced into state housing while the government proposed to sell the last of their heritage to the privileged.

At the same time the politics of racism and anti-racist protest, local and global, spilled over into the sport of rugby, the national game. The first Springbok rugby team to visit New Zealand in 1921 had offended Te Arawa in Rotorua by accepting the tribe's formal welcome and then turning their backs, disgusted at having to play a 'native' team, while a New Zealand Maori side performed the haka. That offence set the tone for subsequent protests, especially given the capitulation to apartheid by the New Zealand Rugby Football Union, which agreed not to send Maori players to South Africa from 1928. Protests were relatively low-key at first. Non-Maori All Black and Springbok rugby tours of South Africa and New Zealand respectively took place in 1949 and 1956, oblivious to objections from Maori MPs and the Maori Women's Welfare League. From the 1960s, however, 'No Maori, no tour' protests featured in national life. South Africa was expelled from the Olympic Games because of apartheid, and in 1973 Kirk ordered the rugby union to cancel the Springbok tour to New Zealand, after violence during an earlier tour of Australia.

Muldoon, however, let South Africa play its game while he played his; he did nothing to stop the 1981 Springbok tour of New Zealand (and arranged a royal tour immediately afterwards) in order to win that year's election. His appeal to law and order secured the National government a majority of one. The tour both damaged the interests of rugby and unleashed protest tantamount to civil war, on a sustained scale unparalleled since the 1860s.

The Springbok tour of 1981 rallied protesters, from treaty activists and gang members to university students, women, the churches, homosexual law reformers and urban middle-class people, with a variety of agendas. In many respects the rugby tour protests signified a popular uprising against this most blatant case of Muldoonism. Once on the streets, worthy citizens were stunned by the police response to their protests. Peaceful demonstrators encountered rings of barbed wire around rugby fields and the violence of the Red Squad, an élite riot squad clad in helmets and bearing batons whose culture 'was as alien to many New Zealanders as was apartheid'. Urban, educated people came face to face with riot police for the first time and found the confrontation and sense of menace frightening, dramatic, and formative. The experience politicised younger baby boomers, while earlier Vietnam and civil rights protests conditioned older ones to join the marches. Thousands flocked to the anti-tour movement, which enjoyed worldwide coverage after protesters stopped the first game at Hamilton in July by invading the pitch. To Nelson Mandela in South Africa it felt as if the sun had come out.

Violence escalated during the tour. In September the scion of a Marxist family halted the test in Auckland by dropping leaflets and smoke bombs from a light plane, just clearing the goal posts. Whole families were riven by conflict, and the entire country became contested ground. The tour secured a narrow victory for National but revealed deep rifts in New Zealand society, shattering its image as a peaceful, homogeneous nation with harmonious race relations. Protesters heard Maori activists denounce not just apartheid in South Africa – chanting 'free Nelson Mandela' – but injustice at home: at stake were competing ideas of New Zealand, its image, identity and future.

Meanwhile the Department of Maori Affairs established a Tu Tangata (stand tall) programme. Senior women prominent in the Maori Women's Welfare League created the idea of kohanga reo, organised as pre-schools to nurture and save the Maori language. Kohanga reo mushroomed from 1982, outpacing officials who rushed to draft the necessary policy and regulations.

Simultaneously, the Waitangi Tribunal mooted in 1975 came to life under Edward T. Durie, the first person of Maori descent to be

10.1 Justice Edward Taihakurei Durie, Chair of the Waitangi
Tribunal, 1981–2003

appointed a judge of the Maori Land Court. As chairman of the
Waitangi Tribunal from 1981, Judge Durie set about redressing
treaty injustices and educating Pakeha about the meaning and significance of the Treaty of Waitangi. Durie himself symbolised a bicultural New Zealand. In 1983 he and the tribunal first attracted public

notice with a decision for Te Ati Awa of Taranaki on the Motunui synthetic fuels plant, a 'Think Big' project that required a sewage outfall to pump effluent into the Tasman Sea. The tribe feared that the outfall would pollute their fishing reefs, and the tribunal agreed.

This decision represented a direct challenge to Muldoonism and won the support of the environmental movement. Indigenous rights in alliance with environmentalist politics saw the outfall proposal dropped. For the first time since 1877, the treaty was 'brought to life', transformed to the status of a constitutional instrument under the 1975 Treat of Waitangi Act, and Maoridom was abuzz. Soon after, Ngati Whatua won a settlement of $3 million through the Waitangi Tribunal while Bastion Point became a public park, vested in the tribe.

With past claims and disputes involving land handled at a political level, inevitably this produced uneven, unfair results. In 1985, therefore, the Lange Labour government opened the way for hundreds of historical claims about breaches of the treaty by settler governments, by making the Waitangi Tribunal's jurisdiction retrospective to 1840 under the Treaty of Waitangi Amendment Act. Koro Wetere, Minister of Maori Affairs, introduced the bill to deal with rising tensions about outstanding grievances. From this moment, iwi and hapu shifted from protest over land claims to litigation, and an expanded tribunal began to channel generations of anger and despair over official wrongs. This transfer of energy also defused extremism and instilled hope for long-sought equality. For some, treaty claims suggested a means to the political goal of advancement of the people through self-determination and establishment of an economic base for tribes. The change called for a national review of indigenous rights through due process of the law.

In 1986 the Waitangi Tribunal declared the Maori language a taonga under article 2 of the treaty, which the state should guarantee to preserve. Consequently Maori acquired the status of an official language, alongside English, and efforts accelerated to save the language from extinction. Maori immersion schools that taught in Maori continued the work of pre-school language nests, and from there students could progress to tertiary education, while state-supported Maori television, designed to appeal to the youthful population of Maori descent, finally screened in 2004.

Critically, questioning of the bases of citizenship by Maori leaders and the formal hearing of treaty claims led to a rewriting of
New Zealand history to include Maori, a process begun by Sinclair
and others in the 1950s, but vastly extended in the 1980s. The
rise of social history, about ordinary people's lives, assisted this
development. Evidence gathered before the tribunal challenged settler narratives skewed by amnesia about 'our' Maori, and undermined assumptions that governments had extinguished indigenous
property rights honourably, through full consent and fair processes of purchase. Further, Rogernomics threw down a challenge
to Maoridom to check settler politicians' use of executive power.
Tribal resistance to the dismemberment and sale of public assets
attracted widespread support because of alarm about the speed and
undemocratic nature of the reform agenda.

The State-Owned Enterprises (SOE) Act 1986 provided the trigger
for a battle in the courts to prevent the privatisation of state assets.
The Act prepared for the transfer of public assets into private ownership, out of reach of treaty claims by tribes and beyond inclusion
in any compensatory settlement package to redress land loss. The
Maori Council challenged the SOE Act in 1987. The nation's most
eminent justices who sat on the Court of Appeal found the Act
contrary to the principles of the treaty. Through this court action
Maoridom successfully challenged the supremacy of parliament.

This initiative highlighted the question of what 'treaty principles'
meant, since politicians had not defined them. The tribunal and
the courts had the task of reinterpreting the treaty concepts of
kawanatanga and tino rangatiratanga and the document's meaning
for modern New Zealand. Accordingly the Court of Appeal introduced the concept of partnership, with the Crown and iwi as treaty
partners, the latter as the identifiable, corporate representatives of
the descendants of the original signatories.

Yet the signatories to the treaty had acted on behalf of their hapu,
not wider iwi. The treaty claims process obliged hapu to organise
into bigger tribal descent groupings to make it easier for governments. Cabinet ministers would only negotiate with iwi; so iwi were
elevated to institutional status, from the 1920s through state-created
and controlled tribal trust boards, and by the end of the twentieth
century on Maori initiative, as private sector iwi corporations. The

Crown stipulated that iwi were its treaty partners in the late 1980s to make it possible to manage and negotiate the surge of claims.

In the Maori Council case, the Court of Appeal found that the principles of the treaty overrode everything else in the SOE Act. The partners had a duty to act reasonably and in good faith, and the supremacy of parliament rested on the treaty because the legitimacy of government depended on it. Maori 'ceded rights of government in exchange for guarantees of possession and control of their lands and precious possessions for so long as they wanted to retain them'. Thus New Zealand justices followed the Waitangi Tribunal's lead and embraced the Maori narrative of the treaty as a 'living, breathing, vital thing'. They saw the purpose of partnership as advancing the welfare of all New Zealanders, subject to the special condition of preserving the integrity of Maoridom.

For the Waitangi Tribunal, now reinforced by the courts, the critical issues revolved around Crown breaches of the treaty in the struggles over land. Conversely, land loss for Maori entailed loss of their mana and place in the nation. If the state were to honour the treaty, the Pakeha–Maori relationship had to be transformed. Major treaty settlements in the 1990s elaborated the issues facing the country. The South Island Ngai Tahu claim, lodged in response to the SOE Act, reflected a long-standing grievance not addressed by the earlier political settlement in 1944 that the state failed to meet undertakings under land purchase agreements made after 1840. In particular, the state neglected to make adequate reserves and ignored the wishes of hapu to retain substantial blocks, for example on the Canterbury plains. Crown agents insisted on taking 'title to the whole of an area' whereas the treaty authorised only purchase of land that 'Maori freely wished to sell'. This resulted in the 'extinguishment' of customary title and denial of access to food-gathering places guaranteed in deeds of purchase. Ngai Tahu were left in poverty, landless and marginalised.

By contrast Tainui had their land in the Waikato confiscated after the wars of the 1860s. Whole communities suffered for the actions of a few, while the government seized the best land, irrespective of whether 'loyal' Maori or 'rebels' were the owners. This injustice not only ensured the continued vigour of the Kingitanga but also hobbled Tainui's participation in national life. Divergent tribal experiences produced similar outcomes of dispossession, poverty and reduced life chances, with accompanying loss of mana. These initial major claims resulted in apologies from the Crown and treaty settlements of $170 million in 1997 and 1995 respectively.

As part of the Ngai Tahu treaty settlement, significant places regained their Maori name. Mt Cook, renamed Aoraki-Mt Cook, returned to the tribe, but on the same day Ngai Tahu, mana restored and acknowledged, gave the mountain to the nation. The tribe quickly developed its new capital base and became an engine of economic growth in the South Island, active in property development and global business.

While native title in land had largely been extinguished, customary rights remained unclear over fisheries. In 1986, as part of the Rogernomics reforms, the Labour government sought to privatise rights in fish by creating property rights that could be traded through a quota management system. The government argued its case in environmental terms, as a response to over-fishing, but Maori perceived that resources were again being sold. Effectively the quota system transferred to others the property right in fishing promised to Maori under the treaty. Maori leaders warned that this breached article 2 of the treaty. In 1987 the Ministry of Agriculture and Fisheries nonetheless began to issue fishing quotas. Maori who had lodged claims with the Waitangi Tribunal moved to halt this process and a pan-Maori injunction succeeded in the High Court. For the first time in 100 years the courts responded positively to the concept of native title, declaring that native title in land might have been extinguished, but not in fish. The quota management system was held to be in conflict with the treaty, obliging the government to negotiate.

From 1989, through the Maori Fisheries Commission, Maori once more became major players in the fishing industry. An imperial instrument, the common law concept of native title had facilitated the recovery of Maori mana and control over resources. The wider community were still adjusting to the idea that article 2 of the treaty was enforceable in the present when the commission's chairman, Tipene O'Regan, Ngai Tahu's shrewd political negotiator, seized a one-off opportunity to deliver fishing quota to iwi. In 1992 he persuaded the government to purchase a block of 27 per cent of the entire fishing quota that had come on the market (known as the Sealord deal), which could be used to settle fisheries claims. The

Treaty of Waitangi Fisheries Commission was established to manage this block of quota and decide a model for distribution of an
increasingly valuable asset, worth $500 million by 1998. Whether to
distribute on the basis of coastline (to the advantage of Ngai Tahu)
or of population (favouring northern tribes) remained contested at
the beginning of the twenty-first century, as did whether distribution
should be to iwi only or include urban Maori groups.

'A WOMAN'S RIGHT TO CHOOSE'

The women's liberation movement similarly sought 'a place to
stand'. The year that the treaty entered legislation – 1975 – marked
International Women's Year. 'Second wave' feminism developed
from shifting family relations and the altered status of women by
the 1970s, as girls increasingly acquired an education, and married
as well as single women moved into the paid workforce. Feminism's
time had come to liberate women from 'patriarchy' and to call adult
women 'Ms'. Family structures and the nature of marriage were
changing; 1975 saw the arrival of 'no fault' divorce. The economy
needed educated people to fill jobs in an expanded tertiary sector,
while continuing to rely on unpaid work in the home. Families also
needed mothers to go out to work since costs of home ownership
and raising children could no longer be met by a breadwinner wage.

Women's lib's objectives paralleled those in Australia and internationally: equal pay (won in legislation in 1972); liberation from
the role of 'housewife'; freedom from 'sex roles' and sexual discrimination; and autonomy over women's bodies and lives. Motherhood and domesticity were no longer imagined as empowering, but
as a prison. In order to claim the self, therefore, feminists set out
to transform society to free women from the bonds of home and
family. The demand for access to safe, legal abortion proved to
be the most contentious issue in the 1970s because it divided the
feminist movement while being opposed strongly by lobby groups
such as the Society for the Protection of the Unborn Child (SPUC),
who had political influence. When it became difficult for women to
have abortions after the passing of the Contraception, Sterilisation
and Abortion Act in 1977, feminist groups in New Zealand and
Sydney co-operated to fly women to Sydney clinics. This restrictive
law demonstrated the social conservatism of the Muldoon years.

While doctors interpreted the law more liberally by the 1980s, the feminist campaign failed to have abortion removed from the Crimes Act.

Management of childbirth, on the other hand, delivered a feminist success with the return of the independent midwife from 1990. Achieved through consensus between midwives, middle-class women's organisations and the Labour government, the return to the idea of birth as a normal, physiological process resulted from changes in the 'political opportunity structure' that favoured midwives over doctors. In contrast to the 1930s, the medical profession's power and influence was challenged following a cervical cancer inquiry in 1988 chaired by Dame Silvia Cartwright, who subsequently became New Zealand's first woman High Court judge (and the second woman Governor-General). The Cartwright inquiry endorsed patients' rights and intensified public questioning of medical authority. The midwife's moment arrived with the Nurses Amendment Act 1990, whereby the midwife regained autonomy as an independent practitioner and won the right to the same pay as a doctor who practised obstetrics.

Rogernomics helped the return of the midwife. State sector reforms redefined birthing women as 'clients', which gave extra weight to patients' rights and to feminist demands that women regain control of birth. Both feminist and economic rationalist agendas favoured the midwife's return. As Helen Clark, then Minister of Health, observed in 1990: 'Even the Treasury could see merit in increased autonomy'. Midwives provided competition for doctors, and midwife-attended births were expected to cut costs. Competition increased but costs duly soared as women opted for shared care by a doctor and a midwife. The result was the Lead Maternity Carer (LMC) scheme from 1996, which obliged the mother to choose a midwife or a doctor, who was paid a capped fee. The scheme was introduced to save money, not to provide choice. By the end of the century most mothers had a midwife-managed birth with a brief stay in hospital. A review of maternity services in 1999 reported the highest levels of satisfied customers among mothers cared for by midwives.

By the late twentieth century nearly half the female population aged 16 to 64 were in paid employment. An independent working life was now a feature of women's life histories. An increasing

10.2 Prime Minister Helen Clark on Hochstetter Dome, Mt Cook National Park, 5 July 2003, southerly clouds spilling over the Main Divide

proportion of married women returned to the workforce, or did not ever leave it, and by 1990 the majority of married women were earners for their families. While equal pay and wealth remained elusive, a United Nations report concluded that New Zealand had one of the highest rankings of gender equality in the world.

A historical question therefore arises of how a country whose 'first wave' feminists extolled motherhood and domesticity as 'colonial helpmeets' appointed women leaders by the end of the twentieth century. New Zealand attained not one but two women prime ministers: Jenny Shipley in 1997, when she toppled Jim Bolger from the leadership of the National coalition government; and Helen Clark, who became the first elected woman prime minister when Labour won the 1999 election. More significantly, the public did not think it odd to have women running the country.

The major continuities are of a liberal feminism, where women worked within the system to influence policy by changing the law, supported by contradictory encouragement from democratic political institutions; and of mother figures (or aunts). The Green Party had a woman co-leader, while the chief justice and attorney-general were both women at the end of the twentieth century. New Zealand chose a woman Governor-General, Dame Catherine Tizard, for the sesquicentennial in 1990, and the popular Aucklander was followed in 2001 by Justice Dame Silvia Cartwright, who embellished the role with regal elegance.

Until the 1970s, women who entered parliament did so through family networks, as did Iriaka Ratana, who became the first Maori woman MP in 1949 after her husband died. Significant change ensued in the early 1980s, spurred by Muldoonism, which drove Clark into politics, when the number of women MPs rose from four to eight. By the centenary of women's suffrage in 1993, women comprised 21 per cent of MPs, rising to 30 per cent in the first MMP parliament in 1996.

Simultaneously, history recovered women's 'herstory'. Unlike the gothic history of gender relations in Australia, played out in the shadow of convictism as a foundational experience, New Zealand women's history was presented as 'standing in the sunshine'. Women's historians recovered Kate Sheppard and the colonial suffragists as heroines, invisible since the early twentieth century, and ambivalent models for post-war baby boomers, who sought to escape the domestic constraints imposed on their mothers and grandmothers. Remembered as an icon for political women and a mother figure representing women's citizenship, Sheppard became the first woman other than the Queen on a banknote.

By the 1990s mother stereotypes stood alongside warrior stereotypes in university lectures and postgraduate theses, just as Zealandia stood with a Maori warrior on the national coat of arms and women began to find a place in the Anzac legend. In the shadow of a colonial past, women who strove to succeed in politics still required a strong, maternal image, whether as the 'great New Zealand mum' or as an authoritative aunt. Meanwhile general histories, quick to include Maori, were slower to include women.

DIVERSITY IN FILM AND PAINTING

Film bid farewell to the Pakeha bloke as the lead character in *Smash Palace*, a road movie, in 1986. The bloke was succeeded by strong and quirky women in *The Piano* (1993), directed by Jane Campion, and *Heavenly Creatures* (1994), directed by Peter Jackson, which re-created the infamous Parker–Hulme murder case of 1954 in Christchurch. It featured the house that was home to schoolgirl Juliet Hulme that became the University of Canterbury staff club. *War Stories Our Mother Never Told Us* (1995), a feature film documentary by Gaylene Preston, brought to life for a younger generation the stories of 'seven old ladies' who talked about World War II. Preston paid tribute to her own mother, who revealed that she married because of a pregnancy, then had an affair during the war, but resumed her marriage for her son's sake.

New Zealand film is also gothic. It often stars the landscape, as if the environment were a character; hence the opening of Lee Tamahori's *Once Were Warriors* (1994) with a classic New Zealand scene, which proved to be a billboard in a grubby urban landscape. This movie reflected the evolution of Kiwi culture to include women and Maori. Based on the grim novel by Alan Duff, son of a Pakeha father and Maori mother, the film shocked audiences but resonated in the national psyche through its tough portrayal of urban Maori and domestic violence. The movie was the product of the deregulation of broadcasting. Tamahori was a commercial television producer with a reputation for slick advertisements, who progressed to Hollywood and to filming James Bond.

If cultural pluralism marked these films, so did a fresh creativity and confidence that farewelled the cultural cringe. Globalisation provided funding for local products and local stories, previously stifled by a tiny domestic market; it also recruited a worldwide audience for stories of universal human interest. Film created a resident creative class who made film in New Zealand, but with international money, and produced a whole new cultural economy.

From the 1970s there was a flowering of art that expressed Maori and Pacific identity. From Ralph Hotere's combining art and poetry to protest against nuclear testing to Julia Morison's post-modern paintings, to Michel Tuffery, who gave sculptural shape to New Zealand's place in the Pacific, New Zealand art was distinguished by diversity, internationally celebrated and yet located here. Shane Cotton drew on Maori history and prophet movements, Euan Macleod's figures walked through abstracted landscapes, while Bill

Hammond portrayed the archipelago as a land of richly clothed birds, and captured the sense of remoteness.

By the time of the sesquicentennial in 1990 the country had become officially bicultural, and 1940 the birthday of the treaty signing rather than of the beginnings of organised white settlement. The spirit of the Treaty of Waitangi emanated from the National Archives in Wellington, where the treaty documents lay in state on permanent public display in a specially commissioned constitution room. Government and the courts were making conscious efforts to provide redress for land improperly acquired, to listen to and accommodate Maori hopes and to ensure fairness in the future. Historians reflected on the emergence of national identity, on Waitangi and Anzac, on being Pakeha and being Maori. Some asked whether there was such a thing as Kiwi culture, while New Zealanders assumed that their way of life had already earned that label.

Was New Zealand still colonial or was it post-colonial? Did Kiwi culture really mean Pakeha culture with token Maori elements added to provide distinctiveness, much like the tiki on the 10 cent coin, or the koru symbol flown by Air New Zealand? Or was this ensemble as bicultural as New Zealand speech? Did national institutions deal fairly with minorities? Race trumped gender as a concern because it always had done. The nation's history pivoted around settler–indigenous relations, and so did sesquicentennial modes of remembrance. In 1990 a Maori woman filmmaker, Merata Mita, made the official film, *Mana Waka*, a documentary that rediscovered forgotten footage of a building project, initiated by Te Puea for the centennial in 1940, to create carved replicas of three ancestral canoes that had brought the first people to Aotearoa. Fifty years later Mita realised Te Puea's vision of restoring pride in Maori traditions.

THE SLOW DEATH OF 'WHITE NEW ZEALAND'

It took longer for New Zealand to become multicultural. The country had first to grow more diverse before acknowledging cultural difference arising from migration. The multicultural idea transferred belatedly, from the 1980s in law and policy, and effectively from the 1990s. Federal Canada had coined the term 'multicultural' to defuse historic tensions with the province of Quebec, whose relations with English Canada in practice followed a bicultural model. Unlike Maoridom, however, Quebec was governed by its own parliament. Some public figures warned that the Treaty of Waitangi created difficulties for biculturalism. They warned that before politicians could imagine New Zealand as a melting pot, like the United States, or the sibling of a multicultural Australia, they should settle treaty grievances and accord indigenous people proper acknowledgement. New Zealand had therefore first to adopt a bicultural model of state development before it could contemplate multiculturalism.

The new national museum, Te Papa (our place), opened on the Wellington waterfront in 1998, presented a history that focused on Maori–European interactions. Since the Treaty of Waitangi had acquired constitutional status culturally (if not in a written constitution) Te Papa showcased the dual texts of the treaty. The first people were acknowledged as tangata whenua, the people of the land. In the museum the treaty structured the politics of memory. It was not this recovery of the treaty and the conscious claiming of Maori as pivotal to national identity that provoked outrage, but the placement within the museum of a painting of an abstract landscape by Colin McCahon alongside a 1950s refrigerator. The debate about the place of popular culture in culture showcased as 'national' touched raw nerves.

Some things stayed the same. As in the past, migrants to this distant and isolated archipelago sought a better life, a hope often expressed by the search for a secure, healthy place to raise their families. Migrant aspirations reinforced the idea of New Zealand as a good place to bring up children that was already embedded in national mythology. But the context changed from the colonial idea of a British nursery to the international concept of a clean, green New Zealand that provided the ideal environment in which to rear flexible, skilled global citizens. Australia and New Zealand continued to operate as a single labour market, as they had done since the nineteenth century. Demographers agreed that trans-Tasman migration, a substantial part of international movement for both countries, represented 'little more than another form of interregional migration within a single labour market'.

Paradoxically, just when New Zealand was becoming more inte-grated with Australia, their populations were growing more diverse. New Zealand's growing Pacific identity owed much to history, but increasingly to a post-war focus on the Pacific Islands as a source of labour and a site of development assistance. Through the 1950s and 1960s Pacific Islanders provided cheap labour for manufactur-ing industry, and immigration authorities tended to ignore those 'overstaying' their work permits. Numbers of Pacific Islanders in New Zealand grew substantially, to over 200,000 in 1996, assisted from the 1970s by the building of airstrips in the Cook Islands, Niue and Samoa. From the 1970s, however, their labour was in less demand. Successive governments launched crackdowns on 'over-stayers', notoriously under the Muldoon government, when the police launched dawn raids on Islanders suspected to carry expired permits.

Samoan New Zealanders also ran into difficulty. In a special case, the Privy Council appeared to confirm that Western Samoans born in Samoa when it was administered by New Zealand as a mandated territory could hold New Zealand citizenship. In 1982 Muldoon warned of the risk of a mass exodus of Samoans to New Zealand. His government thought that they were being generous in granting New Zealand citizenship to all Samoans already in the country. Samoans had a different view of the Citizenship Western Samoa Act 1982. In their understanding, when New Zealand citizenship was introduced in 1948, Western Samoans automatically became New Zealand citizens. So did Cook Islanders, because the Cook Islands were legally part of New Zealand from 1901 to 1965. The Privy Council supported that view.

A change in policy about family reunion after 1986 allowed extended family members to join kin in New Zealand, so that by the 1990s most Pacific Islanders gaining residence, who were not auto-matically New Zealanders, did so not as workers but as family. By the end of the century Pacific Island New Zealanders were no longer immigrants. They were New Zealanders, with multiple identities. They were also transnational citizens, with families spread across the Pacific in New Zealand (mainly Auckland), Australia (Sydney) and the United States (especially Los Angeles). Among Samoans the transnational diaspora overtook the population of Samoa. Twice as many Cook Islanders lived in New Zealand as in the Cook Islands, and the bulk of Niueans had left the coral outcrop for New Zealand. Increasingly scholars described Pacific Island extended family networks as 'transnational corporations', whose multicultural heritages and kin relationships crossed the Pacific.

Islanders travelled the pathways of their ancestors but at the same time created a new trans-Pacific constituency, the largest segment of which became New Zealand residents and citizens. Through mobility they acquired new layers of identity, while their resettlement altered New Zealanders' views of themselves. From hip-hop to the classical drum-driven compositions of Gareth Farr, played at the opening of Te Papa, New Zealand music resonated with a Pacific rhythm and a Pacific sound. Pacific themes embellished fashion stores, interior décor and home gardens.

Externally, the white New Zealand policy yielded to pluralism rapidly and late as globalisation swept aside old prejudices. Following Australia, New Zealand shifted from a policy of immigration restriction to shut out 'Asia' to active encouragement of Asian business migrants and recruitment of international students. With the dramatic reorientation to Asia and the northern Pacific in population and cultural flows, in the economy, travel, and consciousness in the 1980s, immigration policy shed race criteria from 1986 and replaced race barriers with benchmarks of skills and money. Rogernomics, economic integration and transformed links with the world set the new rules that opened the nation to business migrants from Asia and an 'Austral-Asian' future.

Ruptures in total net migration set in by the 1970s as the era of classical British migration ended and the country was exposed to new global pressures that pulled New Zealanders overseas, especially to Australia, and attracted newcomers to New Zealand – this time from Asia. The onset of significant migration swings is shown in figure 4.2, reflecting changes in economic conditions and government policy. A flow of departures in the late 1970s resulted from Muldoonism and better opportunities across the Tasman, and a flow of arrivals in the 1990s from changed global circumstances and economic priorities that accepted Asian migrants who brought skills and capital. By 1999 40 per cent of newcomers were Asian, predominantly from north Asia, while in 1999 as 30 years previously, most permanent and long-term expatriates (57 per cent) departed for Australia.

After the first election under the MMP system in 1996 the New Zealand First Party, headed by Winston Peters, a populist politician of Maori descent, expressed anxieties about Asian immigration. Peters played the power broker in a fragile National–New Zealand First coalition government. Racist rhetoric targeted the most high-profile migrants, who came from Asia. At the same time, minority voices began to be heard in politics and the media. The first MP of Asian ethnic origin, Pansy Wong, from Christchurch, entered parliament as a National list MP in 1996. Between 1986 and 1998, 162,000 Asian people migrated to New Zealand, comprising over half (52 per cent) of the total net gain of non-New Zealanders. This was by no means an 'Asian invasion' as Peters claimed. The 1990s peak did not become a trend. The majority of new arrivals by the end of the century continued to be white, from Australia, Britain and South Africa.

People with global interests and marketable skills increasingly led transnational lives. If Chinese were transnational citizens, so were an increasing proportion of entrepreneurial and educated Maori and Pakeha. For 200 years Sydney had been a Maori town as well as an alluring metropolitan carnival. Australia continued to serve as an extension of home for those who sought new lives, brighter lights, and freedom to be themselves. Descendants of a transient settler society behaved as if they were still following their migrant forebears. Around New Zealand shores, Auckland was the fast-growing new hub for migrants and economic activity, the most Australian of New Zealand cities with its low-density sprawl, the biggest home to Maori and Pacific Islanders, and the centre of business. Three out of ten New Zealanders lived in the Auckland region by the end of the twentieth century.

Transnational society and cultural globalisation showed in sport, turned by media into spectacle. National heroes, most popularly represented by Sir Edmund Hillary, were men of the outdoors, adventurous, frontier types who stride across – and some historians maintain colonise – the landscape. They were men of the land but also the sea. Increasingly they were also women sailors and rowing crews, who rowed to success in the Olympics. The America's Cup, a yachting trophy competed for by rich entrepreneurs who could buy the world's best sailors, became the trophy that New Zealand ought to have, especially once Australia had won it. By implication the nation's mariners were great navigators by birthright, as the heirs of Captain Cook and Polynesian seafarers. Sir Peter Blake, the sailor who skippered the winning America's Cup boat in 1995 (and was murdered on the Amazon), embodied the imperial type sanctioned by the Crown. When his transnational successors lost the cup, and worse, decamped to Switzerland, some read as betrayal the Kiwi sailors' status as mercenaries in world sport.

The commercialisation of sport revived the image of rugby, the national game, by tailoring it for television. Fast-growing Pacific Island and Maori populations, proportionately much younger than the ageing Pakeha population, the cult of the market and the reality that team sports are less expensive, led to a browning of rugby and of the All Blacks. So did white flight from the game as more young men feared being pummelled by early-maturing Pacific Island teenagers. Gaining selection for the All Blacks or for the Silver Ferns, the national netball team, offered a popular chance for Pacific Islanders and Maori to 'get on'. Sports hero Jonah Lomu, a Tongan New Zealander, is an example. The giant wing player became a global brand. In Christchurch, rugby union's premier competition, Super Twelve, comprising twelve provincial teams from New Zealand, Australia and South Africa, generated a new team of local heroes in the 1990s. It was no surprise that they should be called the Crusaders, or that their rivals from Otago should adopt the name Highlanders: colonial paths criss-crossed rugby fields. In such multifarious ways, global forces strengthened local identities.

Milk powder, butter and cheese, timber and articles made from timber remained the major export commodities. Fonterra, the multinational dairy company created from a merger of the Dairy Board and the two largest dairy co-operatives, emerged as the country's major exporter. The settler products of dairy and meat still made a big contribution to the economy, though wool had declined, and good New Zealand milk continued to sustain the nation's global brands. Milk retained vestiges of imperial associations with health and body-building. But the empire's food and medicine to build better bodies had also become post-colonial and feminised through global consumerism at home, as a designer accessory in frothy cappuccinos.

Exports of mechanical machinery overtook fish for the first time in 2003. The country's major trading partners were Australia first; second the United States, and third Japan. In 2000 the United Kingdom, the Republic of Korea, the People's Republic of China, Hong Kong and Germany ranked fourth to eighth after this Pacific Rim trade triumvirate. By 2003 China overtook the United Kingdom and talk of a free trade agreement with China was in the air. In trade, the Pacific Rim was in the ascendant. New Zealand business and policy-makers saw that they increasingly had to work with their best friend Australia in developing relations with China, the world's largest power.

New Zealand defence forces worked equally with Australia as peacekeepers in Bougainville and East Timor in the late 1990s. The truce monitors organised by the New Zealand army in Bougainville displeased Australian officers who read New Zealand brokerage as interference in 'their' Pacific, but the friendly rivalry proved instructive. Maori soldiers mediated with locals and in doing so extended the country's reputation for harmonious race relations. New Zealand warrior peacekeepers were much in demand with the United Nations, so much so that the government could not afford to keep up with requested commitments. The myth of harmonious race relations might have been only partly true, but people believed it wherever the New Zealand army served well. At home, the Anzac legend enjoyed a revival. Myths may inhibit, but can also help to find common ground.

EPILOGUE

Globalisation has always shaken the kaleidoscope of connections between people into new patterns. Much of New Zealand history is about managing global forces. In a world as well as a regional, Pacific context, New Zealand's most important relationship is with Australia. The inaugural Australia–New Zealand Leadership Forum in May 2004 recognised this fact. Given present degrees of interdependence, New Zealand sometimes behaves as if it is a state in a federal Australasia, and at other times performs the role of an independent, sovereign nation, a status that it enjoys politically.

New Zealand became tied early into global economic strategies because European settlement happened so late, and it was isolated from its imperial founder. By the time of establishing a settler society the growth of global consumerism was under way. Successive governments responded by building an edifice of liberal 'state experiments' to manage the social outcomes of exposure to the world, as an export-led economy, by means of colonial democracy and a package that may be summarised as the settler contract. The Antipodean settlement at the turn of the twentieth century pivoted around ethnic solidarity of the 'white races', intended to create a new, improved society that kept out Asia, and assumed that the indigenous people were a dying race. It also ensured that women stayed dependent, through policies that accorded priority to male breadwinners.

In the late twentieth century New Zealand, like Australia, abandoned this model of state development, shaped by late settlement, in favour of an Anglo-American neoliberal one that had become

orthodox worldwide. Consensus reigned about a deregulated economy. After 1950, and especially from the late 1960s, New Zealand
had to adapt to massive, international restructuring, from a kind of
globalisation conducted by empires – in which it bore the status of
a colony and a Dominion of the British Empire – to an economically and, increasingly, culturally integrated world overseen by the
United States. These changes were revolutionary, not just in New
Zealand, so that by the beginning of the twenty-first century relations between the United States, an expanded Europe and Japan
shaped the world order. But in the constitutional monarchy of New
Zealand the ruptures created were extraordinary.

   Since nearly half the country's wealth creation (GDP) came from
exports, it followed that statistics of exports and imports by the
early 2000s showed Australia to be first in importance; the United
States second; Japan third, and the European Union (United Kingdom and Germany) fourth. The People's Republic of China, however, was rapidly catching up with Europe. This pattern of overseas
trade reflected the nature of regional, and world, power relations.
Australia and New Zealand were more integrated than ever, while
China hovered over the horizon as the next global juggernaut.

   In a short space of time, New Zealanders proved to be remarkably
successful at managing globalisation by embracing it. As late as the
1970s, Europeans (and even Australians) despaired at the lack of
coffee, wine, and night life. In food, dress, shelter, and how they
communicate, Kiwis rapidly adapted to be global citizens. Fashion
designers offer one example: labels such as World, Trelise Cooper,
and Karen Walker, hang on boutique racks from New York and
London to Sydney and Wellington. Creatively, designers have made
a watery world part of their distinctive brand.

   New Zealand is a vestigial empire's dairy farm; an efficient
exporter of primary products, it operates within market segments
that are the most protected in the world. It is therefore appropriate
that a breakthrough in world trade talks in 2004 was brokered by
a New Zealand diplomat. Locally, the status of the dairy conglomerate, Fonterra, as the country's largest exporter poses questions of
sustainable development. There is a need to protect the precious
resource of water – in Christchurch, drinking water so pure that it

does not require filtering – from nitrates from animals and fertilisers; and from being diverted to irrigation and power schemes.

Because it is small and remote, the country continues to want to use its voice in promoting international collective security. A certain symbolism attached to the appointment of Mike Moore, Minister of Overseas Trade and (briefly in 1990) the last Labour prime minister of the Rogernomics era, as head of the World Trade Organisation at the close of the twentieth century. Overlapping Moore's tenure, a former National deputy prime minister, Don McKinnon, presided over the British world's twilight years as Commonwealth Secretary-General.

The world changed on 11 September 2001; and there are advantages in being insignificant, perceived as safe, and not a threat to anybody. The ship in the harbour image that once lurked as a menace has been replaced by hijacked aircraft. In New Zealand's case, the most likely terrorist threat is a pathogen that breaches biosecurity. As a word, security now holds more meaning than defence. In terms of both, New Zealand cannot avoid having a unique strategic outlook. The Iraq War illustrated how much had changed, since the government refrained from joining historically 'great and powerful friends', the United States and Britain, in invading Iraq, although engineers were involved in reconstruction efforts.

Key moments and episodes continue to refurbish national myths. Into the slogan '100 per cent pure New Zealand' is folded a mythic collection of ideas of the land and the nation, as a good place to bring up children, from which to buy commodities and expertise, as an Arcadia and a social laboratory. Legends remain the stuff of international marketing exercises.

In every culture, people walk along paths taken by their ancestors. At times the ground moves, rendering old paths perilous, and nowhere is this more clearly seen than in New Zealand. Kiwi icons Captain James Cook and Sir Edmund Hillary 'share a common narrative of discovery and exploration', whereas female icons were rediscovered in the late twentieth century to mark the changed position and status of women. Cook's qualities as a man of action apply to women too. Because of its history, the nation chooses as heroes ordinary people who achieved great heights and world firsts. That these are colonial stereotypes need not denote habits of continued colonialism, if such collectively favoured qualities as ingenuity and quiet achievement are reinterpreted to meet new circumstances.

The filming in New Zealand of J. R. R. Tolkien's *Lord of the Rings* trilogy by director Peter Jackson and his screenwriter partner, Fran Walsh, suggested some possibilities. The three films, launched in December 2001, 2002 and 2003, literally employed a cast of thousands; in a village culture, just about everyone had some degree of association with the movies. New Zealand became Middle Earth during filming, its varied landscape digitally enhanced for special effects. Again the environment performed as a character; 'something beautiful belonging to the land', identified by the artist, the late Colin McCahon, finally belonged to its peoples, and achieved a marketing coup. That New Zealand could pose as Middle Earth confirmed the power of inherited mythology.

So did the New Zealand entry's winning gold at the 2004 Chelsea Flower Show. A picturesque, indigenous garden, embellished by a re-created geothermal landscape of the lost Pink and White Terraces as a historical reference, won acclaim as a showcase for New Zealand. Te Arawa contributed tree ferns and carvings, continuing their people's role of providers of the 'native' element in national trademarks.

New Zealanders need to find equivalent common ground in terms of hopes and expectations for a new era. Divided responses to a speech by Don Brash, leader of the opposition, in January 2004, suggest that to find common ground will call for superior leadership. 'We are one country with many peoples', he expounded, repeating William Hobson's phrase, 'We are one people'. Effectively he presented an article 3 reading of the treaty, which suggested a swing away from the article 2 interpretations dominant since the 1980s. This contradicted the Maori view that the treaty enshrined tribal property rights (native title), and remained a covenant. Explicit in treaty settlements from the 1990s were agreements that Maoridom would participate in shaping the nation's future. Already the MMP electoral system had ushered at least seventeen people of Maori descent into parliament, and they held 14 per cent of the total 120 seats, including seven Maori seats, confirmation that proportional representation was working.

The Labour government, however, triggered the formation of the Maori Party in 2004, by proceeding with a Foreshore and Seabed Bill widely denounced by Maoridom. The government introduced the bill in response to a Court of Appeal decision in 2003 that Maori were entitled to test their claims to the foreshore and seabed in the Maori Land Court. This decision negated the understanding that the foreshore and seabed, for the most part, were owned by the Crown. The government insisted on asserting the supremacy of parliament, while the country's top judges supported the Maori perspective, consistent with treaty jurisprudence since the 1980s, which spoke of a 'partnership' between Maori and the Crown.

Focus on the foreshore reflected global as well as local tides. Struggles for land moved to the foreshore and seabed as the global economy sought fish and energy resources, and the beach as real estate to develop. The furore over the seashore erupted because Maori in the Marlborough Sounds wanted to take up marine farming, and local government refused to co-operate. The foreshore and seabed came into the frame as the 'coast' advanced economically and in ideas of the real New Zealand.

Inevitably that real New Zealand is changing. Births at the end of the twentieth century suggest a future where a little over half of New Zealanders are of European descent; a fifth are of multiple descent, of whom about 60 per cent are European and Maori; 12 per cent are Maori; 8 per cent Pacific Islanders; and 5 per cent Asian. Demographically, as the population ages, more seismic shifts are under way.

A foundational history of late settlement, and rapid development in a brief time span, ensured that New Zealand would be a colonial experiment. Capacity for revolutionary change, if unintended, is embedded in the body politic. It can be exhilarating to be a bit on the side.

GLOSSARY OF MAORI WORDS

Aotearoa	New Zealand (long white cloud)
atua	god, spirit, supernatural being
haka	posture dance, accompanied by a song
hapu	clan, extended family, kin group
hoko	buy, sell
iwi	tribe, people
kai	food
kainga	home, village
katoa	all, whole
kawanatanga	governorship, governance, government
ki (prep.)	to
Kingitanga	Maori King movement
kohanga reo	language nest(s) (pre-schools)
kumara	sweet potato
kupapa	1) 'friendlies', troops who fought on the government's side; 2) independent, neutral (some Maori used the term to state their neutrality)
mahinga kai	In the North Island this meant cultivations, gardens; in the south it had a wider meaning, of food-gathering places (as Ngai Tahu argued in their claim)
mana	influence, prestige, power, psychic force
mana motuhake	self-determination
mana whenua	tribal authority within a region (a late twentieth-century expression)

marae	courtyard, space in front of a meeting house
Maui	mischievous ancestral god of Polynesia credited with pulling New Zealand from the depths of the sea
mere	club
moko	tattoo, mark
Nu Tireni, Nu Tirani (also Niu, Nui)	New Zealand (transliteration of European name)
pa	stockade, fortified village
Paikea	chief who, it is said, came to New Zealand on the back of a whale, or swam (the more usual story)
Pakeha	person of European descent
ponga	tree fern
pounamu	greenstone, New Zealand jade
Rakiura	Stewart Island
rangatira	chief, well-born person
tahi	together, one
tangata	men (nineteenth-century definition), people, humans
tangata whenua	people of the land, indigenous people, original or first peoples
taonga	treasure(s), property, thing(s)
tapu	under religious restriction, sacred
taua	war expedition, raid
Te Ika a Maui	North Island (the fish of Maui)
Te Wai Pounamu	South Island (the river/water of greenstone)
tikanga	custom, the right way of doing things
ti-kouka	cabbage tree
tupuna	ancestor(s), grandparent(s)
utu	repayment, return, reciprocity; to make response, whether by way of payment, blow or answer
wairua	spirit
waka	canoe(s)
whakapapa	genealogy, lineage
whenua	land

TIMELINE

2000 BP	likely arrival of Pacific rat with Polynesian return voyagers
1250–1300	evidence of first Polynesian settlement
1642	visit by Abel Tasman, without landing
1769–70	first visit, of 6 months, by Lt James Cook, second visit 1773–74, third visit 1777
1769	visit by Jean-François de Surville
1772	visit by Marion du Fresne
1793	establishment of Maori relations with Governors of New South Wales; d'Entrecasteaux's search for La Pérouse
1808	sealing rush, Foveaux Strait
1814	arrival from Sydney of Anglican missionaries
1815–40	'musket' or 'land' wars and associated migrations
1820	Hongi Hika visited London and King George IV
1827	commencement of shore whaling stations
1830–32	Te Rauparaha's southern assault
1833	James Busby appointed British Resident, Bay of Islands
1834	New Zealand flag for trans-Tasman Maori shipping
1835	Declaration of Independence by United Tribes of New Zealand; Taranaki Maori invasion of the Chatham Islands

1837	New Zealand Association formed (New Zealand Company 1838)
1838	arrival of Catholic missionaries
1839	boundaries of New South Wales extended to include any ceded lands in New Zealand
1840	Wellington settlement; New Zealand annexed to British Empire as part of Colony of New South Wales; arrival of Lt-Governor William Hobson; Treaty of Waitangi signed; French settlement at Akaroa; Auckland established with migrants from Australia
1841	Crown Colony; Governor William Hobson; Auckland the capital; Wanganui and New Plymouth settlements
1842	Nelson settlement
1843	Governor Robert FitzRoy; Wairau affray
1844	Crown right of pre-emption waived
1845	Governor George Grey
1845–46	northern war; 1846; Te Rauparaha seized
1846–47	conflicts in Wellington region and Wanganui
1848	Otago settlement (Dunedin); purchase of Canterbury block (Kemp's Deed)
1850	Canterbury settlement (Christchurch and port of Lyttelton)
1852	Constitution Act
1853	first elections, of provincial councils; male property vote
1854	part-elected General Assembly
1855	Governor Thomas Gore Browne; earthquake of magnitude 8.2 elevated Wellington
1856	responsible executive; Premiers Henry Sewell, William Fox, Edward Stafford
1858	first Maori king, Potatau Te Wherowhero; Kingitanga established
1860	outbreak of New Zealand wars; Kohimarama conference; European population overtook estimated Maori numbers

1861	discovery of gold in Otago; Premier William Fox; Governor Sir George Grey
1862	Premier Alfred Domett
1863	war in Waikato; New Zealand Settlements Act; Premier Frederick Whitaker
1864	discovery of gold on the West Coast; Premier Frederick Weld
1865	transfer of government from Auckland to Wellington; Premier Edward Stafford; confiscation of Kingitanga land in the Waikato; Taranaki land confiscated; Native Land Court established; Chinese miners invited from Victoria to Otago
1867	first Maori members of parliament; male Maori vote; 'native' schools
1868	Titokowaru's war; Te Kooti's escape from the Chatham Islands
1869	Premier William Fox; first university college (Otago)
1870	secret ballot
1872	Te Kooti took refuge in the King Country; end of New Zealand wars; Premiers Edward Stafford, George Waterhouse
1873	Premiers William Fox, Julius Vogel; free fares to New Zealand
1875	Premier Daniel Pollen
1876	end of provincial government; Premiers Sir Julius Vogel, Harry Atkinson; New Zealand–Australia telegraph cable
1877	Premier Sir George Grey; Prendergast judgment dismissed the treaty; free, compulsory, secular primary education; first woman graduate, Kate Edger
1879	full manhood suffrage; Premier John Hall
1879(?85)–95	the 'Long Depression'
1881	Thermal Springs District Act; assault on Parihaka; Te Whiti and Tohu imprisoned; King Tawhiao made peace
1882	first refrigerated shipment to Britain; Premier Frederick Whitaker

1883	Premier Harry Atkinson
1884	Premiers Robert Stout, Harry Atkinson, Sir Robert Stout; Married Women's Property Act
1885	Women's Christian Temperance Union
1886	Tarawera eruption
1887	Premier Sir Harry Atkinson
1888	introduction of tariffs on imports; immigration restriction against Chinese
1889	abolition of plural voting
1890	Australasian Federation Conference; Australasian Maritime Strike
1891	Liberal Premier John Ballance; Australasian Federation Convention
1892	Kotahitanga movement, Papawai, Wairarapa
1893	Premier Richard Seddon; women's suffrage passed
1894	compulsory arbitration and conciliation; state advances to settlers; first Maori graduate, Apirana Ngata
1895	Kotahitanga boycott of Native Land Court
1896	Brunner mine disaster; National Council of Women; Maori population at lowest; poll tax on Chinese increased to £100
1898	old age pension
1901	Cook Islands and Niue annexed; Department of Tourist and Health Resorts; Department of Public Health
1902	Prime Minister Richard Seddon
1905	state maternity (St Helens) hospitals
1906	Liberal Prime Ministers William Hall-Jones, Sir Joseph Ward
1907	title of 'Dominion'
1908	population reached 1 million; Chinese denied citizenship; completion of main trunk line; Blackball miners' strike; visit of Great White Fleet
1909	Native Land Act removed restrictions on land sales; compulsory military training
1911	home ownership rate reached 50 per cent; launch of HMS *New Zealand*

1912	Waihi strike; Liberal Prime Minister Thomas Mackenzie; Reform Prime Minister William Massey
1913	general strike called by Red Feds
1914	New Zealand soldiers took German Samoa
1915	Anzac landing at Gallipoli; National Prime Minister William Massey
1916	formation of Labour Party; conscription introduced
1917	'6 o'clock closing'
1918–19	influenza pandemic; Ratana movement
1919	women could enter parliament; Reform Prime Minister William Massey
1920	Health Act; Native Trust Office; joined League of Nations; mandate over Western Samoa
1922	Meat Producers' Board
1923	Dairy Export Control Board
1925	Reform Prime Ministers Sir Francis Dillon Bell, J. G. (Gordon) Coates
1926	equal status formula, United Kingdom and Dominions
1928	United Prime Minister Sir Joseph Ward
1929	Arthurs Pass national park
1929–33	Ngata's Maori land development schemes
1930	United Prime Minister George Forbes
1931	independence under Statute of Westminster; Napier earthquake; Coalition Prime Minister George Forbes
1932	Ottawa system of imperial preferences
1933	first woman MP, Elizabeth McCombs
1934	Reserve Bank; first public remembrance of Treaty of Waitangi
1935	Labour Prime Minister Michael Joseph Savage; lowest birth rate
1936	guaranteed prices for dairy farmers; compulsory arbitration restored; formation of National Party
1937	national school milk and housing schemes
1938	import licensing; Social Security Act
1939	free public hospital care

1939–40	Centennial Exhibition, Wellington
1940	Treaty of Waitangi centennial; Prime Minister Peter Fraser
1941	Japanese attack on Pearl Harbor
1942	fall of Singapore naval base; first official representation in the United States; arrival of American forces
1943	High Commission in Canberra
1944	Canberra Pact with Australia; poll tax on Chinese abolished
1945	joined United Nations as 'New Zealand'; Maori Social and Economic Advancement Act; universal family benefit
1946	Samoa a trust territory
1947	adopted Statute of Westminster; South Pacific Commission
1948	New Zealand citizenship defined
1949	first Maori woman MP, Iriaka Ratana; National Prime Minister Sidney Holland
1950	Legislative Council abolished; troops to Korea; Colombo Plan
1951	waterfront dispute; ANZUS Treaty; Maori Women's Welfare League
1952	population 2 million
1953	Edmund Hillary and Tenzing Norgay climbed Mt Everest; Tangiwai rail disaster; Royal tour
1954	SEATO organised
1956	troops to Malaya
1957	National Prime Minister Keith Holyoake; Labour Prime Minister Walter Nash
1959	Antarctic Treaty; opening of Auckland harbour bridge
1960	equal pay in public service; National Prime Minister Keith Holyoake
1961	joined the International Monetary Fund; capital punishment abolished
1962	independence of Western Samoa; New Zealand Maori Council; troops to Malaysia
1964	Cook Strait power cable

1965	NAFTA signed with Australia; troops to Vietnam; Vietnam War protests; Cook Islands self-government
1967	wool price crisis; decimal currency; hotel closing hours extended
1968	*Wahine* storm
1969	end of Maori schools
1970	'Save Manapouri' campaign petition; arrival of Women's Lib
1971	Nga Tamatoa Waitangi Day protest
1972	National Prime Minister John Marshall; Equal Pay Act; Labour Prime Minister Norman Kirk
1973	Britain joined EEC; protest against French nuclear testing; population reached 3 million
1974	Commonwealth Games, Christchurch; voting age lowered to 18; Labour Prime Minister Bill Rowling
1975	Maori land march; Waitangi Tribunal; National Prime Minister Robert Muldoon
1977	National Super scheme; Bastion Point protest
1979	Mt Erebus plane crash
1981	Springbok rugby tour and protests
1982	CER agreement signed with Australia; first kohanga reo established
1982–84	wage, price and rent freeze
1983	CER commenced
1984	Waitangi Day march and protest; Labour Prime Minister David Lange; 20 per cent devaluation of New Zealand dollar
1985	refusal of visit by USS Buchanan; *Rainbow Warrior* sunk by French agents; Treaty of Rarotonga created nuclear free zone in South Pacific; New Zealand dollar floated; Waitangi Tribunal power to hear treaty grievances since 1840
1986	Constitution Act; GST (goods and services tax) introduced; Maori Council challenge in High Court; end of 'white New Zealand' immigration policy

1987	sharemarket crash; Maori an official language; New Zealand legally declared nuclear free
1988	State Sector Act; unemployed over 100,000; Royal Commission on Social Policy
1989	Labour Party split; NewLabour Party formed, Prime Minister Geoffrey Palmer; 'Tomorrow's Schools' education reforms; local government reform; Maori Fisheries Act
1990	New Zealand sesquicentennial; first woman Governor-General, Dame Catherine Tizard; Prime Minister Mike Moore; National Prime Minister Jim Bolger; Commonwealth Games, Auckland; remaining barriers removed under CER; forestry cutting rights sold; welfare benefits cut
1991	Alliance Party; Employment Contracts Act; unemployed over 200,000; troops to Gulf War
1992	'Sealord' fisheries deal; health and state housing reforms
1993	referendum vote for MMP electoral system; National government elected, without a majority
1994	peacekeeping troops in Bosnia
1995	America's Cup victory; Maori protest and occupation of Moutoa Gardens, Wanganui; Waikato Raupatu Claims Settlement Act; renewal of French nuclear tests and New Zealand protests
1996	Waitangi Tribunal recommended settlement of Taranaki land claims; first MMP election; National/New Zealand First coalition government
1997	Ngai Tahu deed of settlement; first woman Prime Minister, Jenny Shipley; Bougainville peace agreement signed at Burnham, near Christchurch
1998	National minority government; new Museum of New Zealand, Te Papa Tongarewa
1999	peacekeeping troops to East Timor; APEC conference, Auckland; Labour government in coalition with Alliance and Green parties; first elected woman Prime Minister, Helen Clark

2001   Government rescue of Air New Zealand
2002   Labour government, in coalition with Progressives
            (rump of Alliance)
2003   foreshore and seabed judgment
2004   end of appeals to Privy Council; first Australia–
            New Zealand Leadership Forum; Maori Party
            formed; Foreshore and Seabed Act

SOURCES OF QUOTATIONS

I WAKA ACROSS A WATERY WORLD

The palaeontologists are Trevor Worthy and Richard Holdaway; the quoted scholar is O'Regan, 'Ngai Tahu and the Crown', 2–3. 'Ancestral genetic trail' from Howe, *The Quest for Origins*, 82; Te Arawa canoe from Evans, *The Discovery of Aotearoa*, 47. Peter H. Buck (Te Rangi Hiroa) relayed the Kupe story in *Vikings of the Sunrise*, New York: Frederick A. Stokes Co., 1938, 268. Ben Finney refuted Andrew Sharp in Sutton, ed. *The Origins of the First New Zealanders*, ch. 2; as did Evans in his record of the voyage by Greg (Matahi) Brightwell and Francis Cowan.

Quotation about whakapapa from Tau, 'Ngai Tahu and the Canterbury Landscape – a Broad Context', 41; 'gods' and 'heroes' from Christine Tremewan, *Traditional Stories from Southern New Zealand*, xvi; 'archetypal images' from Tau, 50; 'rolled up our legends' from O'Regan, 1–2. Paikea story told by Ranginui Walker, *He Tipua: The Life and Times of Sir Apirana Ngata*, Auckland: Viking, 2001, 17–34, quotation from 21. 'Lost tribes of Israel' from Sorrenson, *Maori Origins and Migrations*, 16; 'Caucasian family' in Howe, *Quest for Origins*, 46, citing Smith, 1898 to 1919. The story fashioned by Smith was told in 1940 by Ernest Beaglehole and Pearl Beaglehole, 'The Maori', in *Making New Zealand: Pictorial Surveys of a Century*, ed. E. H. McCormick, Wellington: Department of Internal Affairs, 1940, vol. 1, no. 1, 2–3.

'Sacredness of nature' from Simon Schama, *Landscape and Memory*, London: HarperCollins, 1995, 18. Waitangi Tribunal, *Manukau Report*, Wellington: Government Printer, 1985, 38–9; Waitangi Tribunal, *Ngai Tahu Report*, Wellington: GP Publications, 1991, vol. 2, 201, vol. 3, 879–83. Timothy Flannery, *The Future Eaters*; 'optimal foragers' from Anderson, 'A Fragile Plenty', 20; Diamond, *Guns, Germs and Steel*; 'hunter-gardeners' from Belich, *Making Peoples*, 47.

Predator thesis and quotations from Worthy and Holdaway, *The Lost World of the Moa*, 536; archaeological critique from Anderson, 'A Fragile Plenty', 28. 'Festive fare' from Leach, 'In the Beginning', 23. Ngati Whatua lines quoted in Waitangi Tribunal, *Report of the Waitangi Tribunal on the Orakei Claim (Wai-9)*, Wellington: Waitangi Tribunal, 1987, 13.

2 BEACHCROSSERS 1769–1839

Tasman's views from Salmond, *Two Worlds*, 72, 82. Cook as hero of free trading from Smith, *Imagining the Pacific*, 230. 'Mechanical tinkerers' from E. L. Jones, *The European Miracle: Environments, Economies, and Geopolitics in the History of Europe and Asia*, 2nd edn, Cambridge: Cambridge University Press, 1992, 65. 'Humanist myth' from Obeyesekere, *The Apotheosis of Captain Cook*. Cook quoted in Beaglehole, *The Life of Captain James Cook*, 698, 696–714. Global village from Smith; 'terrible hard biscuits' in Chris Healy, *From the Ruins of Colonialism: History as Social Memory*, Melbourne: Cambridge University Press, 1997.

Sinclair, Beaglehole, Salmond and Belich all cite the Horeta Te Taniwha story, as does Witi Ihimaera; Salmond gives this version in *Two Worlds*, 88. Du Fresne's story is told in Salmond, *Two Worlds*, 387. 'Series of blunders' from Owens, 'New Zealand before Annexation', 30. Governor King in King Papers, 2 January 1806, in *Historical Records of New Zealand*, ed. R. McNab, Wellington: Government Printer, 1908, vol. I, 267; see also Salmond, *Between Worlds*, 351–2, 356, 516. Whalers as agents of contact from Belich, *Making Peoples*, 137. 'Treacherous' Islanders from Salmond, *Between Worlds*, 387; also Moon, *Te Ara Ki Te Tiriti*, 49.

Marsden was known to contemporaries as the 'flogging parson'; on Marsden and Maori, see Salmond, *Between Worlds*, 429–31; Cloher, *Hongi Hika*, 69–91. 'Pocket Parramatta' from Fergus Clunie, 'Kerikeri: A Pocket Parramatta', *Historic Places* no. 85 (May 2002): 24. 'Land wars' from Ballara, *Taua*, 17; wars as 'modern catastrophe' from Head, 'The Pursuit of Modernity in Maori Society', 102.

Wiremu Whiti about 'affrighted and fugitive women' to Captain Sir Everard Home, Kapiti, 1846, quoted in Anderson, *The Welcome of Strangers*, 82. 'Maintenance of tranquillity' by Busby, and his lack of teeth from Hill, *Policing the Colonial Frontier*, vol. 1, 58, 60. Racial hierarchy from Bayly, *Imperial Meridian*, 149, 'independency', 151, 'freeborn Englishmen', 207. Busby to Bourke, 10 October 1835, quoted in Raeside, *Sovereign Chief*, 115. Term 'fatal impact' from Alan Moorehead, *The Fatal Impact: An Account of the Invasion of the South Pacific 1767–1840*, London: Hamish Hamilton, 1966. Imperialism and humanitarianism marched together in Sinclair and Dalziel, *A History of New Zealand*, 70. On 'fatal necessity' see Adams, *Fatal Necessity*. De Thierry is criticised in Vaggioli, *History of New Zealand and Its Inhabitants*, 63, and is quoted in Raeside, *Sovereign Chief*, 183.

'Evils of anarchy' cited in Owens, 'New Zealand before Annexation', 41; British superiority from Porter, ed., *The Oxford History of the British Empire*, vol. 3, 208. On Edward Gibbon Wakefield, see Temple, *A Sort of Conscience*. Hobson's instructions are quoted in Hill, *Policing the Colonial Frontier*, 89. The meeting with 'Warri Podi' and 'Pooni' is from William Mein Smith, Journal of a voyage on board the barque *Cuba* from London to NZ, 5 and 6 January 1840, copy in private possession (original in Alexander Turnbull Library, Wellington).

3 CLAIMING THE LAND 1840–1860

Tareha quoted by Orange, *An Illustrated History of the Treaty of Waitangi*, 16–17; constitutional myth from McHugh, 'Australasian Narratives of Constitutional Foundation', 114. Nopera Panakareao quoted by W. Shortland to Lord Stanley, 18 January 1845, cited in Ward, *An Unsettled History*, 16; article 2 quoted in Ward, 14; Maori text from *Facsimile of the Treaty of Waitangi*, Wellington: Government Printer, 1976; see also Orange, *The Treaty of Waitangi*, 257. Williams quoted in Fitzgerald, ed., *Letters from the Bay of Islands*, 247.

The language scholar is Head, 'The Pursuit of Modernity in Maori Society', 106; innovation from 107. 'Amalgamate' from Ward and Hayward, 'Tino Rangatiratanga', 379; 'friends' as opposed to 'enemies' from Head, 110–11.

'Civilisation' from Pawson, 'Confronting Nature', 63; John Locke quoted in Denoon and Mein Smith, *A History of Australia, New Zealand and the Pacific*, 120. Mixture of classes from Temple, *A Sort of Conscience*, 127. 'Natural abundance' from Fairburn, *The Ideal Society and Its Enemies*; Wakefield quoted in J. B. Condliffe, *New Zealand in the Making*, London: George Allen & Unwin, 1930, 17; and in Edward Gibbon Wakefield, John Ward and Edward Jerningham Wakefield, *The British Colonization of New Zealand*, London: John W. Parker for the NZ Association, 1837, 28–9.

Colonial mothers from Dalziel, 'Men, Women and Wakefield', also Wakefield to Godley, 6 May 1851, quoted by Temple, 419; 'morals and manners' quoted in Temple, 132; description of NZ Company lottery 29 July 1839 from the *Spectator*, 3 August 1839. Last report of W. M. Smith as Surveyor-General, Wellington, 4 April 1842, enclosure in Principal Agent to Secretary, NZC, Wellington, 27 August 1842, CO 208/100, no. 128; Journal, 9 January 1840.

Settler numbers from W. D. Borrie, *The European Peopling of Australasia*, Canberra: Demography, RSSS, ANU, 1994, 95. 'Southern New Zealand' from Tremewan, *French Akaroa*; 'forgotten forty-niners' from Amodeo, *Forgotten Forty-Niners*; 'common working people' quoted in Amodeo, *The Summer Ships*, 44. 'Colonial capitalist class' from McAloon, *No Idle Rich*, 23.

Governor as ruler from Francis, *Governors and Settlers*, 213; appeasement of the 'savage' from McAloon, *Nelson*, 35. Hone Heke quoted by F. R. Kawharu, 'Heke Pokai', in *The Dictionary of NZ Biography* [*DNZB*], vol. 1, 1769–1869, ed. W. H. Oliver, 186–7. 'A show of justice' from Ward, *A Show of Justice*. Gore Browne quoted in Claudia Orange, 'The Covenant of Kohimarama: A Ratification of the Treaty of Waitangi', *New Zealand Journal of History* [*NZJH*], 14, no. 1 (1980): 65.

4 REMOTER AUSTRALASIA 1861–1890

'Returned rebels' from Ballara, 'Introduction', in *Te Kingitanga*, 12. Henry Sewell outlined the Native Land Court's objectives while speaking on the Native Lands Frauds Prevention Bill, in NZ *Parliamentary Debates* [*NZPD*], vol. 9, 29 August 1870, 361. 'Free and exciting life' from Cowan, *The New Zealand Wars*, vol. 1: 1845–64, 266. On the fate of aboriginal title, see Parsonson, 'The Fate of Maori Land Rights', 185.

Te Whiti's walk to captivity from Scott, *Ask That Mountain*, 117. Maori numbers in Pool, *Te Iwi Maori*; migration statistics from Borrie, *The European Peopling of Australasia*. 'Minimally organised society' from Fairburn, *Ideal Society*, 191; Arcadian 'fallacy', 236. 'Disproportion of the sexes' from Macdonald, 'Too Many Men and Too Few Women'.

Millions spent on 'progressive colonisation' from James Belich, 'Presenting a Past', in *Catching the Knowledge Wave*, conference paper, Auckland, 2001. Russell's purchase from Stone, *Makers of Fortune*, 177. Male Maori vote from Atkinson, *Adventures in Democracy*, 50. Share in 'fruits of progress' from Stuart Macintyre, *A Concise History of Australia*, Melbourne: Cambridge University Press, 1999, 115. Alternative given Maori children from James H. Pope, *Health for the Maori: A Manual for Use in Native Schools*, Wellington: Government Printer, 1894. 'Gendered script' from Daley, *Girls & Women, Men & Boys*. Macmillan Brown, 1884, quoted by Gardner, *Colonial Cap and Gown*, 71; percentages of women graduates, 110.

Pamphlet by Charles Flinders Hursthouse, *The Australasian Republic*, Christchurch, 1860s, Archives NZ, Christchurch. Definition of Australasia from Morris, *Austral English*, cited in Denoon, 'Re-Membering Australasia', 293; Russell, 1891, cited in Mein Smith, 'New Zealand Federation Commissioners in Australia', 312, 313; 'different national type' from Russell, in *Official Record of the Proceedings and Debates of the Australasian Federation Conference*, Melbourne, 1890, <http://setis.library. usyd.edu.au/fed>. Quotation from Jebb, *Studies in Colonial Nationalism*, 327; 'dismemberment' from Denoon, 'Re-Membering Australasia', 297.

Depression definition from Hawke, *The Making of New Zealand*, 82–3; borrowing 'frenzy' from Simkin, *The Instability of a Dependent Economy*, 151. Growth of new unionism from Nolan, 'Maritime Strike 1890, Australasia.'

5 MANAGING GLOBALISATION 1891–1913

'State experiments' from Reeves, *State Experiments in Australia and New Zealand*; 'Australian Settlement' from Kelly, *The End of Certainty*; 'domestic defence' from Castles, *Australian Public Policy and Economic Vulnerability*. New Zealand as 'Maoriland' from Keith Sinclair, *A Destiny Apart*, Wellington: Allen & Unwin/Port Nicholson Press, 1986. Belich elaborates his thesis in *Paradise Reforged*.

'Natural resource benefits' from Ville, *The Rural Entrepreneurs*, 7; Maori land loss in Ward, *National Overview*, vol. 2, 246–7; Brooking, *Lands for the People?* 134, 140. Loans as 'reward' from Reeves, *State Experiments*, vol. 1, 330. 'New urban frontier' from Lionel Frost, *The New Urban Frontier: Urbanisation and City-building in Australasia and the American West*, Kensington, NSW: NSW University Press, 1991; see also David Hamer, *New Towns in the New World: Images and Perceptions of the Nineteenth-century Urban Frontier*, New York: Columbia University Press, 1990.

'Man's country' from Jock Phillips, *A Man's Country?* WCTU of New Zealand, 'Sixteen Reasons for Supporting Woman's Suffrage', Christchurch, November 1891; Anna P. Stout, 'The New Woman', in *Women and the Vote*, Dunedin: Hocken Library, 1986, 20.

'Free, prosperous and contented people' from Stuart Macintyre, 'Neither Capital nor Labour', in *Foundations of Arbitration*, eds. Macintyre and Mitchell, 186; Ballance quoted by Hamer, *The New Zealand Liberals*, 53. 'Holding the balance' from Martin, *Holding the Balance*. 'Living wage' cited by Holt, *Compulsory Arbitration in New Zealand*, 105. On Red Feds, see Olssen, *The Red Feds*, and chapters by Olssen and Richardson in Eric Fry, ed. *Common Cause*.

'Maori land grab' from Brooking, *Lands for the People?* 134; 'bursting up', 142. Reform Party supporters cited in *NZ Herald*, 15 May 1906; land in Maori ownership from *Appendices to the Journals of the House of Representatives* [*AJHR*], 1911, G-6, 1–4. Native Land Act 1909 from Ward, *National Overview*, vol. 2, 380; also T. J. Hearn, *Taupo-Kaingaroa Twentieth Century Overview: Land Alienation and Land Administration 1900–1993*, Wellington: Crown Forestry Rental Trust, 2004. Maori blood in Lange, *May the People Live*, 56, Young Maori Party, 122–3. Tregear quoted in Howe, *Quest for Origins*, 169–70, 168.

New Zealanders as non-Australians in Sinclair, 'Why New Zealanders Are Not Australians'. F. L. W. Wood gave his views in 'Why Did New Zealand Not Join the Australian Commonwealth in 1900–1901?', *NZJH* 2, no. 2 (1968): 115–29; the dissenting voice was Adrian Chan, 'New Zealand, the Australian Commonwealth and "Plain Nonsense"', *NZJH* 3, no. 2 (1969): 190–5. Belich suggested that the 'Tasman world' ended in *Paradise Reforged*, 30–1, 52. Barton reported in *Report of the Royal Commission on Federation, Together with Minutes of Proceedings and Evidence, and*

Appendices, AJHR, 1901, A-4, 479, W. Curzon-Siggers, 109. Hall in *Record of the Proceedings and Debates of the Australasian Federation Conference*, 1890, 175.

Chinese as 'archetypal alien' from Manying Ip, ed., *Unfolding History, Evolving Identity*, xi; as outside the mainstream in Charles A. Price, *The Great White Walls are Built: Restrictive Immigration to North America and Australasia 1836–1888*, Canberra: ANU Press, 1974, 254. Ideal society as the 'real enemy' in Moloughney and Stenhouse, '"Drug-Besotten, Sin-Begotten Fiends of Filth"', 64.

Seddon on the Boer War quoted in S. E. [Elizabeth] Hawdon, *New Zealanders and the Boer War or: Soldiers from the Land of the Moa. By a New Zealander*. Christchurch: Gordon and Gotch, *c.* 1902–3, 5; 'fraternal terms', 260. On the 'Learned Eleventh' see Ellen Ellis in Crawford and McGibbon, eds, *One Flag, One Queen, One Tongue*, 140; on New Zealand's interests, McGibbon, ibid., 10. Colonies as 'white men's country' quoted in McGibbon, *The Path to Gallipoli*, 165. 'Best immigrant' quotation from *AJHR*, 1925, H-31, 3. Term 'mother's mutiny' from Belich, *Paradise Reforged*, 181; duty of health aim from Plunket Society, *Annual Reports*; 'educational health mission' by 'Vesta', *Argus*, Melbourne, 19 September 1917. 'Broad hips' quoted in Philippa Mein Smith, *Mothers and King Baby: Infant Survival and Welfare in an Imperial World: Australia 1880–1950*, Basingstoke: Macmillan, 1997, 95. Patriotic scouts from M. Esplin, 'Cossgrove, David. Cossgrove, Selina', in *DNZB*, vol. 3, 117.

6 'ALL FLESH IS AS GRASS' 1914–1929

Making New Zealand: Pictorial Surveys of a Century, ed. E. H. McCormick, Wellington, Department of Internal Affairs, 1940, vol. 1, no. 11, 2; term 'ecological imperialism' from Alfred Crosby, *Ecological Imperialism: The Biological Expansion of Europe, 900–1900*, Cambridge: Cambridge University Press, 1986. Great War quotation from McGibbon, *New Zealand Battlefields and Memorials of the Western Front*, 1. Casualties from McGibbon, *Path to Gallipoli*, 257; Harper, *Massacre at Passchendaele*, 114–15, Harper, ed. *Letters from the Battlefield*, 12; Pugsley, *The Anzac Experience*, 69.

Lieutenant-Colonel Dr Percival Fenwick, *Gallipoli Diary 24 April to 27 June, 1915*, Auckland: Auckland Museum, 1915, 14. Fenwick wrote: 'An order came out naming this bay Anzac Bay . . . Perhaps it will some day be known as Bloody Beach Bay'. Capt. H. S. Tremewan (see 6.3.2) took photos in September 1915 labelled Anzac Beach, Gallipoli. Kevin Fewster, Vecihi Basarin, and Hatice Hurmuz Basarin, *Gallipoli: The Turkish Story*, 2nd edn, Crows Nest NSW, Allen & Unwin, 2003. 'Expression of sorrow' from <http://www.nzhistory.net.nz/Gallery/Anzac/Anzacday.htm>; the 'greatest of all causes' from *The Press*, Christchurch, 11 December

1914; *New Zealand's Roll of Honour 1915*, *Auckland Weekly News*, Illustrated List.

'Neat dress' from C. E. W. Bean, *The Story of ANZAC*, 129, cited by McGibbon, *Path to Gallipoli*, 255; O. Burton, *The Silent Division: New Zealanders at the Front, 1914–1919*, Sydney: Angus & Robertson, 1935; 'digger and cobber' in H. S. B. R., 'War Friends', *New Zealand at the Front: Written and Illustrated by Men of the New Zealand Division*, London: Cassell and Co., 1917; 'Anzacs together' by K. S. Inglis, assisted by Jan Brazier, *Sacred Places: War Memorials in the Australian Landscape*, Melbourne: Melbourne University Press, 1998, 84. Chunuk Bair as 'central' from Shadbolt, *Voices of Gallipoli*, 9; later New Zealand role from Pugsley, *Gallipoli*, 358; 'Daredevil Dan' quoted by Shadbolt, 49; Buck quoted by Wira Gardiner. *Te Mura O Te Ahi: The Story of the Maori Battalion*, Auckland: Reed, 2002, 19; Wilson cited in Harper, *Massacre at Passchendaele*, 10. Capt. Ernest Harston, France, to Mrs Tremewan, 20 September 1916, private collection; obituary in *Wanganui Chronicle*, 31 October 1916, 7. Volumnia quoted by W. H. Triggs, 'New Zealand Mothers and the War', in *Countess of Liverpool's Gift Book of Art and Literature*, Christchurch: Whitcombe & Tombs, 1915, 73.

Te Puea quoted by King, *Te Puea*, 78, and Baker, *King and Country Call*, 213. Megan Hutching, '"Mothers of the World": Women, Peace and Arbitration in Early Twentieth-Century New Zealand', *NZJH*, 27, no. 2 (1993): 173–85. Knitting book quoted in Coney, *Standing in the Sunshine*, 312. *NZ Herald*, 27 April 1925, 11, cited in Worthy, 'A Debt of Honour', 195. Memorial types in Jock Phillips and Ken Inglis, 'War Memorials in Australia and New Zealand', *Australian Historical Studies*, 24, no. 96 (1991): 187; Oamaru's memorial oak trees from Eric Pawson, 'Trees as Sites of Commemoration: The North Otago Oaks', NZHA Conference, Dunedin, 2003.

Truby King quoted in *Argus*, 2 December 1919, 7. 'Modern' women in Linda Bryder, *A Voice for Mothers*, 80–1; Truby King quoted in Mein Smith, *Maternity in Dispute*, 2. Dr Gunn remembered by Barbara Smith, Christchurch (raised in the Manawatu); 'fattening human stock' from Tennant, *Children's Health, the Nation's Wealth*; description of health camp from *Wanganui Chronicle*, 17 November 1922.

Tom Brooking, Robin Hodge, and Vaughan Wood, 'The Grasslands Revolution Reconsidered', in *Environmental Histories of New Zealand*, ed. Eric Pawson and Tom Brooking, 169–82, South Melbourne & Oxford: Oxford University Press, 2002. 'Empire's Dairy Farm' from *NZ Dairy Produce Exporter*, 25 July 1925, 30–1; the films were described at length in *NZ Dairy Produce Exporter*, 29 May 1926, quotation from 21; butter for development, ibid., 43–4; 'housekeeping purse' in 'Interview with Lady (Viscountess) Burnham', *NZ Dairy Produce Exporter*, 29 August 1925, 28–9.

'Maximising income' from Fleming, 'Agricultural Support Policies in a Small Open Economy', 351. King, *The Penguin History of New Zealand*, 313. Prejudice about 'idle' land in Ward, *An Unsettled History*, 159; Ratana in John Henderson, *Ratana: The Man, the Church, the Political Movement*, Wellington: A.H. & A.W. Reed/Polynesian Society, 1972, 88. Nepia described in Spiro Zavos and Gordon Bray, *Two Mighty Tribes: The Story of the All Blacks Vs. The Wallabies*, Auckland & Camberwell, Vic: Penguin, 2003.

7 MAKING NEW ZEALAND 1930–1949
'No pay without work' in McClure, *A Civilised Community*, 49; depression myth in Simpson, *The Sugarbag Years*; Ruth Park quoted in Nolan, *Breadwinning*, 173; 'unfair taxation', ibid; Savage in *Evening Post*, 16 June 1938, quoted in Gustafson, *From the Cradle to the Grave*, 216, election manifesto, 165. On breadwinner wage, H. T. Armstrong interviewed by Mrs E. Freeman, 23 April 1936, L1 3/3/564–1, Archives NZ.
  'Workers' welfare state' from Castles, *The Working Class and Welfare*, wage security, 87; social security goal, Walter Nash cited by McClure, *A Civilised Community*, 80. Painless maternity from Society for the Protection of Women and Children, Auckland, 6 September 1937, Committee of Inquiry into Maternity Services, Evidence, H1 3/7, Archives NZ; *AJHR*, 1938, H-31A, 107.
  Government expenditure from McIntyre, *New Zealand Prepares for War*, 259; 'loyal opposition' from McKinnon, *Independence and Foreign Policy*; Savage's attitude to war in McIntyre, *New Zealand Prepares for War*, 237; broadcast, Radio NZ Sound Archives, D 409, quoted in Wood, *The New Zealand People at War*, 11. Air first, in Fraser to Halsey, 30 August 1943, cited in Wood, 260. War dead in Crawford, ed. *Kia Kaha*, 3. Fraser's reply quoted in Wood, 194, and McIntyre, *New Zealand Prepares for War*, 241.
  'Real settlement' in Department of Tourist and Publicity, *New Zealand Centennial 1840–1940*, Wellington: Government Printer, 1938; exhibition outlined in *Evening Post Centennial Number*, 7 November 1939. Speech delivered by Hon. Sir Apirana Ngata at Waitangi celebrations, 6 February 1940, IA 1, 62/25/6, Archives NZ; also Walker, *He Tipua*, 352. Maori Battalion in Gardiner, *Te Mura O Te Ahi*, 31.
  New Zealand in the Pacific from F. L. W. Wood, *Understanding New Zealand*, New York: Coward-McCann Inc., 1944. Australia–New Zealand co-operation in Kay, ed. *The Australian–New Zealand Agreement 1944*, 146; 'territorial integrity' quoted from Wood, *The New Zealand People at War*, 376. Fraser on equal opportunity in *AJHR*, 1939, E-1, 2–3. Profile of good migrant from McKinnon, *Immigrants and Citizens*, citing *AJHR*, 1946, I-17, 99. Duff quotation from Oliver Duff, *New Zealand Now*, Wellington: Department of Internal Affairs, 1941, 14. 'Legislative (and

intellectual) stagnation' from J. B. Condliffe, *The Eye of the Earth: A Pacific Survey*, ed. Peter G. Condliffe and Michio Yamaoka, Tokyo: International Academic Printed, 2004, 102; 'mother-complex' from J. B. Condliffe, *New Zealand in the Making: A Survey of Economic and Social Development*, London: Allen & Unwin, 1930, 431. Wood on 'mother complex' in *Understanding New Zealand*, 194; foreign policy as 'drama', ibid., 195; 'dual dependency' from McIntyre in Rice, ed. *Oxford History of New Zealand*, ch. 20.

8 GOLDEN WEATHER 1950–1973

Bruce Mason, *The End of the Golden Weather*, revised edn, Wellington: Victoria University Press, 1970, 12–13. This phrase has since entered the New Zealand lexicon. See, for example, its use in Gould, 'The end of the golden weather: 1967–1975', in *The Rake's Progress?* McCahon quoted in Docking, *Two Hundred Years of New Zealand Painting*, 184. Mrs Weston courtesy of Carol Shand (granddaughter), personal communication April 2004.

McIntosh quotation from Alister McIntosh, 'Origins of the Department of External Affairs and the Formulation of an Independent Foreign Policy', in *New Zealand in World Affairs*, 1, Wellington: Price Milburn/New Zealand Institute of International Affairs, 1977, 21; 1951 dispute explained by Green, *British Capital, Antipodean Labour*, 153; McIntosh was aware that injustice had produced the union leader Jock Barnes, who was sacked in 1932 after reporting on the riots of 1932 to a Sydney newspaper; McIntosh to Berendsen, June 1951, quoted in McGibbon, ed., *Undiplomatic Dialogue*, 264–5.

Firth, *Nuclear Playground*; uranium rush and 'atoms for peace' from Rebecca Priestley, Nuclear New Zealand: The Big Picture, PhD thesis, University of Canterbury, in progress; migration statistics from McKinnon, *Immigrants and Citizens*, 39. 'Free association' from Campbell, *Worlds Apart*, 284; 'silent migration' from *The Silent Migration: Ngati Poneke Young Maori Club 1937–1948*. Stories of migration told to Patricia Grace, Irihapeti Ramsden and Jonathan Dennis, Wellington: Huia Publishers, 2001. 'Reserve of industrial labour' from *Labour and Employment Gazette*, 2, no. 2 (February 1952): 16, cited by Woods, 'Dissolving the Frontiers', 119; apprenticeship scheme in Megan C. Woods, Integrating the Nation: Gendering Maori Urbanisation and Integration, 1942–1969, PhD thesis, University of Canterbury, 2002, 77–8, 195–6. Definition of integration in Hunn Report, *AJHR*, 1961, G-10, 15–16; Maori Women's Welfare League quoted in Brookes, 'Nostalgia for "Innocent Homely Pleasures"', 212.

Rangiora pavlova recipe in Jane Teal, 'Recipes for the Renovations: Laurina Stevens and the Pavlova Cake', *History Now*, 9, no. 4 (2004): 13–16; cream advertising on poster, 'Everything tastes better with cream'

(1960s), Archives NZ, Christchurch. The author's great-grandmother and great-uncle were among the dead at Tangiwai. 'Oversexed' girls from *Report of the Special Committee on Moral Delinquency in Children and Adolescents*, Wellington: Government Printer, 1954; 'girls in jeans' quotation from Coney, *Standing in the Sunshine*, 174–5.

Farmer quoted in H. C. D. Somerset, *Littledene: Patterns of Change*, enlarged edn, Wellington: NZ Council for Educational Research, 1974, 126, 220; 'lubricated by trust' from Singleton and Robertson, *Economic Relations between Britain and Australasia*, 11. Wool auction in Easton, *In Stormy Seas*, 73, and Gould, *The Rake's Progress?* 113–14; 'stop-go' in Gould, 113. 'Fight for survival' from John Marshall, *Memoirs: Volume Two: 1960 to 1988*, Auckland: William Collins, 1989, 61; cf. Stuart Ward, *Australia and the British Embrace: The Demise of the Imperial Ideal*, Melbourne: Melbourne University Press, 2001.

9 LATEST EXPERIMENTS 1974–1996

Quotation from Cain and Hopkins, *British Imperialism*, 658; definition of globalisation from Richard Le Heron, in *Changing Places*, 22. Fall in real incomes in Treasury, *New Zealand Economic Growth: An Analysis of Performance and Policy*, Wellington: The Treasury, April 2004; 'misdiagnosis' in Belich, *Paradise Reforged*, 460; 'big government' in Bassett, *The State in New Zealand*, 324.

Muldoon quoted by Gustafson, *His Way*, 6; Muldoon writing in *My Way*, and *The Rise and Fall of a Young Turk*. 'Political ageing' and 'welfare generation' from Thompson, *Selfish Generations?* Muldoon described in Templeton, *All Honourable Men*, 224; 'command economy' in Bassett, 17. Nareen statement (named for Fraser's rural property) in Pamela Andre, Stephen Payton and John Mills, eds, *The Negotiation of the Australia New Zealand Closer Economic Relations Trade Agreement 1983*, Canberra & Wellington: Australian Department of Foreign Affairs and Trade and New Zealand Ministry of Foreign Affairs and Trade, 2003, 1–4, quotation, 2; Anthony in ibid., 5–7.

Michael Cullen, 'Reflecting on the Fourth Labour Government', Conference on the First Term of the Fourth Labour Government, Wellington: Stout Research Centre, Victoria University of Wellington, 30 April–1 May 2004; Lange described by Geoffrey Palmer and John Henderson, ibid. 'Jerry-built economic structure' from Bassett, 23; 'blitzkrieg' from Easton, ed. *The Making of Rogernomics* 171. 'The right thing' quoting Michael Bassett and Roger Douglas, during Conference on the First Term of the Fourth Labour Government; 'long period of deviancy' and margarine example from Palmer and David Caygill, ibid.; change as 'end not the means' from Cullen, ibid. 'Theory driven revolution' in Goldfinch, *Remaking New Zealand and Australian Economic Policy*, 37. There were three finance ministers because of the amount of work that the reforms generated. Assurance that reforms represented the 'answer' from Ron Burgess, former head of Combined Service Unions, Conference on the First Term of the Fourth Labour Government, discussion, session 5.

'Deliver jobs' from Davey, *Another New Zealand Experiment*, 9; 'enormous' concentration quoting Palmer, Conference on the First Term of the Fourth Labour Government; changed processes from Gauld, *Revolving Doors*, 39; 'major limitations' from Barnett and Barnett, 'Back to the Future?'; 'impediment' quoting Gauld, 214.

Quotation about independence and the 'role of power' by McKinnon, *Independence and Foreign Policy*, 278; Merwyn Norrish explained the course of events at the Conference on the First Term of the Fourth Labour Government. The former minister is Michael Bassett; quotation from Michael Bassett, 'The Atom Splitters', *National Business Review*, 8 August 2003, 36. 'Test of principle' in Margaret Wilson, *Labour in Government, 1984–1987*, Wellington: Allen & Unwin/Port Nicholson Press, 1989, 55; quotation ibid., 64; 'triumph for democracy' from Helen Clark, 'A Politician's View', in *Nuclear Free Nation: A Case-Study of Aotearoa/New Zealand*, Hong Kong: International Affairs, Christian Conference of Asia, c.1985, 18. David Lange quoted from '"Nuclear Weapons are Morally Indefensible": Argument for the affirmative during the Oxford Union debate of 1 March', in Ministry of Foreign Affairs, *A Selection of Recent Foreign Policy Statements by the New Zealand Prime Minister and Minister of Foreign Affairs, Rt Hon. David Lange*, Information Bulletin no. 11, March 1985, 15, 16, 21. The speech was written by Margaret Pope, Lange's speechwriter and future wife.

ANZUS 'inoperative' from McIntyre in Rice, ed. *Oxford History of New Zealand*, 535; breach from McMillan, *Neither Confirm Nor Deny*, 88; 'state terrorism' from *The Times*, Leader, 9 July 1986; on 'freedom of the seas', see treaty extracts in McMillan, 168. Quotations from *Defence and Security: What New Zealanders Want*, Wellington: Defence Committee of Enquiry, 1986, 73, 67, 73. 'Crash through' from Goldfinch, *Remaking New Zealand and Australian Economic Policy*, 215.

10 TREATY REVIVAL 1974–2003

Temm, *The Waitangi Tribunal*, 45; <NZHistory.net.nz>, *Waitangi Day: A History*, Ministry for Culture and Heritage, 2004; Maori people 'fed up' from Ward, *National Overview*, vol. 1, 137; 'not one more acre' quoted by Walker in Rice, ed. *Oxford History of New Zealand*, 513. Goal of 'observance' from Treaty of Waitangi Act 1975; Bastion Point protest in Walker, *Ka Whawhai Tonu Matou*, 216; also Waitangi Tribunal, *Report of the Waitangi Tribunal on the Orakei Claim*.

Red Squad culture described by Richards, *Dancing on Our Bones*, 223; Nelson Mandela quoted in ibid., Te Ati Awa [or Te Atiawa] and 'Think Big' from *Evening Post*, 6 April 1983, 6. Treaty 'brought to life' from Temm,

The Waitangi Tribunal, 40, rights ceded in exchange for guarantees of possession, 96, citing Justice Casey, treaty as 'living thing', 97. Tipene O'Regan in Kawharu, ed. *Waitangi*, 242–3; Ngai Tahu's fate outlined in Tau, 'Ngai Tahu – from "Better Be Dead and Out of the Way"'.

Sub-heading from Hayley M. Brown, 'A Woman's Right to Choose': Second Wave Feminist Advocacy of Abortion Law Reform in New Zealand and New South Wales from the 1970s, MA thesis, University of Canterbury, 2004; 'place to stand' quoted in Macdonald, ed. *The Vote, the Pill and the Demon Drink*, 206. Term 'political opportunity structure' from theorist Charles Tilly. Quotation from Helen Clark, 'Opening Address', in *New Zealand College of Midwives Conference Proceedings*, 2–3, Dunedin: New Zealand College of Midwives, 1990.

Gaylene Preston quoted in Shepard, *Reframing Women*, 172; demographic quotation from Bell, 'Comparing Population Mobility in Australia and New Zealand', 190–1. Term 'Austral-Asia' from Denis McLean, *The Prickly Pair: Making Nationalism in Australia and New Zealand*, Dunedin: University of Otago Press, 2003, 307. Under the MMP system people cast two votes: one for a political party, and one for an electorate MP who represents their local electorate. Percentages of party votes determine the number of MPs on a party list (list MPs) elected to parliament. 'Asian invasion' from Bedford et al, 'International Migration in New Zealand', 55.

EPILOGUE

Quotation from Pickles, 'Kiwi Icons', 10. Address by Don Brash, leader of the National Party, to the Orewa Rotary Club, 27 January 2004. Statistics from Statistics NZ website, <www.stats.govt.nz>.

GUIDE TO FURTHER READING

REFERENCE

Kirkpatrick, Russell. *Bateman Contemporary Atlas New Zealand: The Shapes of Our Nation*. Auckland: David Bateman, 1999.

McGibbon, Ian, ed., with Paul Goldstone. *The Oxford Companion to New Zealand Military History*. Auckland: Oxford University Press, 2000.

McKinnon, Malcolm, ed., with Barry Bradley and Russell Kirkpatrick. *New Zealand Historical Atlas*. Auckland: David Bateman/Historical Branch, Department of Internal Affairs, 1997.

Ministry for Culture and Heritage. <NZhistory.net.nz>, New Zealand history website.

—. <www.dnzb.govt.nz>, Dictionary of New Zealand Biography website.

Oliver, W. H., and Claudia Orange, eds. *The Dictionary of New Zealand Biography*. 5 vols. Wellington: Department of Internal Affairs, 1990–2000.

Ward, Alan. *National Overview*. Wellington: Waitangi Tribunal, 1997. Rangahaua Whanui Series, 3 vols.

GENERAL

Belich, James. *Making Peoples: A History of New Zealanders, from Polynesian Settlement to the End of the Nineteenth Century*. Auckland: Allen Lane, 1996.

—. *Paradise Reforged: A History of the New Zealanders from the 1880s to the Year 2000*. Auckland: Allen Lane, 2001.

Coney, Sandra. *Standing in the Sunshine: A History of New Zealand Women Since They Won the Vote*. Auckland: Viking, 1993.

Denoon, Donald, and Philippa Mein Smith, with Marivic Wyndham. *A History of Australia, New Zealand and the Pacific*, The Blackwell History of the World, ed. R. I. Moore. Oxford & Malden, Mass.: Blackwell Publishers, 2000.

Docking, Gil. *Two Hundred Years of New Zealand Painting*. With additions by Michael Dunn covering 1970–90. Revised edn. Auckland: David Bateman, 1990.

Hawke, G. R. *The Making of New Zealand: An Economic History*. Cambridge: Cambridge University Press, 1985.

King, Michael. *The Penguin History of New Zealand*. Auckland: Penguin, 2003.

Rice, Geoffrey W., ed. *The Oxford History of New Zealand*. 2nd edn. Auckland: Oxford University Press, 1992.

Sinclair, Keith, and Raewyn Dalziel. *A History of New Zealand*. Revised edn. Auckland: Penguin, 2000.

Ward, Alan. *An Unsettled History: Treaty Claims in New Zealand Today*. Wellington: Bridget Williams Books, 1999.

I WAKA ACROSS A WATERY WORLD

Anderson, Atholl. *Prodigious Birds: Moas and Moa-Hunting in Prehistoric New Zealand*. Cambridge: Cambridge University Press, 1989.

—. *The Welcome of Strangers: An Ethnohistory of Southern Maori A.D. 1650–1850*. Dunedin: University of Otago Press/Dunedin City Council, 1998.

—. 'A Fragile Plenty: Pre-European Maori and the New Zealand Environment'. In *Environmental Histories of New Zealand*, ed. Eric Pawson and Tom Brooking, 19–34. South Melbourne: Oxford University Press, 2002.

Ballara, Angela. *Iwi: The Dynamics of Maori Tribal Organisation from c.1769 to c.1945*. Wellington: Victoria University Press, 1998.

Coates, Glen. *The Rise and Fall of the Southern Alps*. Christchurch: Canterbury University Press, 2002.

Dacker, Bill. *Te Mamae Me Te Aroha: The Pain and the Love*. Dunedin: University of Otago Press with Dunedin City Council, 1994.

Davidson, Janet. *The Prehistory of New Zealand*. 2nd edn. Auckland: Longman Paul, 1992.

Diamond, Jared. *Guns, Germs and Steel: The Fates of Human Societies*. London: Jonathan Cape, 1997.

Evans, Jeff. *The Discovery of Aotearoa*. Auckland: Reed, 1998.

Flannery, Timothy F. *The Future Eaters: An Ecological History of the Australasian Lands and People*. Melbourne: Reed, 1994.

Howe, K. R. *The Quest for Origins*. Auckland: Penguin, 2003.

King, Michael. *Nga Iwi O Te Motu: 1000 Years of Maori History*. Revised edn. Auckland: Reed, 2001.

Leach, Helen. 'In the Beginning'. In *Te Whenua, Te Iwi: The Land and the People*, ed. Jock Phillips, 18–26. Wellington: Allen & Unwin/Port Nicholson Press, 1987.

O'Regan, Tipene. 'Ngai Tahu and the Crown: Partnership Promised'. In *Rural Canterbury: Celebrating Its History*, ed. Garth Cant and Russell Kirkpatrick, 1–19. Wellington: Daphne Brasell Associates/Lincoln University Press, 2001.

Orbell, Margaret. *Hawaiki: A New Approach to Maori Tradition*. Christchurch: Canterbury University Press, 1991.

—. *The Illustrated Encyclopedia of Maori Myth and Legend*. Christchurch: Canterbury University Press, 1995.

Sorrenson, M. P. K. *Maori Origins and Migrations: The Genesis of Some Pakeha Myths and Legends*. Auckland: Auckland University Press, 1979.

Sutton, Douglas, ed. *The Origins of the First New Zealanders*. Auckland: Auckland University Press, 1994.

Tau, Te Maire. 'Ngai Tahu and the Canterbury Landscape – a Broad Context'. In *Southern Capital: Christchurch*, ed. John Cookson and Graeme Dunstall, 41–59. Christchurch: Canterbury University Press, 2000.

—. *Nga Pikituroa O Ngai Tahu: The Oral Traditions of Ngai Tahu*. Dunedin: University of Otago Press, 2003.

Tremewan, Christine, trans. and ed. *Traditional Stories from Southern New Zealand: He Korero no Te Wai Pounamu*. Christchurch: Macmillan Brown Centre for Pacific Studies, University of Canterbury, 2002.

Wanhalla, Angela. 'Maori Women in Waka Traditions'. In *Shifting Centres: Women and Migration in New Zealand History*, ed. Lyndon Fraser and Katie Pickles, 15–27. Dunedin: University of Otago Press, 2002.

Worthy, Trevor H., and Richard N. Holdaway. *The Lost World of the Moa: Prehistoric Life of New Zealand*. Christchurch: Canterbury University Press, 2002.

2 BEACHCROSSERS 1769–1839

Adams, Peter. *Fatal Necessity: British Intervention in New Zealand 1830–1847*. Auckland: Auckland University Press, 1977.

Anderson, Atholl. *The Welcome of Strangers: An Ethnohistory of Southern Maori A.D. 1650–1850*. Dunedin: University of Otago Press/Dunedin City Council, 1998.

Ballara, Angela. *Taua: 'Musket Wars', 'Land Wars' or Tikanga? Warfare in Maori Society in the Early Nineteenth Century*. Auckland: Penguin, 2003.

Bayly, C. A. *Imperial Meridian: The British Empire and the World 1780–1830*, Studies in Modern History, ed. John Morrill and David Cannadine. London and New York: Longman, 1989.

Beaglehole, J. C. *The Life of Captain James Cook*. London: Adam & Charles Black, 1974.

Cloher, Dorothy Urlich. *Hongi Hika: Warrior Chief*. Auckland: Viking, 2003.

Crosby, R. D. *The Musket Wars: A History of Inter-Iwi Conflict 1806–1845*. 2nd edn. Auckland: Reed, 2001.

Dunmore, John. 'French Navigators in New Zealand 1769–1840'. In *New Zealand and the French: Two Centuries of Contact*, ed. John Dunmore, 8–19. Waikanae: The Heritage Press, 1997.

Head, Lyndsay. 'The Pursuit of Modernity in Maori Society: The Conceptual Bases of Citizenship in the Early Colonial Period'. In *Histories, Power and Loss: Uses of the Past – a New Zealand Commentary*, ed. Andrew Sharp and Paul McHugh, 97–121. Wellington: Bridget Williams Books, 2001.

Hill, Richard S. *Policing the Colonial Frontier: The Theory and Practice of Coercive Social and Racial Control in New Zealand, 1767–1867*, Part I. Vol. 1. Wellington: Historical Publications Branch, Department of Internal Affairs, 1986.

King, Michael. *Moriori: A People Rediscovered*. Auckland: Viking, 1989.

Moon, Paul. *Te Ara Ki Te Tiriti: The Path to the Treaty of Waitangi*. Auckland: David Ling Publishing, 2002.

Obeyesekere, Gananath. *The Apotheosis of Captain Cook: European Mythmaking in the Pacific*. Princeton: Princeton University Press, 1992.

Orange, Claudia. 'The Maori and the Crown'. In *The Oxford Illustrated History of New Zealand*, ed. Keith Sinclair. Auckland: Oxford University Press, 1990.

Owens, J. M. R. 'New Zealand before Annexation'. In *The Oxford History of New Zealand*, ed. Geoffrey W. Rice. Auckland: Oxford University Press, 1992.

Porter, Andrew, ed. *The Oxford History of the British Empire. The Nineteenth Century*. Edited by Wm. Roger Louis. Vol. 3. Oxford: Oxford University Press, 1999.

Raeside, J. D. *Sovereign Chief, a Biography of Baron De Thierry*. Christchurch: Caxton Press, 1977.

Salmond, Anne. *Two Worlds: First Meetings between Maori and Europeans 1642–1772*. Auckland: Viking, 1991.

—. *Between Worlds: Early Exchanges between Maori and Europeans 1773–1815*. Auckland: Viking, 1997.

—. *The Trial of the Cannibal Dog: Captain Cook in the South Seas*. Auckland: Allen Lane/Penguin Books, 2003.

Smith, Bernard. *Imagining the Pacific: In the Wake of the Cook Voyages*. Melbourne: MUP/Miegunyah Press, 1992.

Temple, Philip. *A Sort of Conscience: The Wakefields*. Auckland: Auckland University Press, 2002.

Vaggioli, Dom Felice. *History of New Zealand and Its Inhabitants*. Translated by John Crockett. Dunedin: University of Otago Press, 2000 (first published 1896).

3 CLAIMING THE LAND 1840–1860

Amodeo, Colin. *The Summer Ships*. Christchurch: Caxton Press, 2000.

—, with Ron Chapman. *Forgotten Forty-Niners*. Christchurch: Caxton Press, 2003.

Byrnes, Giselle. *Boundary Markers: Land Surveying and the Colonisation of New Zealand*. Wellington: Bridget Williams Books, 2001.

Dalziel, Raewyn. 'Men, Women and Wakefield'. In *Edward Gibbon Wakefield and the Colonial Dream: A Reconsideration*, 77–86. Wellington: GP Publications/Friends of the Turnbull Library, 1997.

Fairburn, Miles. *The Ideal Society and Its Enemies: The Foundations of Modern New Zealand Society 1850–1900*. Auckland: Auckland University Press, 1989.

Fitzgerald, Caroline, ed. *Letters from the Bay of Islands: The Story of Marianne Williams*. Auckland: Penguin, 2004.

Francis, Mark. *Governors and Settlers: Images of Authority in the British Colonies, 1820–60*. London: Macmillan, 1992.

Hamer, David, and Roberta Nicholls, eds. *The Making of Wellington 1800–1914*. Wellington: Victoria University Press, 1990.

Head, Lyndsay. 'The Pursuit of Modernity in Maori Society'. In *Histories, Power and Loss*, ed. Andrew Sharp and Paul G. McHugh, 97–121. Wellington: Bridget Williams Books, 2001.

McAloon, Jim. *Nelson: A Regional History*. Whatamango Bay: Cape Catley/Nelson City Council, 1997.

—. *No Idle Rich: The Wealthy in Canterbury and Otago 1840–1914*. Dunedin: University of Otago Press, 2002.

McClintock, A. H. *Crown Colony Government in New Zealand*. Wellington: Government Printer, 1958.

McHugh, P. G. 'Australasian Narratives of Constitutional Foundation'. In *Quicksands: Foundational Histories in Australia and Aotearoa New Zealand*, ed. Klaus Neumann, Nicholas Thomas and Hilary Ericksen, 98–114. Sydney: UNSW Press, 1999.

Olssen, Erik. 'Wakefield and the Scottish Enlightenment, with Particular Reference to Adam Smith and His *Wealth of Nations*'. In *Edward Gibbon Wakefield and the Colonial Dream: A Reconsideration*, 47–66. Wellington: GP Publications/Friends of the Turnbull Library, 1997.

Orange, Claudia. *The Treaty of Waitangi*. Wellington: Allen & Unwin/Port Nicholson Press, 1987.

—. *An Illustrated History of the Treaty of Waitangi*. Wellington: Allen & Unwin, 1990. Revised edn 2004.

Parsonson, Ann. 'The Challenge to Mana Maori'. In *The Oxford History of New Zealand*, ed. G. W. Rice, 167–98. Auckland: Oxford University Press, 1992.

Pawson, Eric. 'Confronting Nature'. In *Southern Capital Christchurch*, ed. John Cookson and Graeme Dunstall, 60–84. Christchurch: Canterbury University Press, 2000.

Sharp, Andrew. *Justice and the Maori*. 2nd edn. Auckland: Oxford University Press, 1997.

Sharp, Andrew, and Paul G. McHugh, eds. *Histories, Power and Loss*. Wellington: Bridget Williams Books, 2001.

Sorrenson, M. P. K. 'The Settlement of New Zealand from 1835'. In *Indigenous Peoples' Rights in Australia, Canada, & New Zealand*, ed. Paul Havemann, 162–79. Auckland: Oxford University Press, 1999.

Stone, R. C. J. *From Tamaki-Makau-Rau to Auckland*. Auckland: Auckland University Press, 2001.

Temple, Philip. *A Sort of Conscience: The Wakefields*. Auckland: Auckland University Press, 2002.

Tremewan, Peter. *French Akaroa: An Attempt to Colonise Southern New Zealand*. Christchurch: University of Canterbury Press, 1990.

Ward, Alan. *A Show of Justice: Racial 'Amalgamation' in Nineteenth Century New Zealand*. 2nd edn. Auckland: Auckland University Press, 1995.

—, and Janine Hayward. 'Tino Rangatiratanga: Maori in the Political and Administrative System'. In *Indigenous Peoples' Rights in Australia, Canada, & New Zealand*, ed. Paul Havemann, 378–99. Auckland: Oxford University Press, 1999.

4 REMOTER AUSTRALASIA 1861–1890

Atkinson, Neill. *Adventures in Democracy: A History of the Vote in New Zealand*. Dunedin: University of Otago Press, 2003.

Ballara, Angela. 'Introduction: The King Movement's First Hundred Years'. In *Te Kingitanga: The People of the Maori King Movement*, ed. Dictionary of New Zealand Biography, 1–32. Wellington: Auckland University Press with Bridget Williams Books/DNZB, 1996.

Belich, James. *The New Zealand Wars and the Victorian Interpretation of Racial Conflict*. Auckland: Penguin, 1988 (first published 1986).

—. *'I Shall Not Die': Titokowaru's War New Zealand, 1868–9*. Wellington: Allen & Unwin/Port Nicholson Press, 1989.

—. *The New Zealand Wars*. Video. Auckland: TVNZ/Landmark Productions, 1998.

Binney, Judith. *Redemption Songs: A Life of Te Kooti Arikirangi Te Turuki*. Auckland: Auckland University Press/Bridget Williams Books, 1995.

Borrie, W. D. *The European Peopling of Australasia*. Canberra: Demography, RSSS, ANU, 1994.

Breward, Ian. *A History of the Churches in Australasia*. Oxford: Oxford University Press, 2001.

Cain, P. J., and A. G. Hopkins. *British Imperialism, 1688–2000*. 2nd edn. Harlow: Longman, 2002.

Cowan, James. *The New Zealand Wars: A History of the Maori Campaigns and the Pioneering Period*. Vol. 1: 1845–64. Wellington: Government Printer, 1922 (reprinted 1983).

—. *The New Zealand Wars*. Vol. II: The Hauhau Wars, 1864–72. Wellington: Government Printer, 1922 (reprinted 1983).

Cox, Lindsay. *Kotahitanga: The Search for Maori Political Unity*. Auckland:
Oxford University Press, 1993.

Daley, Caroline. *Girls & Women, Men & Boys: Gender in Taradale 1886–
1930*. Auckland: Auckland University Press, 1999.

Dalziel, Raewyn. *Julius Vogel: Business Politician*. Auckland: Auckland
University Press/Oxford University Press, 1986.

Denoon, Donald. 'Re-Membering Australasia: A Repressed Memory'.
Australian Historical Studies 34, no. 122 (October 2003): 290–304.

Dow, Derek A. 'Springs of Charity? The Development of the New Zealand
Hospital System, 1876–1910'. In *A Healthy Country: Essays on the Social
History of Medicine in New Zealand*, ed. Linda Bryder, 44–64. Welling-
ton: Bridget Williams Books, 1991.

Durie, Mason. *Whaiora: Maori Health Development*. 2nd edn. Auckland:
Oxford University Press, 1998.

Elsmore, Bronwyn. *Mana from Heaven: A Century of Maori Prophets in
New Zealand*. Auckland: Reed, 1999.

Evans, Julie, Patricia Grimshaw, David Philips, and Shurlee Swain. *Equal
Subjects, Unequal Rights: Indigenous Peoples in British Settler Colonies,
1830–1910*, Studies in Imperialism, ed. John M. MacKenzie. Manchester
& New York: Manchester University Press, 2003.

Fairburn, Miles. *The Ideal Society and Its Enemies*. Auckland: Auckland
University Press, 1989.

Fraser, Lyndon, ed. *A Distant Shore: Irish Migration and New Zealand
Settlement*. Dunedin: University of Otago Press, 2000.

—. '"No One but Black Strangers to Spake to God Help Me": Irish Women's
Migration to the West Coast, 1864–1915'. In *Shifting Centres: Women
and Migration in New Zealand History*, ed. Lyndon Fraser and Katie
Pickles, 45–62. Dunedin: University of Otago Press, 2002.

Gardner, W. J. *Colonial Cap and Gown: Studies in the Mid-Victorian Universities of Australasia*. Christchurch: University of Canterbury, 1979.

Hill, Richard S. *The Colonial Frontier Tamed: New Zealand Policing in
Transition, 1867–1886*. 2 vols. Wellington: Historical Branch/GP Books,
1989.

Ip, Manying. *Dragons on the Long White Cloud: The Making of Chinese
New Zealanders*. Auckland: Tandem Press, 1996.

Jebb, Richard. *Studies in Colonial Nationalism*. London: Edward Arnold,
1905.

Lovell-Smith, Margaret. *Easily the Best: The Life of Helen Connon (1857–
1903)*. Christchurch: Canterbury University Press, 2004.

Macdonald, Charlotte. *A Woman of Good Character: Single Women as
Immigrant Settlers in Nineteenth-Century New Zealand*. Wellington:
BWB/Historical Branch, 1990.

—. 'Too Many Men and Too Few Women: Gender's "Fatal Impact" in Nineteenth-Century Colonies'. In *The Gendered Kiwi*, ed. Caroline Daley and Deborah Montgomerie, 17–35. Auckland: Auckland University Press, 1999.

May, P. R. *The West Coast Gold Rushes*. Christchurch: Pegasus Press, 1962.

—. 'Gold on the Coast (1) and (2)'. *New Zealand's Heritage* 3, no. 31 & 32 (1971).

Mein Smith, Philippa. 'New Zealand Federation Commissioners in Australia: One Past, Two Historiographies'. *Australian Historical Studies* 34, no. 122 (October 2003): 305–25.

Morrell, W. P. *The Provincial System in New Zealand 1852–76*. 2nd edn. Christchurch: Whitcombe and Tombs Ltd, 1964.

Munro, Jessie. *The Story of Suzanne Aubert*. Auckland: Auckland University Press/Bridget Williams Books, 1996.

Ng, James. *Windows on a Chinese Past*. 4 vols. Dunedin: Otago Heritage Books, 1993.

Nolan, Melanie. 'Maritime Strike 1890, Australasia'. In *St James Encyclopedia of Labor History Worldwide*, ed. Neil Schlager. Chicago: Gale Group, 2003.

Olssen, Erik. *A History of Otago*. Dunedin: McIndoe, 1984.

—. 'Families and the Gendering of European New Zealand in the Colonial Period, 1840–80'. In *The Gendered Kiwi: Pakeha Men and Women, 1840–1990*, ed. Caroline Daley and Deborah Montgomerie, 37–62. Auckland: Auckland University Press, 1999.

Parsonson, Ann. 'The Challenge to Mana Maori'. In *The Oxford History of New Zealand*, ed. Geoffrey W. Rice. Auckland: Oxford University Press, 1992.

—. 'The Fate of Maori Land Rights in Early Colonial New Zealand: The Limits of the Treaty of Waitangi and the Doctrine of Aboriginal Title'. In *Law, History, Colonialism: The Reach of Empire*, ed. Diane Kirkby and Catharine Coleborne, 173–89. Manchester: Manchester University Press, 2001.

Pool, Ian. *Te Iwi Maori: A New Zealand Population Past, Present and Projected*. Auckland: Auckland University Press, 1991.

Richardson, Len E. *Coal, Class and Community: The United Mineworkers of New Zealand 1880–1960*. Auckland: Auckland University Press, 1995.

Riseborough, Hazel. *Days of Darkness: Taranaki 1878–1884*. Revised edn. Auckland: Penguin, 2002.

Scott, Dick. *Ask That Mountain: The Story of Parihaka*. Auckland: Heinemann/Southern Cross, 1975.

Simkin, C. G. F. *The Instability of a Dependent Economy: Economic Fluctuations in New Zealand 1840–1914*. Oxford: Oxford University Press, 1951.

Simon, Judith, and Linda Tuhiwai Smith, eds. *A Civilising Mission? Perceptions and Representations of the Native Schools System.* Auckland: Auckland University Press, 2001.

Simpson, Tony. *The Immigrants: The Great Migration from Britain to New Zealand, 1830–1890.* Auckland: Godwit Publishing, 1997.

Sinclair, Keith. *A Destiny Apart: New Zealand's Search for National Identity.* Wellington: Allen & Unwin/Port Nicholson Press, 1986.

Star, Paul, and Lynne Lochhead. 'Children of the Burnt Bush: New Zealanders and the Indigenous Remnant, 1880–1930'. In *Environmental Histories of New Zealand,* ed. Eric Pawson and Tom Brooking, 119–35. Melbourne: Oxford University Press, 2002.

Stone, R. C. J. *Makers of Fortune: A Colonial Business Community and Its Fall.* Auckland: Auckland University Press/Oxford University Press, 1973.

Tennant, Margaret. *Paupers and Providers: Charitable Aid in New Zealand.* Wellington: Allen & Unwin/Historical Branch, 1989.

Thomson, David. *A World without Welfare: New Zealand's Colonial Experiment.* Auckland: Auckland University Press/BWB, 1998.

Wevers, Lydia. *Country of Writing: Travel Writing and New Zealand 1809–1900.* Auckland: Auckland University Press, 2002.

5 MANAGING GLOBALISATION 1891–1913

Brooking, Tom. *Lands for the People?* Dunedin: University of Otago Press, 1996.

—, and Roberto Rabel. 'Neither British nor Polynesian: A Brief History of New Zealand's Other Immigrants'. In *Immigration and National Identity in New Zealand,* ed. Stuart W. Greif, 23–49. Palmerston North: Dunmore Press, 1995.

Castles, Francis G. *The Working Class and Welfare: Reflections on the Political Development of the Welfare State in Australia and New Zealand, 1890–1980.* Wellington: Allen & Unwin/Port Nicholson Press, 1985.

—. *Australian Public Policy and Economic Vulnerability: A Comparative and Historical Perspective.* Sydney: Allen & Unwin, 1988.

Crawford, John, and Ian McGibbon, eds. *One Flag, One Queen, One Tongue: New Zealand, the British Empire and the South African War 1899–1902.* Auckland: Auckland University Press, 2003.

Curnow, Jenifer, Ngapare Hopa, and Jane McRae, eds. *Rere Atu, Taku Manu! Discovering History, Language and Politics in the Maori-Language Newspapers.* Auckland: Auckland University Press, 2002.

Daley, Caroline, and Melanie Nolan, eds. *Suffrage and Beyond: International Feminist Perspectives.* Auckland: Auckland University Press, 1994.

Dalziel, Raewyn. 'The Colonial Helpmeet: Women's Role and the Vote in Nineteenth-Century New Zealand'. In *Women in History: Essays on European Women in New Zealand*, ed. Barbara Brookes, Charlotte Macdonald and Margaret Tennant, 55–68. Wellington: Allen & Unwin/Port Nicholson Press, 1986.

Fry, Eric, ed. *Common Cause: Essays in Australian and New Zealand Labour History*. Wellington: Allen & Unwin/Port Nicholson Press, 1986.

Greasley, David, and Les Oxley. 'Globalization and Real Wages in New Zealand 1873–1913'. *Explorations in Economic History* 41, no. 1 (January 2004): 26–47.

Grimshaw, Patricia. *Women's Suffrage in New Zealand*. Auckland: Auckland University Press, 1987.

Hamer, David. *The New Zealand Liberals: The Years of Power, 1891–1912*. Auckland: Auckland University Press, 1988.

Holt, James. *Compulsory Arbitration in New Zealand: The First Forty Years*. Auckland: Auckland University Press, 1986.

Ip, Manying. *Dragons on the Long White Cloud: The Making of Chinese New Zealanders*. Auckland: Tandem Press, 1996.

—, ed. *Unfolding History, Evolving Identity: The Chinese in New Zealand*. Auckland: Auckland University Press, 2003.

Kelly, Paul. *The End of Certainty: The Story of the 1980s*. Sydney: Allen & Unwin, 1992.

Lange, Raeburn. *May the People Live: A History of Maori Health Development 1900–1920*. Auckland: Auckland University Press, 1999.

McGibbon, Ian. 'Australia–New Zealand Defence Relations to 1939'. In *Tasman Relations*, ed. Keith Sinclair, 164–82. Auckland: Auckland University Press, 1987.

—. *The Path to Gallipoli: Defending New Zealand 1840–1915*. Wellington: GP Books, 1991.

Macintyre, Stuart, and Richard Mitchell, eds. *Foundations of Arbitration: The Origins and Effects of State Compulsory Arbitration 1890–1914*, Australian Studies in Labour Relations. Melbourne: Oxford University Press, 1989.

Martin, John E. *Holding the Balance: A History of New Zealand's Department of Labour 1891–1995*. Christchurch: Canterbury University Press, 1996.

Meaney, Neville. *The Search for Security in the Pacific, 1901–14*. Sydney: Sydney University Press, 1976.

Mein Smith, Philippa. 'New Zealand'. In *The Centenary Companion to Australian Federation*, ed. Helen Irving, 400–5. Melbourne: Cambridge University Press, 1999.

Moloughney, Brian, and John Stenhouse. '"Drug-Besotten, Sin-Begotten Fiends of Filth": New Zealanders and the Oriental Other, 1850–1920'. *New Zealand Journal of History* 33, no. 1 (1999): 43–64.

Nolan, Melanie. *Breadwinning: New Zealand Women and the State.* Christchurch: Canterbury University Press, 2000.

O'Connor, P. S. 'Keeping New Zealand White, 1908–1920'. *New Zealand Journal of History* 2, no. 1 (1968): 41–65.

Olssen, Erik. *The Red Feds: Revolutionary Industrial Unionism and the New Zealand Federation of Labour 1908–14.* Auckland: Oxford University Press, 1988.

—. *Building the New World: Work, Politics and Society in Caversham 1880s–1920s.* Auckland: Auckland University Press, 1995.

Orbell, Margaret, ed. *He Reta Ki Te Maunga: Letters to the Mountain: Maori Letters to the Editor 1898–1905.* Auckland: Reed, 2002.

Phillips, Jock. *A Man's Country? The Image of the Pakeha Male, a History.* Revised edn. Auckland: Penguin, 1996.

Reeves, William Pember. *State Experiments in Australia and New Zealand.* 2 vols. London: George Allen & Unwin, 1902.

Ross, Angus. *New Zealand Aspirations in the Pacific in the Nineteenth Century.* Oxford: Clarendon Press, 1964.

Sinclair, Keith. *William Pember Reeves: New Zealand Fabian.* Oxford: Clarendon Press, 1965.

—. 'Why New Zealanders Are Not Australians: New Zealand and the Australian Federal Movement, 1881–1901'. In *Tasman Relations: New Zealand and Australia, 1788–1988*, ed. Keith Sinclair, 90–103. Auckland: Auckland University Press, 1987.

Ville, Simon. *The Rural Entrepreneurs: A History of the Stock and Station Agent Industry in Australia and New Zealand.* Cambridge: Cambridge University Press, 2000.

6 'ALL FLESH IS AS GRASS' 1914–1929

Baker, Paul. *King and Country Call: New Zealanders, Conscription and the Great War.* Auckland: Auckland University Press, 1998.

Boyd, Mary. 'The Record in Western Samoa to 1945'. In *New Zealand's Record in the Pacific Islands in the Twentieth Century*, ed. Angus Ross, 115–88. London & New York: Longman Paul, 1969.

Bryder, Linda. *A Voice for Mothers: The Plunket Society and Infant Welfare, 1907–2000.* Auckland: Auckland University Press, 2003.

Daley, Caroline. *Leisure & Pleasure: Reshaping & Revealing the New Zealand Body 1900–1960.* Auckland: Auckland University Press, 2003.

Ferguson, Gael. *Building the New Zealand Dream.* Palmerston North: Dunmore Press/Historical Branch, 1994.

Fleming, G. A. 'Agricultural Support Policies in a Small Open Economy: New Zealand in the 1920s'. *Economic History Review* 52, no. 2 (1999): 334–54.

Harper, Glyn. *Massacre at Passchendaele: The New Zealand Story.* Auckland: HarperCollins, 2000.

—, ed. *Letters from the Battlefield: New Zealand Soldiers Write Home 1914–18*. Auckland: HarperCollins, 2001.

King, Michael. *Te Puea: A Biography*. Auckland: Hodder and Stoughton, 1977.

McGibbon, Ian. *The Path to Gallipoli: Defending New Zealand 1840–1915*. Wellington: GP Books/Historical Branch, 1991.

—. *New Zealand Battlefields and Memorials of the Western Front*. Auckland: Oxford University Press/History Group, Ministry for Culture and Heritage, 2001.

Mein Smith, Philippa. *Maternity in Dispute: New Zealand 1920–1939*. Wellington: Historical Branch, Department of Internal Affairs, 1986.

Pugsley, Christopher. *Gallipoli: The New Zealand Story*. Auckland: Sceptre, 1990.

—. *Te Hokowhitu a Tu: The Maori Pioneer Battalion in the First World War*. Auckland: Reed, 1995.

—. *The Anzac Experience: New Zealand, Australia and Empire in the First World War*. Auckland: Reed, 2004.

Rice, Geoffrey. *Black November: The 1918 Influenza Epidemic in New Zealand*. Wellington: Allen and Unwin/Historical Branch, 1988.

Shadbolt, Maurice. *Voices of Gallipoli*. Auckland: Hodder and Stoughton, 1988.

Tennant, Margaret. *Children's Health, the Nation's Wealth: A History of Children's Health Camps*. Wellington: Bridget Williams Books/Historical Branch, 1994.

Walker, Ranginui. *He Tipua: The Life and Times of Sir Apirana Ngata*. Auckland: Viking, 2001.

Worthy, Scott. 'A Debt of Honour: New Zealanders' First Anzac Days'. *New Zealand Journal of History* 36, no. 2 (2002): 185–200.

7 MAKING NEW ZEALAND 1930–1949

Bassett, Michael, and Michael King. *Tomorrow Comes the Song: A Life of Peter Fraser*. Auckland: Penguin, 2000.

Clark, Margaret, ed. *Peter Fraser: Master Politician*. Palmerston North: Dunmore Press, 1998.

Crawford, John, ed. *Kia Kaha: New Zealand in the Second World War*. Auckland: Oxford University Press, 2002.

Easton, Brian. *The Nationbuilders*. Auckland: Auckland University Press, 2001.

Gardiner, Wira. *Te Mura O Te Ahi: The Story of the Maori Battalion*. Auckland: Reed, 2002.

Gustafson, Barry. *From the Cradle to the Grave: A Biography of Michael Joseph Savage*. Auckland: Reed Methuen, 1986.

Hanson, Elizabeth. *The Politics of Social Security*. Auckland: Auckland University Press/Oxford University Press, 1980.

Hilliard, Chris. 'Stories of Becoming: The Centennial Surveys and the Colonization of New Zealand'. *New Zealand Journal of History* 33, no. 1 (1999): 3–19.

Hutching, Megan, ed. *'A Unique Sort of Battle': New Zealanders Remember Crete*. Auckland: HarperCollins/History Group, Ministry for Culture and Heritage, 2001.

Kay, Robin, ed. *The Australian–New Zealand Agreement 1944*. Vol. 1, Documents on New Zealand External Relations. Wellington: Historical Publications Branch, Department of Internal Affairs, 1972.

McClure, Margaret. *A Civilised Community: A History of Social Security in New Zealand 1898–1998*. Auckland: Auckland University Press/Historical Branch, 1998.

McGibbon, Ian. *New Zealand and the Second World War: The People, the Battles and the Legacy*. Auckland: Hodder Moa Beckett, 2004.

McIntyre, W. D. *The Rise and Fall of the Singapore Naval Base, 1919–1942* Cambridge Commonwealth Series. London and Basingstoke: Macmillan, 1979.

—. *New Zealand Prepares for War: Defence Policy 1919–39*. Christchurch: University of Canterbury Press, 1988.

McKinnon, Malcolm. *Independence and Foreign Policy: New Zealand in the World since 1935*. Auckland: Auckland University Press/Historical Branch, 1993.

—. *Immigrants and Citizens: New Zealanders and Asian Immigration in Historical Context*. Wellington: Institute of Policy Studies, Victoria University of Wellington, 1996.

Montgomerie, Deborah. *The Women's War: New Zealand Women 1939–45*. Auckland: Auckland University Press, 2001.

Nolan, Melanie. *Breadwinning: New Zealand Women and the State*. Christchurch: Canterbury University Press, 2000.

Simpson, Tony. *The Sugarbag Years*. 2nd edn. Auckland: Penguin, 1990.

Taylor, Nancy M. *The New Zealand People at War: The Home Front*. 2 vols. Official History of New Zealand in the Second World War 1939–45. Wellington: Government Printer, 1986.

Wood, F. L. W. *The New Zealand People at War: Political and External Affairs*, Official History of New Zealand in the Second World War 1939–45. Wellington: War History Branch, Department of Internal Affairs, 1958.

8 GOLDEN WEATHER 1950–1973

Brookes, Barbara. 'Nostalgia for "Innocent Homely Pleasures": The 1964 New Zealand Controversy over *Washday at the Pa*'. In *At Home in New Zealand*, ed. Barbara Brookes, 210–25. Wellington: Bridget Williams Books, 2000.

Burnett, Alan, and Robin Burnett. *The Australia and New Zealand Nexus*. Canberra: Australian Institute of International Affairs/NZ Institute of International Affairs, 1978.

Campbell, I. C. *Worlds Apart: A History of the Pacific Islands*. 4th edn. Christchurch: Canterbury University Press, 2003.

Easton, Brian. *In Stormy Seas: The Post-War New Zealand Economy*. Dunedin: University of Otago Press, 1997.

—. *The Nationbuilders*. Auckland: Auckland University Press, 2001.

Firth, Stewart. *Nuclear Playground*. Sydney, 1987.

—. 'A Nuclear Pacific'. In *The Cambridge History of the Pacific Islanders*, ed. Donald Denoon, Stewart Firth, Jocelyn Linnekin, Malama Meleisea and Karen Nero, 324–58. Cambridge: Cambridge University Press, 1997.

Gould, J. D. *The Rake's Progress? The New Zealand Economy since 1945*. Auckland: Hodder and Stoughton, 1982.

Green, Anna. *British Capital, Antipodean Labour: Working the New Zealand Waterfront, 1915–1951*. Dunedin: University of Otago Press, 2001.

Guest, Morris, and John Singleton. 'The Murupara Project and Industrial Development in New Zealand 1945–65'. *Australian Economic History Review* 39, no. 1 (1999): 52–71.

Gustafson, Barry. *The First Fifty Years: A History of the New Zealand National Party*. Auckland: Reed Methuen, 1986.

Haines, Nicolas, ed. *The Tasman: Frontier and Freeway?* Canberra: Centre for Continuing Education ANU, 1972.

Ip, Manying. 'Redefining Chinese Female Migration: From Exclusion to Transnationalism'. In *Shifting Centres: Women and Migration in New Zealand History*, ed. Lyndon Fraser and Katie Pickles, 149–65. Dunedin: University of Otago Press, 2002.

McGibbon, Ian. 'Forward Defence: The Southeast Asian Commitment'. In *New Zealand in World Affairs Volume II 1957–1972*, ed. Malcolm McKinnon, 9–39. Wellington: NZIIA/Historical Branch, 1991.

—, ed. *Undiplomatic Dialogue: Letters between Carl Berendsen and Alister McIntosh 1943–52*. Auckland: Auckland University Press/MFAT/Historical Branch, 1993.

McIntyre, W. David. *Background to the Anzus Pact: Policy-Making, Strategy and Diplomacy, 1945–55*. Macmillan's Cambridge Commonwealth Series, ed. D. A. Low. Houndmills, Basingstoke/Christchurch: St Martin's Press/Canterbury University Press, 1995.

McKinnon, Malcolm. *Independence and Foreign Policy: New Zealand in the World since 1935*. Auckland: Auckland University Press, 1993.

—. *Immigrants and Citizens: New Zealanders and Asian Immigration in Historical Context*. Wellington: Institute of Policy Studies, Victoria University of Wellington, 1996.

Martin, John E., ed. *People, Politics and Power Stations: Electric Power Generation in New Zealand 1880–1998*. Wellington: Electricity Corporation/Historical Branch/Bridget Williams Books, 1998.

Nolan, Melanie. *Breadwinning: New Zealand Women and the State*. Christchurch: Canterbury University Press, 2000.

Phillips, Jock. *Royal Summer: The Visit of Queen Elizabeth and Prince Philip to New Zealand, 1953–54*. Wellington: Historical Branch/Daphne Brasell Associates, 1993.

Pickles, Katie. 'Workers and Workplaces – Industry and Modernity'. In *Southern Capital Christchurch: Towards a City Biography 1850–2000*, ed. John Cookson and Graeme Dunstall, 138–61. Christchurch: Canterbury University Press, 2000.

Rolfe, Mark. 'Faraway Fordism: The Americanization of Australia and New Zealand During the 1950s and 1960s'. *New Zealand Journal of History* 33, no. 1 (1999): 65–91.

Singleton, John, and Paul L. Robertson. *Economic Relations between Britain and Australasia 1945–1970*, Cambridge Imperial and Post-Colonial Studies, ed. A. G. Hopkins. Houndmills, Basingstoke: Palgrave, 2002.

Stocker, Mark. 'Muldoon's Money: The 1967 New Zealand Decimal Coinage Designs'. *History Now* 7, no. 2 (2001): 5–10.

Walker, Ranginui. *He Tipua: The Life and Times of Sir Apirana Ngata*. Auckland: Viking, 2001.

Wood, F. L. W. 'New Zealand Foreign Policy 1945–1951'. In *New Zealand in World Affairs*, 1, 89–113. Wellington: Price Milburn/New Zealand Institute of International Affairs, 1977.

Woods, Megan. 'Dissolving the Frontiers: Single Maori Women's Migrations, 1942–1969'. In *Shifting Centres: Women and Migration in New Zealand History*, ed. Lyndon Fraser and Katie Pickles, 117–34. Dunedin: University of Otago Press, 2002.

9 LATEST EXPERIMENTS 1974–1996

Barnett, Ross, and Pauline Barnett. 'Back to the Future? Reflections on Past Reforms and Future Prospects for Health Services in New Zealand'. *GeoJournal* 59, no. 2 (2004): 137–47.

Bassett, Michael. *The State in New Zealand 1840–1984: Socialism without Doctrines?* Auckland: Auckland University Press, 1998.

Cain, P. J., and A. G. Hopkins. *British Imperialism, 1688–2000*. 2nd edn. Harlow: Longman, 2002.

Castles, Frank, Rolf Gerritsen, and Jack Vowles, eds. *The Great Experiment: Labour Parties and Public Policy Transformation in Australia and New Zealand*. Auckland: Auckland University Press, 1996.

Dalziel, Paul, and Ralph Lattimore, eds. *The New Zealand Macroeconomy: A Briefing on the Reforms*. Auckland: Oxford University Press, 1999.

Davey, Judith A. *Another New Zealand Experiment: A Code of Social and Family Responsibility.* Wellington: Institute of Policy Studies, 2000.

Easton, Brian, ed. *The Making of Rogernomics.* Auckland: Auckland University Press, 1989.

—. *In Stormy Seas: The Post-War New Zealand Economy.* Dunedin: University of Otago Press, 1997.

—. *The Commercialisation of New Zealand.* Auckland: Auckland University Press, 1997.

Gauld, Robin. *Revolving Doors: New Zealand's Health Reforms.* Wellington: Institute of Policy Studies/Health Services Research Centre, Victoria University of Wellington, 2001.

Gibbs, Alan, and Hospital and Related Services Taskforce. *Unshackling the Hospitals: Report of the Hospital and Related Services Taskforce.* Wellington: The Taskforce, 1988.

Goldfinch, Shaun. *Remaking New Zealand and Australian Economic Policy.* Wellington: Victoria University Press, 2000.

Gustafson, Barry. *His Way: A Biography of Robert Muldoon.* Auckland: Auckland University Press, 2000.

Hazledine, Tim. *Taking New Zealand Seriously: The Economics of Decency.* Auckland: HarperCollins, 1998.

James, Colin. *The Quiet Revolution.* Wellington: Allen & Unwin, 1986.

Le Heron, Richard, and Eric Pawson, eds. *Changing Places: New Zealand in the Nineties.* Auckland: Longman Paul, 1996.

McKendry, C. G., and D. Muthumala. *Health Expenditure Trends in New Zealand: Update to 1993.* Wellington: Ministry of Health, 1994.

McKinnon, Malcolm. *Independence and Foreign Policy: New Zealand in the World since 1935.* Auckland: Auckland University Press, 1993.

McMillan, Stuart. *Neither Confirm Nor Deny: The Nuclear Ships Dispute between New Zealand and the United States.* Wellington: Allen & Unwin/Port Nicholson Press, 1987.

Muldoon, R. D. *The Rise and Fall of a Young Turk.* Wellington: A. H. & A. W. Reed, 1974.

—. *My Way.* Wellington: Reed, 1981.

Templeton, Hugh. *All Honourable Men: Inside the Muldoon Cabinet 1975–1984.* Auckland: Auckland University Press, 1995.

Thompson, David. *Selfish Generations? How Welfare States Grow Old.* Revised edn. Cambridge, England: White Horse Press, 1996.

10 TREATY REVIVAL 1974–2003

Bedford, Richard D. 'International Migration, Identity and Development in Oceania: Towards a Theoretical Synthesis'. In *International Migration at Century's End: Trends and Issues.* Liege: IUSSP, 1997.

Bedford, Richard, Elsie Ho, and Jacqueline Lidgard. 'International Migration in New Zealand: Context, Components and Policy Issues'. In

Populations of New Zealand and Australia at the Millennium. A Joint Special Issue of the Journal of Population Research and the New Zealand Population Review, ed. Gordon A. Carmichael, with A. Dharmalingam, 39–65. Canberra and Wellington: Australian Population Association/Population Association of New Zealand, 2002.

Bell, Martin. 'Comparing Population Mobility in Australia and New Zealand'. In *Populations of New Zealand and Australia at the Millennium*, ed. Gordon A. Carmichael, with A. Dharmalingam, 169–93. Canberra and Wellington: Australian Population Association/Population Association of New Zealand, 2002.

Coates, Ken S., and P. G. McHugh. *Living Relationships: Kokiri Ngatahi: The Treaty of Waitangi in the New Millennium*. Wellington: Victoria University Press, 1998.

Dann, Christine. *Up from Under: Women and Liberation in New Zealand 1970–1985*. Wellington: Allen & Unwin/Port Nicholson Press, 1985.

Denoon, Donald, with Stewart Firth, Jocelyn Linnekin, Malama Meleisea, and Karen Nero, eds. *The Cambridge History of the Pacific Islanders*. Cambridge, New York and Melbourne: Cambridge University Press, 1997.

Durie, Mason H. *Te Mana Te Kawanatanga: The Politics of Maori Self-Determination*. Auckland: Oxford University Press, 1998.

Evison, Harry C., ed. *The Treaty of Waitangi and the Ngai Tahu Claim*, Ka Roimata Whenua Series: No. 2. Christchurch: Ngai Tahu Maori Trust Board, 1988.

Greif, Stuart W., ed. *Immigration and National Identity in New Zealand: One People, Two Peoples, Many Peoples?* Palmerston North: Dunmore Press, 1995.

Havemann, Paul, ed. *Indigenous People's Rights in Australia, Canada, and New Zealand*. Auckland: Oxford University Press, 1999.

Kawharu, I. H., ed. *Waitangi: Maori and Pakeha Perspectives of the Treaty of Waitangi*. Auckland: Oxford University Press, 1989.

King, Michael. *Being Pakeha Now: Reflections and Recollections of a White Native*. Auckland: Penguin, 1999.

Macdonald, Charlotte, ed. *The Vote, the Pill and the Demon Drink: A History of Feminist Writing in New Zealand 1869–1993*. Wellington: Bridget Williams Books, 1993.

Mein Smith, Philippa. 'Midwifery Re-Innovation in New Zealand'. In *Innovations in Health and Medicine: Diffusion and Resistance in the Twentieth Century*, ed. Jennifer Stanton, 169–87. London & New York: Routledge, 2002.

Nolan, Melanie. 'Unstitching the New Zealand State: Its Role in Domesticity and Its Decline'. *International Review of Social History* 45 (2000): 252–76.

Parsonson, Ann. 'Ngai Tahu – the Whale That Awoke: From Claim to Settlement (1960–1998)'. In *Southern Capital Christchurch: Towards a*

City Biography 1850–2000, ed. John Cookson and Graeme Dunstall, 248–76. Christchurch: Canterbury University Press, 2000.

Richards, Trevor. *Dancing on Our Bones: New Zealand, South Africa, Rugby and Racism*. Wellington: Bridget Williams Books, 1999.

Shepard, Deborah. *Reframing Women: A History of New Zealand Film*. Auckland: HarperCollins, 2000.

Tau, Te Maire. 'Ngai Tahu – from "Better Be Dead and Out of the Way" to "to Be Seen to Belong"'. In *Southern Capital Christchurch: Towards a City Biography 1850–2000*, ed. John Cookson and Graeme Dunstall, 222–47. Christchurch: Canterbury University Press, 2000.

Temm, Paul. *The Waitangi Tribunal: The Conscience of the Nation*. Auckland: Random Century, 1990.

Walker, Ranginui. *Ka Whahai Tonu Matou: Struggle without End*. Auckland: Penguin Books, 1990. Revised edn 2004.

EPILOGUE

Cain, P. J., and A. G. Hopkins. *British Imperialism, 1688–2000*. 2nd edn. Harlow: Longman, 2002.

Pickles, Katie. 'Kiwi Icons and the Re-Settlement of New Zealand as Colonial Space'. *New Zealand Geographer* 58, no. 2 (2002): 5–16.

INDEX

accent, New Zealand 81
advances to settlers 100
aerial top dressing 195, 197
ageing, political 204
Air New Zealand 196
Anglo-Japanese alliance 119
Anthony, Doug 205
Anzac Day 123, 126, 128
Anzac legends, Australian and
    New Zealand 95, 127
  Diggers 127
  Kiwis 127
ANZUS alliance 179, 180, 194,
    200, 216, 217, 218, 219, 220,
    222, 223, 224, 225
Aoraki, *see* Mt Cook
Aotearoa 7, 8, 9, 13, 15, 17
Arbitration Court 151, 155
arbitration, compulsory 105
art 241
Auckland, as capital 49
Auckland, as largest city 246
Australasia 92
Australia New Zealand Closer
    Economic Relations Trade
    Agreement (CER) 205, 207,
    215, 223
Australia, defence relations 220
  effects of ANZUS split 223

Australian federation, *see*
    Commonwealth of Australia
Australia–New Zealand Agreement
    168
Australia–New Zealand Leadership
    Forum 249

baby boomers 176, 188, 191, 192,
    193, 194, 195
Ballance, John 100, 105
Bastion Point 229, 230, 233
Beaglehole, J. C. 25
Beeby, C. E. 170
Bennett, Rev. Frederick 148
biculturalism 226, 243
births, by ethnicity 253
Blake, Sir Peter 247
Boer War 118, 119
Bolger, James 213, 214
Brash, Donald 252
Buck, Sir Peter, *see* Te Rangi
    Hiroa
Busby, James 39, 40, 41, 43
Buzzy Bee 170

Californian bungalow 141, 142
Canberra Pact, *see* Australia–New
    Zealand Agreement
Cartwright, Dame Silvia 238, 240

centennial, 1940 164, 165, 172, 173
Chatham Islands invasion 37
Chelsea Flower Show 252
childbirth, free 157
childbirth, management of 140, 238
  Lead Maternity Carer scheme 238
  midwife, return of the 238
China 250
Chinese 82, 116, 117
Chisholm, Caroline 62
Choie Sew Hoy 82
Citizenship Western Samoa Act 244
citizenship, New Zealand 172
Clark, Helen 218, 238, 239
Coates, J. G. 146, 148, 153, 154, 159
Cold War 178, 179, 180, 181, 182, 188, 193
Colombo Plan 179
colonisation 54
  Arcadian ideas 54
  Canterbury Association 61
  Canterbury settlement 61–62
  lottery of land orders 56
  Manawatu 64
  Nelson 63
  New Plymouth 63
  New Zealand Company settlers 59
  Otago 61
  pastoralism 68
  systematic 54–55
  Wanganui 63
Commonwealth of Australia 112
  White Australia 114
Condliffe, J. B. 172
confiscation, Waikato 72
Connon, Helen 88, 89
Cook Islands 116

Cook, Captain James 23–27
  voyages 27
Cooper, Whina 228
Cossgrove, David 122
Crozet, Julien 28

dairying 143
  Dairy Export Control Board 143
  feminine consumers 145
  milk 143, 144
de Surville, Jean-François 28
de Thierry, Charles 41
decimals 197
  decimal currency 197
defence 159, 161, 162, 164
defence policy 178
democracy, early 86
depression 92–94, 150–151
  effects 152
  recovery 154, 156
  relief schemes 152
  unemployment 150, 151, 153, 157
Domett, Alfred 64
Dominion of New Zealand 124
Dominion status 119
Douglas, Roger 208, 210, 211
du Fresne, Marion 28
Durie, Edward T. 231, 232

economic liberalisation 203, 208
economy, export-led 98
Edger, Kate 88
education 86–88
  native schools 87
electoral reform 225
electoral system 252
Elizabeth II, Queen 190
Employment Contracts Act 213
entrepreneurial state 84, 94
environment movement 194
equal opportunity 170, 171
European Economic Community 198, 199, 200, 202

export diversification 203
exports 247, 250
  to Britain 142
External Affairs, Department of
  168

family wage 106
fauna 3, 5, 9, 14
  kiwi 5
  moa 5, 14, 15, 16, 17
feminism, *see* Women's Liberation
  Movement
feminism, 'second wave' 237,
  239
feminism, colonial 102
Fenwick, Percival 125
fertility decline 120
film 240, 241
FitzRoy, Governor Robert 64
flora 4, 9, 14
Forbes, George 151
Foreshore and Seabed Bill 253
Fraser, Malcolm 207
Fraser, Peter 157, 160, 162, 165,
  167, 169, 170, 171

geology 3–4
globalisation 95, 96, 97, 106, 107,
  249
  definition of 202
gold rushes 79–82
gold-seekers 78, 79, 81, 82
Gondwana 1, 3, 5
Gore Browne, Governor Thomas
  68, 71
government 65
  Constitution Act 66
  first election 67
  provincial 67
  representative 66
  responsible 67
grasslands revolution 143
Great White Fleet 119
Greer, Germaine 192

Grey, Governor Sir George 65, 70,
  71
Gunn, Elizabeth 138

Hall, Sir John 103, 115
Hartley, Dinah 64
Harvester judgment 106
Hauhau, *see* Pai Marire
Hawaiki 6, 7, 9, 10, 11
health policy 124, 135, 136, 137,
  138, 139, 141, 143, 147
  health camps 138
  maternal deaths 139
  open-air schools 138
  school medical inspections 138
Health, Department of 137
Hillary, Sir Edmund 190
Hobson, Captain William 42, 43,
  44, 45, 46, 47, 48 49, 50, 51,
  52, 53, 59, 64
Holland, Sidney 177, 199
Holyoake, Keith 180
home ownership 100, 102, 188
Hone Heke 46, 64
Hongi Hika 32, 33, 34, 35, 36
  and Thomas Kendall 33
  and Waikato 33
Horeta Te Taniwha 26, 27
Hursthouse, Charles 91
Huru 29
hydroelectric power 182

immigration 183, 244, 245, 246
  Asian 245
  Australian 184
  British 183
  Chinese 184
  Dutch 183
  Immigration Amendment Act
  184
  Indian 184
  Pacific Islanders 184, 185, 186,
  244, 246, 247
  refugees 184

immigration policy 141, 171, 172
Immigration Restriction Act 117
income inequality 215
infant mortality 111, 121
infant welfare movement 136
influenza pandemic 137, 147

Kawiti 64, 65
Kerikeri 32
King movement, *see* Kingitanga
King, Sir Frederic Truby 121, 135,
    136, 137
King, Governor Philip 29
Kingi, Wiremu 68, 71
Kingitanga 67, 68, 69, 71, 72, 76
Kingston, Charles C. 105
Kirk, Norman 193
kohanga reo 231
Kohimarama conference 68
Korean War 178, 180, 197
Kotahitanga 110

La Pérouse, Galaup de 27
Labour government, first 150,
    154
    school milk scheme 155
    state houses 158
Labour government, fourth 203,
    208, 214, 216
labour militancy 107
Labour Party, New Zealand
    133
land ownership 70, 99
    Maori 78, 99
    settlers 99
Lange, David 208, 209, 211, 217,
    218, 219, 221, 222
Langlois, Jean François 61
Legislative Council, abolition of
    177
liberalism, new 95
    liberalism, social 96
life expectancy 176, 187
liquor licensing laws 192
Lomu, Jonah 247

McCahon, Colin 177
McCombs, Elizabeth 104, 153
McCrae, John 123
Macmillan Brown, John 88
Macquarie, Governor Lachlan 32
Malayan Emergency 179
Malone, Colonel W. G. 128
manhood suffrage 86
Maori 1, 4, 6, 7, 8, 9, 11, 12, 13,
    14, 15, 16, 17, 18, 19, 20,
    108, 227
    Christianity 38
    crafts 18
    Declaration of Independence 41
    explorers 18
    first contact 23
    fisheries claims 19, 236
    flag 40–41
    gardening 17–18
    health 111
    Land Councils 110
    land loss 108
    Land March 228
    language 19
    leases 109
    pa 19
    perceptions of Indigenous
        Australians 29
    protest 228
    reserves 109
    tribes 122
    urbanisation 228
Maori Council 227, 234, 235
Maori Social and Economic
    Advancement Act 171
Maori wars, *see* New Zealand wars
Maori Women's Welfare League
    186, 187
Maritime Strike 94
married women, paid work 191
Marsden, Rev. Samuel 31–32
Mason, Bruce 176
Massey, William Ferguson 124,
    141, 146, 148
Meat Producers' Board 146

Mein Smith, Captain William 44, 56, 57, 58, 59
survey of Wellington 57
Middle Earth 252
migrations, tribal 5, 9, 16
missionaries 30
Church Missionary Society 32
Roman Catholic 42
Moriori 37
Mt Cook 4
Muldoon, Robert 204, 205, 206, 207, 208, 209, 213, 217
multiculturalism 227, 242, 243, 245
musket wars 33–35
effects 37–38

Nanto-Bordelaise Company 61
National Council of Women 103
National government 204, 213, 214, 217
health reforms 214
national heroes 246, 251
National Party 175, 177, 180
nationalism, colonial 92, 96, 112, 117
Native Land Act 111
Native Land Court 73, 74, 77, 90, 91
navigators, Polynesian 5, 6, 7, 12
fleet, organised 13
Kupe 9, 11, 13
Paikea 11
Tupaia 9
Nene, Tamati Waka 46, 53, 64, 65, 67
Nepia, George 148
New Zealand Company 37, 44, 50, 54, 56, 59, 61, 63, 64
New Zealand First Party 246
New Zealand Settlements Act 72, 75
New Zealand wars 70, 78, 84, 92
New Zealand–Australia Free Trade Agreement (NAFTA) 199

Nga Tamatoa 227, 228
Ngata, Sir Apirana 110, 148
Niue 116
nuclear free nation 216, 217, 221, 224
nuclear free zone 221
nuclear power 182
nuclear weapons 177, 181, 182
bomb tests 181
opposition to 194

O'Regan, Tipene 236
oil shocks 202, 205
Ottawa conference 153

Pacific identity 185
Pacific Islands 184
decolonisation 185
Pacific Ocean 21, 23, 25, 26, 27, 30, 31, 32, 39, 41, 43
Pai Marire 72, 74
Palmer, Geoffrey 211, 218
Parihaka, invasion of 75
Patuone 46, 53, 67
pavlova 189
peacekeepers 248
Pember Reeves, William 95, 104, 105
Peters, Winston 246
Pill, the 191
Plunket Society 121
political system 214, 215, 225
Pomare, Maui 111
Pomare, Miria 134
Pompallier, Bishop J. B. F. 42, 46, 47, 65
population 70, 77, 78
British migration 78
growth 79
Maori 70
structure 80
trends 78
Prebble, Richard 211, 217

predators 5, 14
   Pacific rat 14, 15
provincial government, end of 86
Public Health, Department of 111

race relations policy 186
   integration 187
racial template 12
   Maori, Aryan 12
Rainbow Warrior, bombing of
   221
Rata, Matiu 229
Ratana Church 147
Ratana movement 226, 227
Ratana, Iriaka 240
Ratana, T. W. 147
'recolonisation' 96, 118
Reeves, Maud 104
Reform Party 146
refrigeration 96, 97, 107
religion 30–32, 38, 74, 86
Reserve Bank 153, 154, 156, 158
Rewi Maniapoto 72
Richardson, Ruth 213
Ringatu 74
Rogernomics 208, 209, 210, 212,
   213, 215, 216, 218, 224
   financial deregulation 211
   labour market reform 212
   privatisation 212
   public sector reforms 211
   social costs 213
   state-owned enterprises 212
   tax reform 211
Ross, Hilda 177
Rotorua 77, 90, 91
Rua Kenana 134
Ruatara 31, 32
Russell, Captain William 92

St Helens Hospitals 120
Samoa 114, 116
Samoa, Western 124, 137
Savage, Michael Joseph 154
scouting movement 122

sealers 30
security 251
Seddon, Richard John 82, 114,
   115, 120
Select Committee on Aborigines,
   House of Commons 43
Select Committee on New Zealand,
   House of Lords 43
sesquicentennial 240, 242
settlement, time of 6
Sheppard, Kate 102, 103, 240
Shipley, Jenny 239
Sinclair, Keith 185
six o'clock closing 141
Smith, S. Percy 13
social security 154, 156, 159, 169
   family benefit 170
   old age pension 159
Somerset, H. C. D. 195
South Pacific Commission 169
Southeast Asia Collective Defence
   Treaty 179
sport, commercialisation of 247
Springbok tours 230, 231
state development, Australasian
   model 95
Statute of Westminster 172
sterling area 196
stock and station agents 98
Stout, Anna 103
Strutt, William 59, 60
suburbia 100, 186, 187, 188, 191
   suburban ideal 101
superannuation, national 204

Talboys, Brian 207
Tangiwai 190
Taranaki 70, 71, 72, 73, 75
Tasman Empire Airways Limited
   196
Tasman Pulp and Paper Company
   199
Tasman, Abel 23
Tawhiao 71, 75
Te Heuheu Tukino 91

Te Kooti Arikirangi Te Turuki 74
Te Maiharanui 36
Te Papa 243, 245
Te Pehi Kupe 36
Te Puea 133, 148
Te Puni 44, 56
Te Rangi Hiroa 12
Te Rangihaeata 63, 64
Te Rauparaha 35, 36, 37, 63, 64, 65
    attack on Kaiapoi 37
Te Ua Haumene 72
Te Wharepouri 37, 44, 56
Te Wherowhero 47, 67
Te Whiti 75
telegraph 71, 85
Thermal Springs District Act 90
'Think Big' development projects 205
Thomas, Captain Joseph 62
Thompson, Henry 63
Titokowaru 73, 75
Tizard, Dame Catherine 240
Tohu 75
Toi 11
tourism 90
Tourist and Health Resorts, Department of 90
trade 203, 207, 212
trading partners 248
traditions 5, 8, 9, 10, 11, 17
Treaty of Waitangi 45–53, 226, 228, 229, 232, 233, 237, 242, 243
    article 1 50
    article 2 51
    article 3 52
    documents 47
    Maori narratives 50
    neglect of 49
    settler narratives 49
    treaty principles 234
Treaty of Waitangi settlements 149, 171

Tregear, Edward 111
Tremewan, Captain H. Spencer 131
Tuki 29

Union Steam Ship Company 94
unionism 94
United Nations 169
United States of America, relations with 211, 216, 217, 218, 219, 220, 221
urbanisation, Maori 186
    Hunn Report 187

Vaggioli, Dom Felice 42
Vietnam War 179, 180, 192, 193
    protests 193
Vogel, Julius 79, 82, 84, 85
vote, Maori 86

Waikato, invasion of 71
Wairau dispute 63
Waitangi Day 226, 227
Waitangi Tribunal 13, 14, 231, 232, 233, 235, 236
    treaty settlements 235, 236
Waitangi, Treaty of, *see* Treaty of Waitangi
Waitara 68, 69, 70, 71, 72
Wakefield, Captain Arthur 63
Wakefield, Colonel William 44, 55
Wakefield, Edward Gibbon 44, 54, 55, 58, 67
Walsh, F. P. 180
waterfront dispute 180
    Federation of Labour 180
welfare, colonial 89
Wellington 56
    site of 57
    tenths reserves 58
Wellington, as capital 85
Weston, Agnes Louisa 177
Wetere, Koro 233
whakapapa 9, 10, 11, 20
whalers 29

Williams, Henry 45, 46, 50, 51
Wilson, Margaret 218, 219
women in paid employment 238
women members of parliament
    240
Women's Christian Temperance
    Union 103
Women's Liberation Movement
    192
women's suffrage 102, 103, 104
    reasons for 104
Wong, Pansy 246
World War I 124
    1st Maori Contingent 129
    Anzacs 125
    Battle of the Somme 129
    casualty rate 124
    Chunuk Bair 128
    conscientious objectors 133
    conscription 132, 133, 134
    expeditionary forces 124
    Gallipoli 125
    Great Sacrifice 127
    maternal sacrifice 132
    Messines 129
    New Zealand Division
        129
    nurses 134

Passchendaele 125, 129, 130
Pioneer Battalion 129
war memorials 135
Western Front 123, 124, 125,
    129
women peace activists 134
women's war effort 134
World War II 160, 163, 170, 171,
    172
    2 NZEF 161
    28 (Maori) Battalion 165
    Americans, presence of 168
    deaths 161
    Japanese 159, 162, 163, 164,
        167, 168
    Maori War Effort Organisation
        165
    Pearl Harbor 162
    rationing 167
    rehabilitation scheme 171
    Singapore, fall of 162
    United States 161, 162, 163,
        164, 167, 168, 169, 174
    Women's War Service Auxiliary
        167

Young Maori Party 110, 111
youth culture 190